The Publisher screen

Using

MW00748201

New to Publisher? This handy quick-reference card fills you in on all the basic features on the screen.

Quick Start

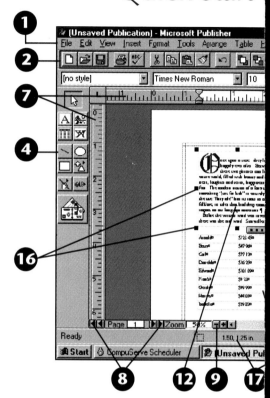

❶ Menu bar

Give Publisher your orders from here.

❷ Standard toolbar

The commands you'll use most often: Cut, Paste, Save, Print, the all-important Undo, Send to Front, Send to Back, Help, and more. See inside for details.

❸ Formatting toolbar

Depending on what kind of object you're working with, you'll see various buttons here that can help you format text and tables, change colors, and otherwise dress up your publication.

❹ Publisher toolbar

Use these buttons to draw text, table, graphics, and WordArt frames, access the PageWizards and Design Gallery, insert objects from other programs and add boxes, circles, lines, and custom shapes.

❺ Scroll arrows

Click to scroll up and down the page you're working on.

❻ Scroll box

Drag the box for fine adjustments to the positioning of your page; click on either side of it to move a whole screen.

❼ Rulers

Move these up and down or across the screen to help you precisely position text frames, tables, graphics, or WordArt.

❽ Page selection

Use these buttons to move to the next page, the previous page, the first page, or the last page of your publication, or click on the text box to directly enter the page you want to go to.

❾ Zoom

Click these buttons to zoom in to or out from the page, or click on the text box to select what percentage of full-size you want to view the page at.

ublisher for Windows 95

o Publisher Perfection!

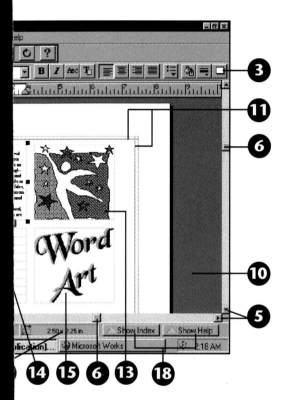

que®

201 W. 103rd Street Indianapolis, IN 46290
(317) 581-3500
Copyright© 1995 Que Corporation

⑬ Graphics frame

Graphics frames contain the artwork that brings your publication to life.

⑭ Table

To present some information properly, just put it in table form.

⑮ WordArt

When plain text just won't cut it, WordArt lets you create text with extra flair—thanks to plenty of built-in special effects.

⑯ Selection handles

When you select an object, these little black handles appear around it. Grab them and drag them to change the shape and size of the object.

⑰ Status bar

This bar shows you, on the left, the precise position of your mouse arrow on the page, and, on the right, the dimensions of the currently selected object.

⑱ Show Index/Help

Click Show Help to bring up the built-in Help files; click Show Index if you need help getting around Help!

⑩ Scratch area

Use this area as a virtual tabletop on which to place text frames, tables, graphics, and WordArt until you're ready to precisely position them in your publication.

⑪ Layout guides

Layout guides mark the margins you've established for your page and any columns you want to indicate.

⑫ Text frame

Text frames hold text: the meat and potatoes of your publication.

Using

Microsoft Publisher for Windows® 95

Using

Microsoft Publisher for Windows® 95

Edward C. Willett

with
Kathy Ivens

Using Microsoft Publisher for Windows®95

Copyright© 1995 by Que® Corporation

Library of Congress Catalog No.: 95-71416

ISBN: 0-7897-0635-0

97 96 95   6 5 4 3 2 1

Interpretation of the printing code: the rightmost double-digit number is the year of the book's printing; the rightmost single-digit number, the number of the book's printing. For example, a printing code of 95-1 shows that the first printing of the book occurred in 1995.

All terms mentioned in this book that are known to be trademarks or service marks have been appropriately capitalized. Que cannot attest to the accuracy of this information. Use of a term in this book should not be regarded as affecting the validity of any trademark or service mark.

Screen reproductions in this book were created using Collage Plus from Inner Media, Inc., Hollis, NH.

Composed in *ITC Century* and *Highlander* by Que Corporation.

Credits

President
Roland Elgey

Vice President and Publisher
Marie Butler-Knight

Associate Publisher
Don Roche, Jr.

Director of Marketing
Lynn E. Zingraf

Editorial Services Director
Elizabeth Keaffaber

Managing Editor
Michael Cunningham

Senior Series Editor
Chris Nelson

Publishing Manager
Brad R. Koch

Acquisitions Editors
Elizabeth South
Nancy Stevenson

Product Director
Lisa D. Wagner

Production Editors
Theresa Mathias
Thomas F. Hayes

Editor
Julie A. McNamee

Assistant Product Marketing Manager
Kim Margolius

Technical Editor
Nancy Jacobs

Acquisitions Coordinator
Tracy M. Williams

Operations Coordinator
Patty Brooks

Editorial Assistant
Carmen Phelps

Book Designer
Ruth Harvey

Cover Designer
Jay Corpus

Production Team
Kim Cofer, Jennifer Eberhardt,
Tricia Flodder, David Garratt,
Joe Millay, Erika Millen,
Erich J. Richter, Gina Rexrode,
Christine Tyner, Karen Walsh,
Robert Wolf

Indexer
Brad Herriman

This book is dedicated to my parents, James and Nina Willett, who always told me I could do anything I put my mind to...although I'm not at all sure this is what they had in mind.

For Debby, Bev, and Judy, just because I love them.

About the Authors

Edward Willett is a freelance writer living in Regina, Saskatchewan, Canada. Born in New Mexico, he moved to Weyburn, Saskatchewan from Texas as a child but returned to the U.S. for college. He graduated from Harding University in Searcy, Arkansas, with a degree in journalism. Edward was a newspaper reporter, photographer, cartoonist, columnist and eventually, editor for the weekly *Weyburn Review* for nine years, then for five years worked as the communications officer for the Saskatchewan Science Centre. Working at the Science Centre led directly to the weekly science column he now writes for several Canadian newspapers; he's also a regular guest on radio and TV programs to talk about science.

In addition to writing about science, Edward writes everything from plays and TV scripts to science fiction and fantasy. In addition, he's a singer and actor who has performed in numerous plays, musicals, and operas across Saskatchewan.

Kathy Ivens has been a computer consultant since 1984, and teaches diverse computer courses at a variety of institutions. She has authored and coauthored a number of books on computer subjects. She is a frequent contributor to national magazines, writing articles and reviewing software.

Before becoming an expert in computing, Ms. Ivens spent many years as a television producer, where she had fun producing sports and was moderately amused producing news and entertainment programs. Preceding that career was some time spent as a community organizer for social agencies in the Philadelphia, Pennsylvania, area. She still doesn't know what she wants to be when she grows up.

Ms. Ivens has three grown daughters, none of whom has ever figured out precisely what she does for a living.

We'd Like to Hear from You!

As part of our continuing effort to produce books of the highest possible quality, Que would like to hear your comments. To stay competitive, we *really* want you, as a computer book reader and user, to let us know what you like or dislike most about this book or other Que products.

You can mail comments, ideas, or suggestions for improving future editions to the address below, or send us a fax at (317) 581-4663. For the online inclined, Macmillan Computer Publishing has a forum on CompuServe (type **GO QUEBOOKS** at any prompt) through which our staff and authors are available for questions and comments. The address of our Internet site is **http://www.mcp.com** (World Wide Web).

In addition to exploring our forum, please feel free to contact me personally to discuss your opinions of this book: I'm **lwagner@que.mcp.com** on the Internet.

Thanks in advance—your comments will help us to continue publishing the best books available on computer topics in today's market.

Lisa D. Wagner
Product Development Specialist
Que Corporation
201 W. 103rd Street
Indianapolis, Indiana 46290
USA

Contents at a Glance

Table of Contents

Before you begin...

see page 11

I've used Publisher before

see page 16

*Working
with
frames*

see page 29

*On your
mark, get
set,...*

see page 38

4 Doing It Yourself   61

HELP!!

see page 55

*What are
layout
guides?*

see page 65

*Adding
and
deleting
pages*

see page 79

Part II: Working with Words

*What's the
difference
between
indents
and tabs?*

see page 94

Everything you've always wanted to know about fonts

see page 116

Adding special characters

see page 125

Styles save you lots of time

see page 144

Part III: Graphics

10 Adjusting Graphics   163

11 Let's Table That   177

What all's in the ClipArt Gallery

see page 154

ROTATE

Can I use data from another program?

see page 181

Part IV: Special Effects

12 Borders and Shadows and Fills, Oh My!   195

13 Getting Creative with Shapes   205

Adding a drop shadow

see page 202

Circles and ovals

see page 210

Adding color to shapes

see page 218

Oh-lay

Lining up objects

see page 258

Quality control

see page 274

Printing in color

see page 294

I need to install the software

see page 303

Introduction

When I became a full-time freelance writer, one of the first purchases I made was a laser printer. The second was Microsoft Publisher 2.0.

A journalist by training, I have huge respect for the printed word. But there's something else you learn in the newspaper business: almost as important as the words themselves are the way they look on the page. You have to entice the readers, draw them in, capture with a first glance, make them welcome. There are a lot of distractions in the world today—if you want a reader to look at your publication before he or she turns on the TV, your publication had better look good.

I learned desktop publishing as communications officer for the Saskatchewan Science Centre. But when I became a freelance writer, I was on my own. I needed a program powerful enough to allow me to create the kind of documents people would pay me for. I shopped around and, based on price and features, I finally chose Publisher—just like you have.

But then I faced a new challenge. Nobody was talking about Publisher. Nobody was writing about it. There were no books on how to use it. Even online, in desktop publishing newsgroups and forums, I couldn't find much about it.

So I had to teach myself to use it…and I discovered that Publisher was a powerful, flexible program that could do almost anything I asked of it. Pretty soon, people *were* paying me to do desktop publishing jobs for them.

Now you have the latest version of Publisher—and I don't want to see you in the same boat I was, paddling furiously with no help in sight. That's why I wrote this book. It's about time Publisher got the recognition it deserves—and it's about time Publisher users got the help they need.

So join me for a step-by-step exploration of Microsoft Publisher 3.0. We'll investigate every aspect of this terrific program. We'll have some fun along the way. And when we're done, you'll know exactly what you need to use Publisher to its full potential—and keep those restless readers away from the TV.

What makes this book different?

Using Microsoft Publisher for Windows 95 guides you through the features of Publisher 3.0 in the same order you are likely to use them: from text to graphics to tables; to embellishments that make your publication sparkle; to a final check of the layout and printing.

Along the way, you find **tips** to help you design a better document, **plain-English explanations** of some of the mysterious jargon of printing and publishing, **sidebars** full of interesting tidbits of additional information, and **question and answer segments** to solve mysteries before they lead to mayhem in your document.

Users experienced with Publisher 2.0 will find a host of new features to learn about and explore. And those coming to Publisher for the first time will find that it's easier to create great-looking documents than they ever thought possible.

Publisher has features you can't find in some top-end desktop publishing programs, yet it costs hundreds of dollars less. It's no wonder that for more and more users, it's the program of choice.

How do I use this book?

That's up to you; but however you choose to use it, you'll find that it works.

If you're just looking for quick help on a particular topic, turn to the Table of Contents at the front of the book first. There's a good chance you'll find it there. If you don't, turn to the Index at the back for more detailed help.

If you're a browser, flip through the book and take a look at the start of each chapter. You'll find a short list of the topics covered, plus a summary statement of what the chapter's about.

There are also large, clear headings throughout the book that divide chapters into sections. Browse until you see a section heading that interests you, and plunge in.

Finally, you might even want to read the whole thing from beginning to end. I wrote *Using Microsoft Publisher for Windows 95* with that possibility in mind, so each chapter flows logically into the next. It might not be the latest

Stephen King thriller, but if you're interested in getting the most out of Publisher, you won't be bored.

How this book is put together

A desktop publishing document is made up of many elements. So is a desktop publishing program like Publisher—and so, too, is this book. In fact, it's divided into seven parts.

Part I: Getting Started

If you let it, Publisher will take you by the hand and practically design your publication for you. After a quick tour of the Publisher workspace and tools, you learn about all the different types of publications the PageWizards have up their sleeves, from newsletters to paper airplanes (check out the AM radio option on the deluxe model). Visit the Design Gallery and find out how its selection of snazzy design elements can perk up your publication. And if you get lost, don't be afraid to cry for help—Publisher provides plenty.

If you'd rather do it yourself, find out how to get started and how to customize Publisher's tools to suit your needs. Explore a few more basic Publisher principles, then move on to…

Part II: Working with Words

A picture might be worth a thousand words, but for really effective communication, most people still find words pretty useful. Find out how to put words into your publication, format them, edit them, and bring them in from and export them to other programs. Have fun with fonts, in more ways than you might expect: Publisher has a whole chest full of new formatting tools.

Part III: Graphics

If you just wanted to use text, you'd have stuck with your word processor, right? Find out how to add the perfect pictures to your publication, whether they come from the built-in ClipArt Gallery, a disk, or a CD. Learn how to relocate graphics, resize them, recolor them, and rotate them. Move on to try your hand at tables: find out how to build one, how to fill one, how to decorate one, and how to bring one in from Excel or another program.

Part IV: Special Effects

The tools to make your publication shine just keep on coming. Add borders, shadows, and fills to any sort of Publisher object. Draw lines, boxes, ovals, star bursts, and more. Twist, stretch, flip, and color text with WordArt. And if that's still not enough, learn to add just about anything you can create on the computer to your document via OLE.

There are so many ways to tweak your publication that you might have to force yourself to quit playing with shapes and text and drawings and get back to "work." (That's something I noticed right away when I started learning desktop publishing, but which seldom gets mentioned: it's a heck of a lot of fun!)

Part V: Putting it Together

Text frames, picture frames, tables, WordArt, and more: what happens when they all end up on the same Publisher page together? Can they peacefully coexist?

You bet they can—with a little help from this part. Learn how to control frames even if you have to lasso them with a mouse. Line them up and give them a nudge if they step out of line. Group them the way you want them. Keep that text flowing. And finally, check your layout—use your own eyes first, then let Publisher loan you a second pair. Then take the big step: print your document, or prepare it for an outside printing service.

Appendix

But wait! I don't even have it installed yet!

If this is the case, this appendix shows you what kind of equipment you need to run Publisher and what it takes to install it. You'll find clear, step-by-step instructions and answers to your common installation questions.

Index

Finally, two very special indexes allow you to look up a problem you need to solve or find a task you want to do, then flip immediately to the page where you can find the answer. And of course, the book closes with a plain old index to look things up in.

Special book elements

This book contains a number of special elements and conventions to help you find information quickly—or skip stuff you don't want to read right now.

TIP **Tips either point out information often overlooked in the** documentation, or help you use your software more efficiently, like pointing out a shortcut. Some tips help you solve or avoid problems.

CAUTION **Cautions alert you to potentially dangerous consequences of a** procedure or practice, especially if it could result in serious or even disastrous results, such as loss or corruption of data.

Q&A *What are Q&A notes?*

Cast in the form of questions and answers, these notes provide you with advice on ways to avoid or solve common problems.

66 *Plain English, please!*

These notes explain the meanings of technical terms or computer jargon in language you can easily understand. 99

Throughout this book, I use a comma to separate the parts of a pull-down menu command. For example, to start a new document, you choose <u>F</u>ile, <u>N</u>ew. That means, "Pull down the <u>F</u>ile menu, and choose <u>N</u>ew from the list."

And if you see two keys separated by a plus sign, such as Ctrl+X, that means to press and hold the first key, press the second key, then release both keys.

Sidebars are interesting nuggets of information

Sidebars provide interesting, nonessential reading, side-alley trips you can take when you're not at the computer or when you just want some relief from "doing stuff." Here you might find more technical details, funny stories, personal anecdotes, or interesting background information.

Part I:

Getting Started

1

Basics of Desktop Publishing

● In this chapter:

● So just what exactly is desktop publishing?

● How do I get started?

● The dos and don'ts of good design

Desktop publishing puts the awesome power of the printing press in your hands. . . . . ●

n 1984, a new kind of personal computer appeared: the Apple Macintosh. Graphically oriented, controlled primarily not with a keyboard but with something called a mouse, featuring easy-to-use pull-down menus and commands, the Mac was unlike anything else on the market. Two years later, Apple Computer introduced the Laserwriter laser printer, and just like that, **desktop publishing (DTP)** was born. In just two pieces of equipment, you had everything you needed to print anything you wanted, with far more precision and far less effort than had ever been possible before.

Because it was so easy to use, the Macintosh became the standard tool of desktop publishers. IBM-compatible personal computers (PCs, for short) were far less "user-friendly." Keyboards and lots of arcane commands were how users communicated with PCs in the late 1980s. (The same year the Macintosh appeared we got new computers at the newspaper I edited. Drawing a box required a string of commands that looked like mathematical equations. Drawing a box in a desktop publishing program on a Macintosh required only pointing, clicking, and moving the hand slightly.) But the Macintosh's advantage was narrowed in the early 1990s with the introduction of the Windows operating system. Now PC-owners, too, could start programs and call up commands by just pointing and clicking—and publish documents with the same ease Macintosh users had always known. A Mac user could sit down at a Windows-based PC and feel pretty well right at home (at least, I did when I made the switch in 1993).

And now, there's Windows 95: even easier to use than Windows. Less clicking, for one thing. Much easier to install new programs on. And there are lots of new programs coming out that take advantage of its new features: Microsoft Publisher 3.0, for one.

With powerful software and high-quality printers now available for a fraction of what similar tools would have cost even 10 years ago, the ability to prepare and mass-produce a document that powerfully presents your message is now at the fingertips of anyone with a computer.

Whether you purchased Microsoft Publisher to create professional-looking documents for your small business or to produce a magazine devoted to Rhodesian Ridgebacks, Publisher has all the tools you need—and then some!

Why use DTP?

Desktop publishing offers distinct advantages over more traditional methods, including these features:

- **You eliminate the middleman.** A lot of the cost of traditional publishing arises because there are so many people involved: artists, typesetters, designers, printers, even receptionists and cleaning people (a big print shop is a pretty dirty place, with all that ink flying around). With desktop publishing, although you can involve all those people if you want, you can also do the entire job yourself. And unlike in a traditional print shop, where many jobs are underway at the same time, your job is always at the top of the priority list.

- **You save time.** Your computer is literally at your fingertips. A couple of clicks, and Publisher is at your command. You can create your document, print it, and move on to your next task without ever leaving your desk. It's simple efficiency: achieving the greatest result with the least amount of work.

- **Your message remains clear.** A published document—any published document—is an attempt to communicate something. Who has a better idea of what you want to communicate than you do? With desktop publishing you do it "your way"—just like Frank Sinatra.

- **You can easily modify your publication.** Making changes in a publication that's been prepared by a traditional printer isn't easy—or cheap. You have to clearly communicate the changes you want made and double-check them after they're made—if they can be made at all. With a DTP document, you can make a change with a click of the mouse.

Play by the rules

Desktop publishing gives everyone the capability to create a publication. The downside to that is obvious—DTP gives *everyone* this capability, whether they're up to the task or not. Bad design abounds. Just because you *can* add that clip art you found of a pig dancing the tango with an ostrich doesn't mean you *should*.

A lot of the bad desktop publishing that plagues the computerized world can be avoided by following one simple rule:

Plan ahead

A good way to run the risk of creating an ugly document is to simply plunge into it without any forethought.

Before they paint a masterpiece, most artists spend a lot of time thinking about it. They consider the size of the canvas, what colors to use, maybe even where the finished painting will hang. More than likely, they'll make a few pencil sketches before ever lifting a brush.

That's a good rule for desktop publishers, too. Before you begin a publication, take time to think about it—and maybe even make a sketch.

Know your goal

The first thing to consider is the purpose of the publication. Do you want to sell things? Promote an event? Educate the public? Lay out an agenda for a meeting? Inform the members of an organization?

Knowing your goal helps you determine the overall look of the publication. Every publication has its own tone or mood, the general feeling you get when you look at it. It might shout for your attention or whisper suggestively; attract you with its beauty; intrigue you with an air of mystery; or simply make you laugh. A brochure about a clown who performs at children's parties is going to have a very different look than a flyer advertising a coffin sale at the undertaker's (I hope).

The audience you hope to reach also determines the overall look. A publication designed to impress the board of directors of IBM will look very different from a flyer intended to attract potential buyers of your old Harley-Davidson.

Ask yourself these questions...

After you know the mood you want, you can ask yourself more specific questions.

1 What font should I use?

2 What kind of artwork do I want to include, and how much of it?

3 Do I want color? A lot or a little? What colors?

4 What size should my publication be?

5 Should it be a single page? Folded once down the middle? Folded three times, to make a brochure? Folded some other way?

With these and similar questions in mind, sketch out your publication before you begin. Indicate where you'll put text and graphics, where you want a table or a drawing, where you don't want anything at all.

Always keep in mind that your goal is to *communicate*. Don't get so carried away with fancy design ideas that you obscure the message you're trying to get across.

 TIP   **Graphics should highlight text, or text should clearly explain** graphics; tables should be clear, concise, and convey real information; and you should place all of these elements on the page in a logical, well-thought-out way that emphasizes the most important elements of your message and de-emphasizes the less-important elements (without obscuring them completely).

But be creative

With sketch in hand, you'll find it's really easy to create a publication that does what you want it to do. But don't make the mistake of being too devoted to a preliminary sketch: it's just a beginning. As you assemble the elements of your publication, you might find, for example, that the graphic you originally thought looked perfect at the top of the page actually looks better at the bottom. Go ahead and make the improvements to the initial sketch that suggest themselves during the design process.

Remember that desktop publishing makes it easy to make changes. That's one of its greatest strengths—it allows you to fine-tune your design to achieve the maximum impact.

Which brings you, finally, to the moment you've been waiting for: the moment when you get to learn how to use Microsoft Publisher, a program that offers you so many ways to create great-looking documents you might feel like a kid in a candy store. (Only this is even better—Microsoft Publisher is fat- and calorie-free, too!)

Welcome to the amazing world of desktop publishing.

2

Introducing Microsoft Publisher

In this chapter:

- I've used Publisher before; just tell me what's new in this version
- What're all those things on my screen?
- Understanding frames
- Safety first: saving your work
- Opening and closing publications

I've never even pretended to be an artist. But thanks to Publisher, I can produce slick, professional publications just like the folks on Madison Avenue. And now, so can you . . . . .

I f you've never used Publisher before, you're off on a great ad venture. You can produce professional-looking publications of almost any kind, from a one-page flyer to a complicated multi-page brochure.

What's new?

If you're a Publisher veteran, there are some features new to Publisher 3.0 that you'll love. For newcomers, the new features give you a hint of the power you'll find in Publisher.

 Plain English, please!

When you use Publisher, the data files you create are called **publications**. If you've used word processors, you probably referred to those files as documents, but we'll be using the Publisher terminology in this book, publications.

More toolbar power!

Now Publisher has the same Standard toolbar as most other windows applications. If you aren't familiar with it, it means there are buttons available at the top of your screen. Click a button once to open, save, and print files, cut and paste text, and do many other common tasks.

More graphics tools!

When you're working with pictures and shapes, you'll find new and powerful features. There's instant access to lots of design elements, like borders and boxes, by clicking the new Design Gallery button.

You can rotate pictures, spinning them clockwise or counterclockwise. You can flip shapes, turning a triangle upside down so it rests on its point or making a mirror image of a more complicated shape—one click and it's facing the other way.

And, after you format something so it's absolutely perfect, you can transfer that same formatting scheme to another element in your publication, saving lots of time and energy.

More color tools!

There's a much wider choice of colors, and if you're sending your publication to an outside printer, there's full access to the standard color schemes used by professional printers. There's also spot coloring available, which lets you print a bright color in one spot to highlight an element in your publication. Great for adding zip to logos or headlines or artwork in the middle of a black and white publication.

Outside printing support!

Use the built-in features to get your publication ready for an outside printer, and then send it off to the printer right from the menu bar.

Better Help!

Help is always one click away, with a Help button always on your Publisher window. Complicated chores are easier with the help of Wizards and demos.

Long file names

Because this version of Publisher is written for Windows 95, you can use long file names. There's no limit of eight characters for a file name with a three character extension. You can even use spaces in your file names, so you can name a file **My Secret Resume**.

 TIP **Most of the buttons on your Publisher window explain themselves** with the help of a nifty feature called **ToolTips**. If you hold your mouse pointer on a button for a couple of seconds (don't click, just pause), a little yellow message appears explaining the use of that element (see fig. 2.1). The message only hangs around for a few seconds, so read fast.

Fig. 2.1
"Hello," says this ToolTip, "I'm the Print button."

Getting things done in Publisher

There's a profusion of buttons and text all over the Publisher window. Each of these items gives you easy access to Publisher's features and functions.

Publisher toolbar
All sorts of special effects at the click of a mouse button. Click a button to create artwork, add fancy designs around your words, or put a picture into your publication.

Menu bar
Each item on the menu bar has a menu that drops down, where you find commands that let you get various tasks accomplished.

Standard toolbar
Click a button to perform the functions you use frequently, like saving your work or moving text and graphics around.

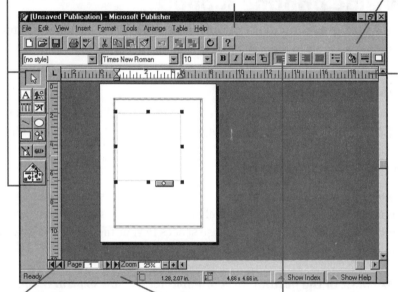

Rulers
Rulers help you create guides for page layout, in addition to providing a way to judge the size of objects on the page. They're marked every quarter inch, so you can always figure out where you are. Your mouse pointer's position is always indicated on both rulers by a thin line.

Status bar
This is a mini road map that shows you which part of your publication you're working on right now. The arrows and zoom controls let you move around all the parts and pages of your publication quickly.

Status line
On the Status line, the Help buttons are always available so you can get quick advice as you work. The information boxes let you keep an eye on the size of the individual parts of your publication.

Formatting toolbar
Here are the buttons you click to change the way your text or artwork looks. For example, you can change the way a sentence looks to make it stand out, or you can turn your artwork upside down.

Toolbars give you point-and-click access to common tasks

You will normally find two toolbars on your Publisher window: the Standard toolbar and the Publisher toolbar. You can also use another toolbar, the Formatting toolbar, when you work with text or graphics in your publication.

 TIP **Don't worry about memorizing all these buttons right now.** When you need a certain button to do something discussed in the book, I'll remind you what it looks like in the margin, like the Print button shown here. Still, you might want to dog-ear this page so you can quickly find the whole list a week—or a year—from now.

66 *Plain English, please!*

A **frame** is a container for an element in your publication. Everything you do in Publisher starts with a frame. You can create a frame of any type and any size. To add text, artwork, or shapes, first you have to create a frame. All the types of frames you need are available on the Publisher toolbar. (You'll find out a lot more about frames later in this chapter.)

An **object** is an element in a publication. You can identify, select (click on) and manipulate it. A frame, for example, is an object. And, frames can have more than one element, such as text and art, and each individual element in the frame is also an object. 99

The Standard toolbar, up close and personal

A familiar part of most Windows software, the Standard toolbar has buttons that give you one-click access to functions you probably use a lot (see fig. 2.2).

Fig. 2.2
The Standard toolbar probably looks familiar—most of these are common to all Windows programs.

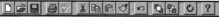

 New
Opens a new publication

 Paste
Places the contents of the Clipboard where your pointer is when you select the Paste button

 Open
Opens an existing publication

 Format Painter
Takes the formatting of an item and applies the same formatting to another item

 Save
Saves the current publication

 Undo/Redo
Reverses your last action

 Print
Prints the current publication

 Bring to Front
Brings an object in the background to the foreground

 Spelling
Performs a spell check on text in the publication

 Send to Back
Takes a foreground object and places it in the background

 Cut
Removes the selected item from your publication and places it on the Clipboard

 Rotate
Rotates a graphic element

 Copy
Makes a copy of the selected item and places it on the Clipboard

 Help
Opens the Help window

The Publisher toolbar, a closer look

The toolbar on the left side of your screen is the Publisher toolbar (see fig. 2.3). It has buttons specific to the work you do in Publisher.

Fig. 2.3
The Publisher toolbar is the Mission Control center for any publication you're working on.

Pointer
Click here to return your pointer to its normal shape after you use other buttons on the toolbar

Picture
Places a picture in your publication

Text Frame
Click this button and then click the place in your publication where you want to insert a frame to hold text

WordArt
Bend and twist text for a special effect by using WordArt

Table Frame
This button inserts a Table frame in your publication

Circles and Ovals
Click here, then draw a circle or an oval

Line
Allows you to draw a line

Custom Shapes
Click this button to choose a frame shaped just the way you want it

Rectangle
Click this button to draw a rectangle in your publication, which can hold text or artwork

Insert Object
Use this button to place an object, such as clip art, an icon, or a special graphic into your publication

PageWizards
Click here to have the PageWizards help you insert special items such as logos or clip-and-send coupons

Design Gallery
This opens the Publisher gallery of art work where you can find designs to embellish your publication

The Text Formatting toolbar, appearing when needed

When you're working on text, a special toolbar appears below the Standard toolbar. This Text Formatting toolbar helps you format your layout so you present just the right message (see fig. 2.4).

[no style]
Times New Roman
10

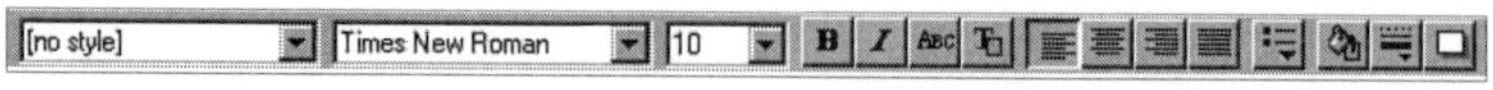

Fig. 2.4
The Text Formatting toolbar helps you handle text without a lot of hassles.

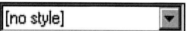

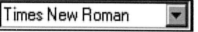

[no style]
Times New Roman
10
Style list box
Put together a group of formatting commands and save them as a style—then you can choose it from the Style list box when you need it
Font list box
Choose a font (typeface)
Size list box
Make your text larger or smaller
Bold
Make your text bold—it stands out because it's darker
Italic
Choose Italic to make your text lean to the right
Small Capitals
Make the lowercase letters small versions of uppercase letters
Font Color
Pick a new color for your text
Align Left
Your text lines up neatly on the left margin, with an uneven right margin
Align Center
Centers each line of text
Align Right
The right edge of every line aligns against the right margin and the left edge is uneven
Justify Text
The text lines up at both the left and right margins
Bullet or Number List
Create a neat list, with bullet marks or numbers
Color
Pick a color to fill the area in which your text appears
Border
Change the border around your text to a different thickness or pattern
Shadows
You can put a shadow effect around the border that surrounds your text

The Formatting toolbar for graphic shapes

If you're working on a graphic shape, like a circle or an oval, you can put text or artwork inside the shape. The Formatting toolbar changes to give you the buttons you need to manipulate the graphic (see fig. 2.5).

Fig. 2.5
Flip, rotate, color, and otherwise play with your graphic objects using the Graphics Formatting toolbar.

 Flip Horizontal
Flip your graphic from left to right, like a mirror image

 Object Color
Opens a color palette so you can add color to the graphic

 Flip Vertical
Flip the graphic so the top is at the bottom and the bottom at the top

 Border
Create or change the border of the graphic

 Rotate Right
Rotate the graphic clockwise

 Add/Remove Shadow
Add a shadow around the graphic's shape or get rid of a shadow you added earlier

 Rotate Left
Spin the graphic in a counter-clockwise direction

The Formatting toolbar for pictures

When you work with pictures, the Formatting toolbar changes to add a few specific buttons you can use to make pictures fit perfectly in your publication (see fig. 2.6).

Fig. 2.6
The Picture Formatting toolbar is like the Graphics Formatting toolbar, but its tools are more specific to working with artwork instead of basic shapes.

Crop Picture
You can eliminate part of the picture and save just the part you need

Wrap Text to Picture
Text around the picture follows the contours of the picture—not the frame

Wrap Text to Frame
The text around your picture follows the contours and margins of the frame that holds the picture

Navigating around your publication

As you work in your publication, moving from place to place isn't accomplished in the same way as most of the other software you use.

For example, if you use a word processor, you can use the Page Down and Page Up keys to move through your publication, crossing from one page to another as you do so. In Publisher, those keys don't permit you to move between pages. There are, however, tools available to help you navigate.

The Status bar: Publisher's path finder

The Status bar, directly beneath your workspace, has the tools that let you navigate through your publication (see fig. 2.7).

Fig. 2.7
The Status bar has the controls you use to navigate through your publication.

First Page
Moves to the first page of your publication

Zoom Out
Move the page further away from you incrementally

Previous Page
Moves to the page before the current page

Zoom In
Move the page closer to you incrementally

Change Pages
You can choose a specific page to move to

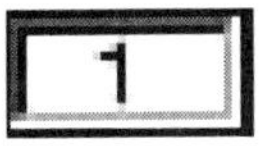

Left Horizontal Scroll bar arrow
Use the arrow to move to the left side of the page

Next Page
Move to the next page

Right Horizontal Scroll bar arrow
Use this arrow to move to the right side of the page

Last Page
Move to the last page

Zoom
You can specify the size of the view, using a percentage of the page size

TIP For a shortcut, the F9 key toggles you between whatever the current zoom percentage is and a 100 percent view. This means you can move in to work on text or formatting and then move out to see the overall effect easily.

The Status line: more tools and information

Just below the Status bar, the Status line provides information about the elements of your publication, and holds the buttons that summon help when you need it (see fig. 2.8).

Fig. 2.8
The Status line tells you about the size and position of objects.

Object Position box   *Object Size box*

In the center of the Status line are the Object Position box and the Object Size box.

- When you select a frame or a portion of a frame, its position appears on the Object Position box. When you haven't selected anything, it tells you the position of the pointer.

- The Object Size box tells you the size of a selected object.

 Plain English, please!

> **Selecting** a frame or an object means choosing it to work on. You select one object at a time, work on it, then select another object. To select an object, click on it. This changes the object's frame to a dark line with squares appearing on all sides and in the corners. The squares are called **selection handles.**

The right side of the Status line holds buttons for Publisher Help. You can show or hide the Help Index and Help Contents. If you click the Show Index button, the Help Index appears in its own window. As you select topics, the information about that topic displays in the Help window to the right of the Index window (see fig. 2.9). The buttons on the Status line changed to Hide Index and Hide Help; click them to close the Help windows.

Fig. 2.9

You can open the Help Index and Help Contents windows with a click of a button.

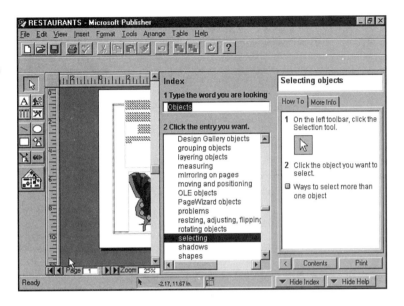

Understanding frames

When you use Publisher, **frames** are your life. They are the *sine qua non* (that's Latin for "without that, nothing") of creating publications; they are the basis of all life—well, life as a Publisher user; they are the foundation of everything you build; they are the cornerstones…okay, you get the idea. Every element in your publication is enclosed in a frame. There are text frames, picture frames, table frames, WordArt frames, and so on.

Because everything is framed, it's really the frames you manipulate to put together your publication. It's just like decorating a wall with pictures. You get a friend to hold the pictures up at various places on the wall while you stand back and look. When a picture looks right on a certain place, you hang it. Then you take the next picture, which might be a different size, and go through the same steps. Then the next picture, and the next, and so on. By the time your helper gets muscle cramps, you have a gallery of pictures. They're of varying sizes and differing content. Maybe some are thin line drawings and others are fulsome, colorful oils. You might even have some "text" pictures: posters or samplers.

Of course, you didn't really hang the pictures, you hung the frames. Some of the pictures inside the frames might be oval in shape, or square, or irregular. The contents might be surrounded by a raised mat or pasted onto a colorful background. It's quite possible you made a gallery of pictures of all shapes, but all were enclosed in frames of the same shape.

Frames have a shape and a function

Rather than using your mind's eye, take a look at some frames in a publication. Figure 2.10 is an illustration of a page that uses frames. This page has three frames on it:

- A WordArt frame. WordArt is a program (connected to Publisher) that lets you twist text into various shapes.

- A Text frame.

- A ClipArt frame.

Fig. 2.10
Viewing a page with three different frames can help you visualize the way you use frames.

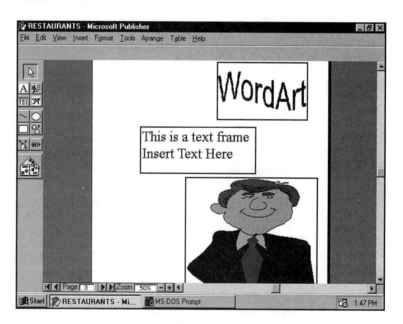

When you actually place frames in a publication, there aren't any lines around each frame—unless you specifically want to have a border (which is usually only used around text). Take a look at figure 2.11 to see the effect of different frames on a single page.

Fig. 2.11

You don't see the frames of a finished page—just the contents of the frames display and print.

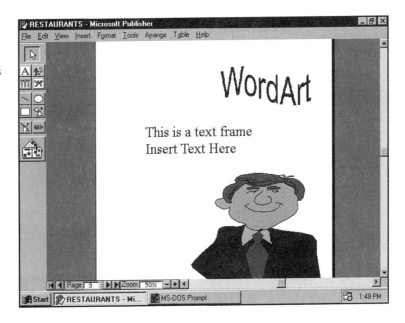

Working with frames

When you begin creating your own publications and inserting frames on pages, there are several tools you use.

- Selection handles
- Resizers
- Frame movers

You can find specific information about manipulating and filling frames throughout this book. For now, I'll just discuss the concepts and go over some of the things you'll do with frames.

Selection handles

When you want to work with the frame's shape, size, or placement, you need to select it (click on it). When you select a frame, small squares appear around the frame's perimeter. These are called the frame's **selection handles** (see fig. 2.12).

Fig. 2.12
Use these selection handles to manipulate the frame and move it around the page.

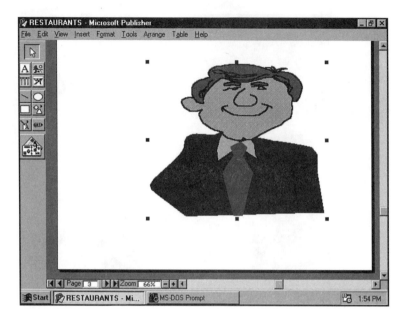

Resizing frames

If you place your mouse pointer on one of the selection handles, the pointer changes to a **resizer**—a double-headed arrow (see fig. 2.13). You can drag the handle to change the size of the frame.

Fig. 2.13
To change the size of a frame, you first need to see the resizer pointer.

If you move your pointer to one of the corner handles, the resizer is a double-headed arrow that points at an angle. When you drag the mouse, the two sides that meet at the corner move simultaneously.

Sometimes this causes the frame to change its proportions. You can control the corner resizer's actions by using special keys while you're dragging.

- To keep the proportions of the frame, hold down the Shift key as you drag the corner frame handle. Don't let go of the Shift key until after you release the mouse button.

- To keep the center of the frame in place, hold down the Ctrl key as you drag. Don't let go of the Ctrl key until you release the mouse button.

- To do both, hold both keys while you drag.

Sometimes you resize a frame and don't like the effect it produces on the contents. Squished up graphics can look pretty awful. Just click the Undo button.

Moving frames

While you select a frame, if you put your mouse pointer inside the frame, the pointer turns into a moving van (see fig. 2.14). Drag the mouse to move the frame (and its contents) anywhere on the page.

Fig. 2.14
When the moving van shows up, you can move your whole frame around the page.

CAUTION **Moving a text frame is a bit different from moving any other type** of frame. If you want to move a text frame, your mouse pointer has to be on the outside edge of the frame to make the pointer turn into a moving van. Imagine a line connecting all the selection handles. Move your mouse pointer anywhere on that imaginary line and the pointer changes its shape to a moving van. Now you can move the frame.

Deleting frames

To delete a frame, select it and press the Delete key. If you didn't mean to do it, after you finishing screaming "oh no," immediately click the Undo button on the toolbar.

Save your work

Like any other computer file, to make your publication available for future use, you have to save it. But waiting to save until you finish all your work is an invitation to disaster. The disaster fairies somehow learn that you've been working for hours without saving your work, and just when you're almost done with a large, complicated publication, they strike. Something happens to the electricity or to your computer.

That might sound like I just worked for 30 straight hours, but it actually happens!

TIP **Save early and often. I save a publication as soon as I enter a line** of data. This establishes the file name and makes subsequent saves a one-click maneuver (by clicking the Save button). Then I save again every time I do anything significant (which, to me, means I finish a paragraph, create a frame, or place something in a frame). Come to think of it, every time I do anything more than type a couple of sentences, I consider it significant enough to save.

You can save a publication by:

- Choosing the Save button on the Standard toolbar

- Choosing File, Save

- Pressing Ctrl+S

I get caught up in my work and forget to save often enough

It never fails. Every time there's rain in the forecast, I can count on my phone ringing. It's Mom, of course, reminding me to take my umbrella if I'm going out. Although it can be a little annoying, that's what Moms do. They remind you, often, to do the things you should.

Publisher does the same thing when it comes to saving your work. If you haven't saved the file during the last 15 minutes, Publisher nags, er, reminds you to do so (see fig. 2.15).

Fig. 2.15
Publisher reminds you that you haven't saved your work in a while.

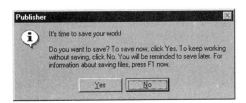

 CAUTION **The file reminder is only that—a reminder. If you answer Yes**, Publisher saves the file. If not, it doesn't. This is not an automatic save function you can find in other applications. Here, the burden's on you.

If you work fast and could lose a lot of work if you wait the full 15 minutes, or if you work slowly and find the interruption annoyingly frequent, you can change the length of time between reminders.

1 Choose Tools, Options to open the Options dialog box.

2 Choose More Options to open the More Options dialog box, which has the Remind To Save Publication check box (see fig. 2.16).

3 Click in the Every box and then specify the time period between reminders you want.

Fig. 2.16
You can specify the duration of time between reminders to save your work.

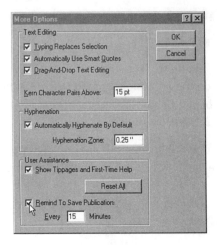

Opening and closing publications

When you launch Publisher, it's not always to start a new publication. You frequently want to work on an existing publication. Or, during a Publisher session, you might finish working on one publication and then want to move to another existing publication do to some more work on it.

Not a problem where Publisher is concerned.

Opening a publication when Publisher first launches

When you start Publisher, you see the opening Microsoft Publisher screen that has three tabs (see fig. 2.17).

- Choose the PageWizard tab to create a new publication with the help of the Wizard.

- Choose the Blank Page tab to create a new publication on your own.

- Choose the Existing Publication tab to open a publication you already saved.

The last option lets you open one of a publications you've already saved. The Existing Publication dialog box appears, listing all the publications in your system.

Fig. 2.17
The Publisher opening screen lets you choose what you want to do.

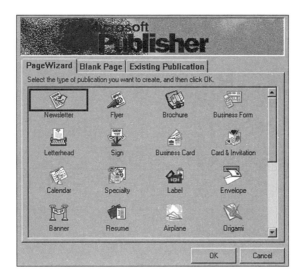

Closing a publication

Closing a publication means you remove it from your workspace, clearing your screen to make room for the next publication you want to work on. It isn't the same as exiting, which closes Publisher completely.

To close a publication, choose File, Close Publication. If you made any changes since the last time you saved the publication, Publisher asks if you want to save those changes before you close the publication.

One at a time, please

You can only have one publication open at any one time. This differs from many other software packages where you can open multiple publications and switch between them.

If you want to open an existing publication or start a new one, you must first close the current publication.

If you choose to open a new publication and you haven't saved recent changes in the current publication, you are given the opportunity to save the publication before it closes.

How to work on two publications at once

If you need to work on two publications at the same time, usually because you're cutting and pasting between them, launch another copy of Publisher.

Just click the Start button, choose Programs, Microsoft Publisher. Open the other publication (you can't load the same publication in two separate sessions).

If you don't have sufficient memory or resources and an error message appears to that effect, close any other applications that are open and try again.

Let Publisher Give You a Hand

● **In this chapter:**

- **PageWizards give step-by-step assistance**

- **Look at all these different types of publications!**

- **Special elements to put into publications**

- **A visit to the Design Gallery**

- **How can I get some help?**

Creating polished, professional documents is remarkably easy—the PageWizard does the grunt work for you. . . . . . . ▶

When I travel to someplace new (even when I have a map), sometimes I make a lot of U-turns, stop in lots of gas stations to ask directions, and generally meander around.

Sometimes I have trouble following the routes and lines on the map. Besides, driving and reading a map at the same time is a dangerous form of multi-tasking. A knowledgeable tour guide in the passenger seat would be a great help.

When I first started using Publisher, I did find a tour guide in my passenger seat: PageWizard. Not only does PageWizard get me from the starting point to the finish line, it provides additional help for all the stops along the way. This makes developing a creative, effective publication remarkably easy.

Cut your design time in half with PageWizard

Take a quick look at what PageWizard can do for you as you design and create a publication. I'll create one publication as an example, so you can get the idea. Then take a quick look at all the other types of publications available. You can see the general layout for each publication type, which makes it easier to decide on a type when you're ready to fly solo.

Abracadabra!

The first group of chores PageWizard performs is to set up the general design of the publication. As an example, I'll show you what PageWizard does with a newsletter. If you want, you can follow along with your own copy of Publisher.

Start a new publication

When you first start Publisher, you can have PageWizard work with you to design a publication by picking a publication type. If you're already working in Publisher, you can see the opening screen and have the same choices available by following these steps:

1 Save any current publication you're working on.

2 Choose File, Create New Publication.

3 Choose Newsletter, and then choose OK.

Designing a newsletter

When you start out, PageWizard gives you a number of styles to choose from. Figure 3.1 illustrates the available styles for a newsletter. You can click each style to see a description in the bottom-left corner of the dialog box and a preview of the style above the description. When you decide on a style, click Next.

 TIP **Even if you don't see exactly what you're looking for, you can** choose a style that's close, then modify it to your heart's content.

Fig. 3.1
There are lots of types of publications to choose from, and there are plenty of styles for each of them. You can find exactly what you need.

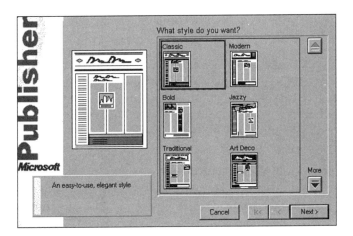

The Wizard's questions depend on what you're doing

The questions you answer and the decisions you make depend on the type of publication you create. For example, if you create a brochure, PageWizard asks about the ratio of text to pictures you prefer. For a business card, decide whether you want to print your e-mail address and your home telephone number.

CAUTION **The following newsletter styles are pre-configured—you won't have an opportunity to make the design decisions discussed for the newsletter in this book:**

Water Color

Influential

Holiday

Holiday Book-fold

Graphic Headline

School News

The PageWizard begins the setup of the pages, based on the publication. For a newsletter, these decisions are as follows:

1 PageWizard asks how many columns you want and says three columns is the most popular format for newsletters. Pick a number and click Next.

2 Now PageWizard asks how many stories there will be on the front page. The suggestion is two stories, but you can pick one, two, or three. Now choose Next.

 TIP **When you create a publication, try to imitate similar publications.** A newsletter is like a newspaper or magazine, so pick up the periodicals lying around your home or office and look at the way they're designed and assembled. For example, don't devote the entire first page to only one story (unless you're breaking some important international news, which is not a likely prospect) because that won't evoke as much interest.

Making decisions about design and layout

It's important to keep in mind the job the publication is going to do and make decisions about the layout accordingly. A brochure (usually a detailed booklet about a single subject), presents a different image than a flyer, which is a sales item that has to grab attention immediately.

A newsletter should be filled with information in the form of stories, instead of being blatantly sales oriented (although nothing stops you from using the story content to sell a concept or product in a subtle way).

3 Now you need to give your newsletter a title or a name. Enter the information and click Next (see fig. 3.2).

Fig. 3.2
Your newsletter needs a name—pick something clever or profound, depending upon the image you want to project.

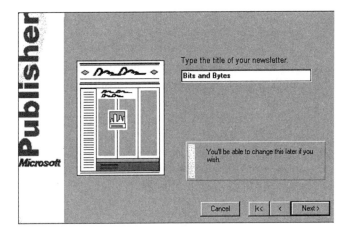

4 Now choose the optional information you want to print in the newsletter and click Next.

- A Table of Contents
- The Date
- Volume and Issue Information

 Plain English, please!

Volume and **Issue** are old publishing terms that indicate the year of publication. Volume one is the first year the publication appears; each year's birthday changes the volume number and the issue in that year. The scheme is based on a mental image of keeping each year's issues together (in some sort of volume or binder) in the proper order (by issue number). For a monthly magazine that started in January of 1994, the magazine published in November of 1995 would be Volume 2, Issue 11.

TIP **The date and volume information can be helpful for readers and** also for your own image. If your newsletter is issued monthly, you can use just the name of the month as the date. You can use the Volume and Issue portion to indicate the year (Roman numerals can be impressive) instead of a real volume number, and just omit the Issue information.

5 Tell PageWizard how many pages you want for this newsletter—don't worry, you can always change your mind and add or remove pages. PageWizard suggests four pages. Choose Next when you specify the number of pages you want.

6 Tell PageWizard if you want space allotted for a mailing label on the back of the newsletter. Do this to avoid the time, labor, and expense of putting the newsletter into an envelope in order to mail it. Then choose Next.

7 Indicate whether you want to print on both sides of the paper, or have a separate paper for each page. I've never seen a newsletter that wasn't printed on both sides. Choose Next after you select the option.

Q&A *My printer doesn't have duplex printing to print on two sides. How do I do it?*

The old-fashioned way: by inserting paper twice. Print the odd pages, then insert page one upside down to print page two and repeat that tactic to print page four on the back of page three.

Now PageWizard has all the information it needs to create your newsletter. Well, the stories aren't there yet, but you can easily take care of that. Just click Create It and sit back while PageWizard does the work.

You finished the design, now add the content

In a minute or so (depending on the speed of your computer), PageWizard announces that the design is complete, and offers to continue assisting you as you add text and graphics (see fig. 3.3). There's no good reason to turn down expert help when it's offered, so answer in the affirmative and click OK. (After you've worked in Publisher for a while, you might decide to decline the invitation. Just select No and click OK.)

Fig. 3.3
The grunt work is done and the basic design is established—now you just have to add the contents.

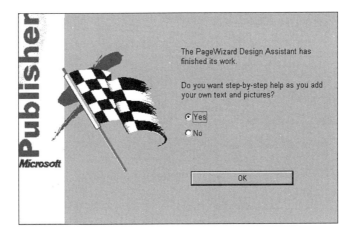

Publisher Help goes into action, listing all the steps you need to take to complete your publication (see fig. 3.4). You can get assistance on any individual task, and you don't have to select the topics or the work in any particular order.

Fig. 3.4
You can accomplish every step you need to take to finish your publication with the assistance of the on-screen Help windows.

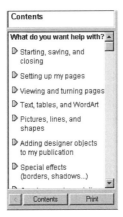

Look at the Setting Up My Pages topic. Click the arrow next to that topic to select it. Help asks you what exactly you want help with (see fig. 3.5).

Fig. 3.5
Pick a specific question to ask and you'll get an instant answer.

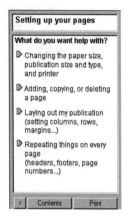

Click the arrow next to the topic on setting up headers and other repeating text. Wow! As you can see from figure 3.6, there's plenty of help here. You can learn to perform several specific tasks, or you can see a demo explaining what the background is. Click the arrow next to the topic on how to repeat everything in the same place on every page.

Fig. 3.6
The Help box is right on the screen—you can read the Help contents as you perform the tasks.

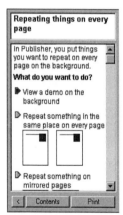

First, Help wants to know whether you already entered the object you want on every page. If you answer Yes, the instructions tell you how to turn the object into a background object and place it on all the pages in the newsletter. If you answer No, the instructions tell you how to create an object in the background.

TIP **Need even more detailed help? Many of the Help windows have a** tab labeled More Info. Click that tab to see additional explanations and some suggestions for troubleshooting problems.

The process of letting PageWizard create your publication, followed by the appearance of Publisher Help next to your workspace, always works the same way, no matter what type of publication you create.

There's a template for almost any project

There are quite a few types of publications available, and there are plenty of format choices in each type. I won't show you all of them here, but feel free to explore on your own. PageWizard can help you put together any of these:

- **Newsletter.** (Been there, done that.)

- **Brochure.** For information or marketing (see fig. 3.7).

Fig. 3.7
Scare up more business for your company with a three-panel brochure.

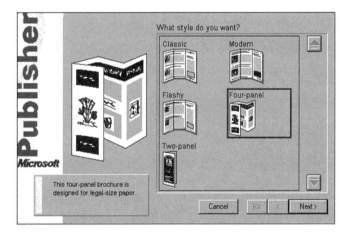

- **Flyer.** Tell the world about an event or sale, get political and endorse a candidate, or start a protest movement.

- **Letterhead.** Pick a style to match (or create) your image, then pick a layout that provides the information you want.

- **Business card.** Lots of choices, lots of styles, lots of elements to include (see fig. 3.8).

Fig. 3.8
Traditional or unconventional, Publisher can help you design a business cards to suit your style.

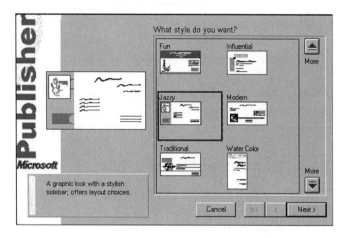

• **Envelope.** Plenty of different styles, with lots of interesting design elements.

• **Business forms.** A form for every purpose—or invent a purpose for a form you like.

• **Labels.** Plenty of styles and design elements—no matter what you need to label, you can print it easily (see fig. 3.9)

Fig. 3.9
Before you know it, you'll be creating labels for your underwear.

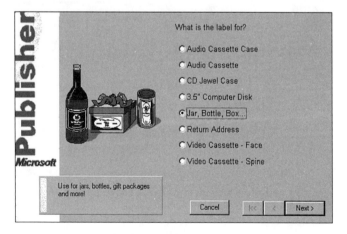

• **Signs.** For everything from wet paint warnings to "Keep Out" to sale notices.

• **Banners.** Across the hallway, between your house and the neighbor's, across the front porch to celebrate the dog's birthday—you'll never run out of occasions, and you can customize the publication so it's perfect for the banner's message.

- **Resumes.** This is one you probably shouldn't work on in the office unless you're alone. All the design elements you need to create the perfect impression.

- **Cards.** For every occasion, when you care enough to create the very best. Even put cards in cards for RSVP messages.

- **Calendars.** Monthly or yearly, you design the layout so you have everything you need—room to write notes if you want, include art work. Horizontal or vertical layouts for all styles.

- **Airplanes.** Yes, you read that right! You can publish a paper airplane, and it'll fly! Decorate the plane with designs that express your personality (or the plane's). The finished product has all the lines drawn for folding, and an instruction page prints right behind it (see fig. 3.10).

Fig. 3.10
Publisher's not only a
great office assistant,
it's a baby-sitter too!

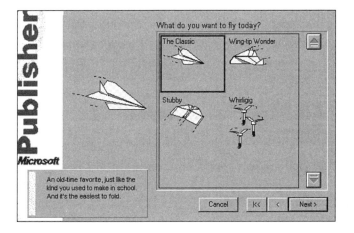

 TIP **Publisher has a wry sense of humor. You can choose options for** your paper airplane while you're designing it, such as the tail's shape, types of wing flaps, and whether you want an AM/FM radio on board. Sounds cool! But if you choose the radio, Publisher asks you to be serious—this is just a paper airplane. (And they say programmers are propeller heads without humor!)

- **Origami.** Become a designer in the ancient art of paper folding. Plenty of shapes and design options, plus instructions—but it's still challenging (see fig. 3.11).

Fig. 3.11
The cup even holds water—really!

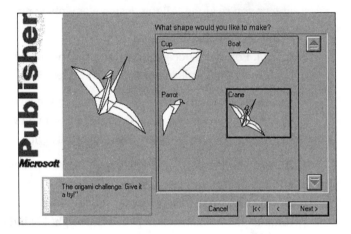

- **Specialty Publications.** For every business or personal need, there's something in this category that will be the perfect solution, from gift tags to menus. Tons of design elements and layout choices for each style.

Add special elements to a publication you already started

Even after you've got your publication underway, PageWizard can help you over some rough spots. For example, what if you want to add a calendar to your newsletter? It's easy to add any of the following to your publication:

- Calendars
- Ads
- Coupons
- Logos

To get to these features, click the PageWizard button on the Publisher toolbar and choose the one you want.

Create a calendar

There are lots of reasons to add a calendar to your publication. A flyer or brochure for an organization might need to show all the events the organization is sponsoring. A company newsletter might have a calendar listing staff birthdays or deadlines for company projects.

1 Click Calendar on the PageWizard menu.

2 Place your pointer at the position on the page where you want the left top edge of the calendar to appear. Then drag to the right and down until you have the size you think fits best (you can always change the size later).

3 When you release the mouse button, the Calendar PageWizard appears (see fig. 3.12).

Fig. 3.12
Inserting a calendar into a publication is a one-click operation with the Help of the PageWizard.

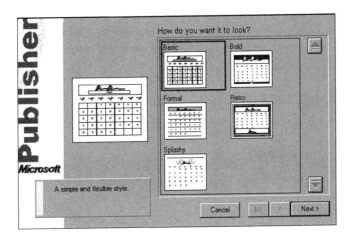

4 Choose a style and click Next. Then continue to make choices until the calendar is complete and Publisher inserts it in your publication (see fig. 3.13).

Fig. 3.13
Poof! A completed calendar, with all the elements you need.

Add an ad

You can place ads in your publication, using graphics or text (for classified ads). The Ad Wizard even helps you come up with catchy titles and slogans, then inserts the finished ad in your publication (see fig. 3.14).

 TIP **You might even want to sell some advertising space to other** companies—a great way to offset the costs of producing and mailing a newsletter.

Fig. 3.14
Where would the world be today without advertising?

Create the coupon and logo elements similarly.

Design Gallery: Guggenheim at your door!

The Design Gallery is a collection of objects that add a little zing, a little something extra, to a publication. There are fancy borders with ornate scrolls or modern lines that you can use around titles or lists; color background patterns to put behind important text boxes; even ornamental drawings you can place here and there to fill space.

To visit the gallery, click the Design Gallery icon on the Publisher toolbar. There are a number of design elements available (see fig. 3.15).

- **Headlines.** Backgrounds and borders to make your headlines special.

- **Ornaments.** Artwork to draw attention or fill space.

- **Pull Quotes.** Fancy boxes to use when you pull a line from your text and insert it in a box as a come-on to attract interest in your article.

- **Sidebars.** A box for placing additional text outside the main body of text, to highlight information.

- **Table of Contents.** Fancy backgrounds and borders to make your TOC more artistic.

- **Titles.** Borders, lines, and backgrounds to put behind titles.

Fig. 3.15
Go to the Design Gallery and choose some doo-dads from the category that matches your publication's image.

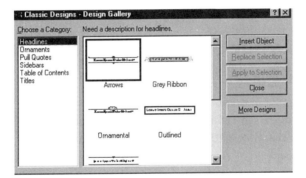

Scroll through the categories to get an idea of the range of design elements available.

You can also click <u>M</u>ore Designs to see a menu of different types of gallery exhibits that are really different "moods." When you change design groups, the categories of the design elements remain the same, but the overall styles change to match the new group.

The Classic Designs group always appears when you first open the gallery, but you can choose other design groups. For example, figure 3.16 shows some of the design elements available in the Modern Designs part of the gallery. The slick, clean look of the backgrounds and borders is quite different from the fancy scrollwork you'd find in the Classic Designs group.

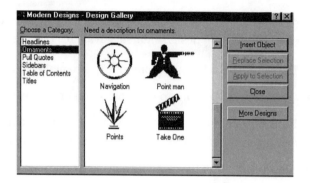

Inserting elements from the Gallery

To insert a design element from the Design Gallery into your publication,
highlight it and choose Insert Object (or, double-click the design element).
The Design Gallery dialog box closes and the object appears in your
workspace. Drag it to any position you want in the publication.

Add your own masterpieces to the Gallery

When you have a publication open in your workspace, you can put together a
group of design elements just for that publication. This becomes a **design
set** for that publication, and you can put multiple design elements in it. You
can include existing design elements gathered from all the Gallery sections
and categories. You can even edit an existing design element and save that in
your own design set.

1 Open the Design Gallery by clicking its icon.

2 Choose a category and a design element. For now, choose Sidebars as
the category (these are fancy boxes you can use to add flair to things
like a business card, letterhead, or page) and Bowtie as the design
element (see fig. 3.17).

Fig. 3.17
Choose an element to begin building a new design set.

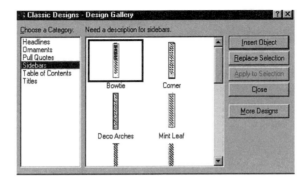

3 Insert the design element into your publication, then select it.

4 Open the Design Gallery and choose <u>M</u>ore Designs. The menu now has two new choices:

- Designs for Your Current Publication

- Add Selection to Design Gallery

5 Choose Add Selection to Design Gallery. Publisher asks if you want to start a new design set. Answer Yes, of course. The Adding an Object dialog box appears (see fig. 3.18).

6 Type a name for the element in the <u>O</u>bject Name text box and choose a <u>C</u>ategory to place it in. Choose OK.

Fig. 3.18
You can add objects to a new design group that you form for a specific publication.

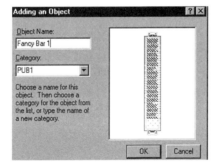

7 The Create New Category dialog box opens. Type an explanation of this new category in the Type a <u>D</u>escription text box and choose OK.

8 The Design Gallery now has a new category for your publication (see fig. 3.19). You can return to the other category sets by selecting <u>M</u>ore Designs.

Fig. 3.19
After you select a name for your new category, it's always available in the Design Gallery.

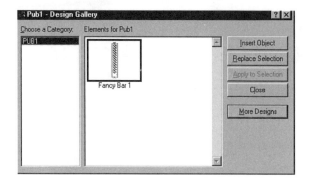

Changing a design element

I like the background pattern in one of the designs I use for headlines, but the border is a little too old fashioned for my taste. And, I love the Title design with the mint leaves but I think it needs a color background behind the text. Luckily, changing the design elements to match my own taste is no problem.

Grouping: Objects that lay together and stay together

When you select certain design elements, in addition to seeing the handles, you see an icon below the frame. That icon is called a Group button and it indicates that the design element is composed of several individual elements grouped together—they behave as a single unit when you move, copy, or insert them. You probably can't make it out, even on your own screen, but the shape of the group button is that of a button coming through a buttonhole. It's buttoned up, so to speak. When you click it, it unbuttons and you can manipulate the individual parts using their individual handles.

Another characteristic of a grouped design element is that if you move your pointer around the frame and click, you probably see small, individual frames outlined. Each of these is an element in the group.

You can take individual design elements you created or inserted and group them together. Grouping and ungrouping are functions that allow you to use a great deal of creativity.

You can find more detailed information about grouping in Chapter 16, "When Elements Overlap."

You can change any design element you insert in a publication; you can resize it or change the color scheme. And, for some design elements, you can take the design apart and use the individual parts as elements. You can also put design elements together. (See the preceding sidebar on grouping for more details.)

 TIP **Of course, you can add the newly remodeled design elements to** the Design Gallery so you don't have to reinvent the wheel every time you want that slightly different look.

I need help!

No matter how easy a program is to learn and use, there's always time when you can use a little coaching. Fortunately, as you learned earlier, there's an enormous amount of help in Publisher. In addition to handy tools like PageWizard, help on every Publisher function is never more than a click or two away.

Quick Demos

For many concepts and functions, Publisher provides a Quick Demo. Demos are listed in the Help window and the arrow that points to a demo is colored (arrows that sit next to other help items are gray). Click a demo listing's arrow to see the demo.

When the first page of the demo appears, it indicates the number of pages in the demo and provides buttons for moving around the pages. Figure 3.20 shows the first page of the Layout Guides demo.

Fig. 3.20
Demos don't just tell you about Publisher features—they show you. Don't forget the popcorn!

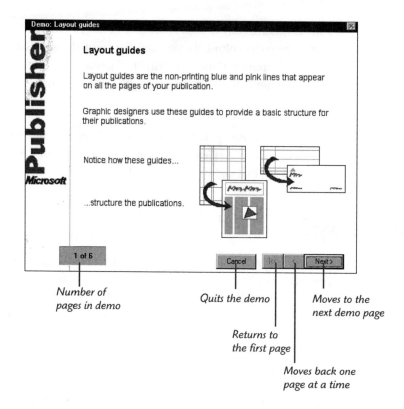

Number of pages in demo

Quits the demo

Moves to the next demo page

Returns to the first page

Moves back one page at a time

Help Index and Help Content buttons

You got a taste of how Help worked when you worked through the PageWizard. But what if you aren't using the PageWizard? Does that mean you can't get back to those handy little helpers? Of course not. Quick access to help is always available from the Status line, using the Show Index and Show Help buttons.

Click the Show Index button and both the Index and Help windows open (see fig. 3.21).

Fig. 3.21
Scroll through the
topics in the Index.
When you click a
topic of interest, the
contents of the Help
window change to
match the topic.

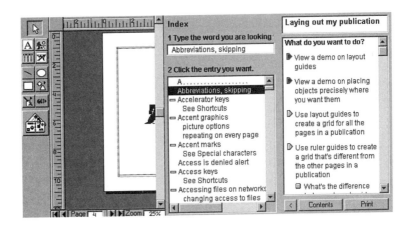

You can also enter a word in the Type the Word You Are Looking For text
box in the Index window to move immediately to the subjects connected to
that word.

When the Help windows are open, the buttons on the Status Line change to
Hide Index and Hide Help. Click them to remove the Help windows from
your workspace.

 TIP   **It can be handy to leave the Help window open while you're**
working in a particular function so you can easily get plenty of help for
each step.

What's This?

That isn't a question, it's a feature. You can find it in dialog boxes that want
you to fill in fields or enter data. For example, figure 3.22 shows the Text
Styles dialog box, which has a bunch of different choices available.

Say you want to create a new style, but you're not really sure what will
happen if you do. Placing the mouse pointer over a button or text of a choice,
and click the right mouse button. A little box opens with the message
What's This? displayed (see fig. 3.23).

Fig. 3.22

Dialog boxes some-
times offer choices or
want information you
might not understand.

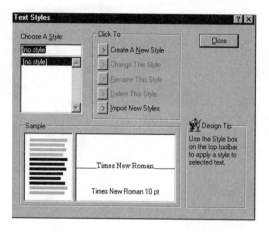

Fig. 3.23

Anytime you're not
sure about a choice in
a dialog box, just ask
Publisher "What's
This?" by clicking the
right mouse button on
the choice.

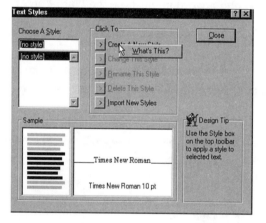

You can either type a **W** (because that's the underscored letter in the message) or click anywhere on the What's This message box to see an explanation (see fig. 3.24).

Fig. 3.24
The answer to "What's
This" gives an in-depth
explanation of the
option.

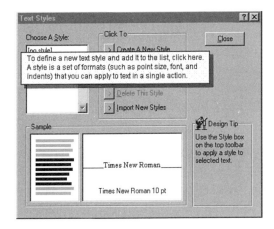

First-time help

The first time you use a feature in Publisher, Publisher explains the feature
and offers detailed explanations and help about the feature if you want it (see
fig. 3.25). If not, just click Continue.

Fig. 3.25
I wanted to change a
text style and look what
I got!

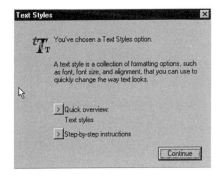

TIP **If you like the first time tips, you can reset your system so the next**
time you use a feature, you'll get the tip again:

  1 Choose Tools, Options, More Options.

  2 In the User Assistance area, click Reset All.

  3 Click OK, and then click OK again in the Options menu.

Tippages

Tippages are Help features that are really polite ways of telling you you're trying to do something incorrectly. Instead of displaying a message such as "No, fool, you can't do that!" or—even worse—just beeping at you rudely, Publisher tells you a suggestion or gives you advice about a better way to do what you're trying to do.

For example, if you enter text in a text frame that's too small for the font size you chose, Publisher tells you about the problem (see fig. 3.26). Other times, Publisher will explain a problem you created and offer to help you work through it.

Fig. 3.26
If you do something wrong, or create a problem in your publication, a Publisher Tippage appears to help you straighten things out.

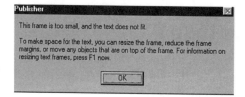

Doing It Yourself

● In this chapter:

- **I'm ready to start a new publication**

- **How can I customize the way things look while I work?**

- **Tell me how to use the tools in Publisher**

- **What do I need to know about backgrounds and foregrounds?**

- **I need to add more pages**

After you understand the theory, it's time to go to work and create a publication. There's plenty of help and lots of tools that make your work easier. . . . . **>**

Okay, you've been introduced to Publisher, you've gotten an idea of what it does and how it does it. It's time to do some hands-on work!

Now start a publication and go over some of the basic functions and elements you need.

Starting a new publication

If you're just launching Publisher, you'll land in the right place to start a new publication. If you already have Publisher open, choose File, Create New Publication. Either way, the PageWizard appears on your screen, basically asking what you want to work on next (see fig. 4.1).

Fig. 4.1
The PageWizard is waiting to walk you through every step of setting up a publica-tion, as soon as you decide what kind of publication you want to create.

I'm going to do a newsletter, but you can do whatever you want. Although, if you want to work along, choose the Newsletter, too—if you don't need one for work, write one anyway and send it to all your family and friends you owe letters to.

After you set up the basic newsletter, with the help of the PageWizard (see Chapter 3), you're ready to configure the layout of the publication so it's just perfect.

Page setup

One of the first things to do is fine-tune the setup of the pages for the publication. Some of the things to think about are:

- The size of the paper

- The size of the printed area of the paper

- Size and placement of columns and rows

- Spacing between columns

- Margins

Take a closer look at each of these issues.

First, determine the paper size and printing area

You have to decide on the paper size and the part of the paper that will actually have printing on it. Choose File, Page Setup. The Page Setup dialog box appears (see fig. 4.2).

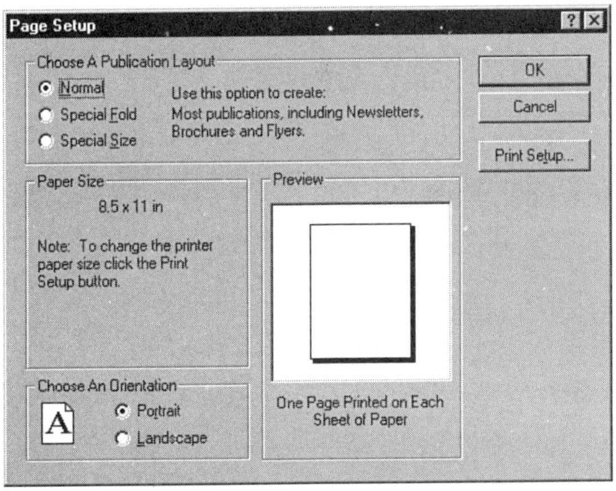

Fig. 4.2
Use the Page Setup dialog box to pick a paper size and a layout scheme.

If you're creating a publication that goes on normal paper, there's nothing much to change. However, if you're creating a card or a publication that has a special size and has to be folded just so, choose the appropriate option. The dialog box reflects that information (see fig. 4.3).

Fig. 4.3

If you have to use special paper to print your publication, the Page Setup dialog box lets you specify paper, paper folding schemes, and other special needs.

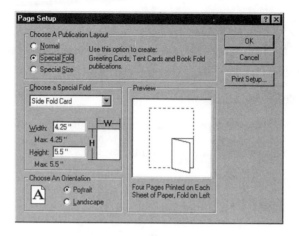

Page layout varies depending on the publication type

After the PageWizard set up my newsletter, I wanted to take a close look at it and decide for myself where to put illustrations, headlines, and so on. Figure 4.4 shows what the workspace looks like after PageWizard sets it up. I don't know about you, but my eyes can't tell a headline from text at that size!

Fig. 4.4

The newsletter is ready for me to work on, but I can't tell what's what with this display size.

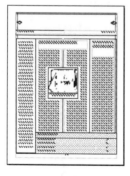

Using the Zoom feature, I can click different portions of the page and move in to see what the layout looks like (or I can zoom in on the total page and use the scroll bars to move around). Then I can use the Resize and Move options on the various frames until the layout is exactly what I want. (More information about using these functions is found in earlier chapters of this book.)

What are layout guides?

To make sure you lay out your publication in a professional and consistent manner, use **layout guides**. These are lines that appear on the pages, but they only display on the screen—they don't print. Using these guides offers some real advantages.

- Headlines, headers, the bottom lines on a page, or any other element in the publication will line up at the same place on every page.

- Graphic elements will be properly placed instead of landing just a bit too far left or right in relation to the columns.

- If you change margins, you can make sure they will be consistent for every page.

To use layout guides, choose Arrange, Layout Guides. The Layout Guides dialog box opens (see fig. 4.5). There are several sections in the dialog box, and each section has choices you can make to establish the guides you want.

Publication size

There's a difference between paper size and publication size. For some types of publications, this is obvious and easy to understand. For example, if you are printing a newsletter or flyer or letterhead on paper that is 8.5 by 11 inches, the area you use for publication is at least 1/4 inch less than that on all sides. First, most laser printers don't print along the very edges of paper; and second, it would look terrible to have text running to the absolute edge of the paper.

However, it isn't just a matter of having a little blank, unused space. Think about printing labels or business cards. You don't use a separate piece of paper stock for each item, and you might arrange several duplicates of a card side-by-side. Then, after you print, you can cut the paper. Even letterheads are printed this way at professional print shops, with duplicates put next to each other and then printed on large paper.

On the opposite end of the spectrum are banners. You might have a banner that's three feet long, but the paper size you use is still probably 8.5 by 11 inches (in this case, you paste paper together).

Fig. 4.5
Use the Layout Guides dialog box to divvy up your page so you can place objects with precision.

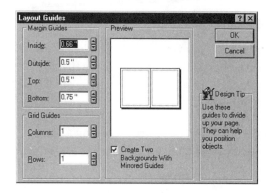

 Q&A *Why does my Layout Guide setup show only one column and one row when I'm doing a three-column newsletter?*

The multiple columns you need should be individual frames, and you deal with the columns by dealing with the frames. The layout guide deals with the setup of the page. The margins are page margins and are there to make sure the edges of the publication are consistent—that the white space between the end of text and the physical edge of the paper remains constant for every page.

Some hints about professional appearance

The mirrored margins are an important issue, and if your publication has facing pages, it won't look right without them. Picture two facing pages in a book with left margins of a half inch and right margins of three quarters of an inch. That's not usually how professional publications are put together. Instead, the left page would have those margins, but the right page would reverse the margins. That way, the distance between the center of the two pages and the point at which text appears would be equal. The distance from the outside edge of the paper to the text area would also be equal.

Another design element is that text for such publications is usually justified on both the left and right sides. Otherwise, careful consideration about margin widths would be irrelevant.

Mirrored guides

At the bottom of the Preview area of the Layout Guides dialog box is the Create Two Backgrounds With Mirrored Guides check box. This is an important issue when your publication has facing pages, because you need to mirror the margins, not duplicate them.

 Plain English, please!

Facing pages are the two pages that are side by side in a book or other publication that has printing on both sides. The page on the left is always an even-numbered page, and the page on the right is always odd-numbered. There is no facing page for the first or last page of a multi-page publication.

 Plain English, please!

The space between the pages is called the **gutter** (where the binding or fold is). You should always plan your gutter width to accommodate any binding devices (real binding, three-ring punch holes, staples, whatever) with white space left over.

Margin guides

In the Layout Guides dialog box, you can set margins for the Inside, Outside, Top, and Bottom of the page layout.

 Plain English, please!

An **inside margin** is the one next to the gutter; an **outside margin** is the one next to the other side of the page. This only applies to mirrored pages (when you print on both sides of the paper). For example, the left page's right margin is the inside margin.

Grid guides

You can have grid guides for columns and rows. You can make column guides equal or uneven in width, depending on the publication type and the effect you want to create.

You establish row guides when you want horizontal control over the placement of the text and design elements in your publication. You can have equally spaced or uneven rows.

To understand the best use of these guides, picture the way a magazine looks, using a page that has a story and also has advertisements around the story. You'll notice that every page in the magazine places the edge of advertisements at the same place on every page. If there are ads to the right of the columns that contain the story, the left edge of every ad is in the same spot, and the right column of every line in the story is in the same spot.

What display options do you want?

The way the workspace looks as you create and fine-tune your publication is important, because you need to create an environment you find easy to work in.

Also, there are some aspects of your work that need specific parameters. For example, if you're looking at inches but the project (and the printer) require points, you need to do something about that.

You set display options by choosing Tools, Options. The Options dialog box opens (see fig. 4.6).

Fig. 4.6
Use the Options dialog box to design a set of working conditions you're comfortable with. You can specify the way everything in your Publisher workspace looks and works.

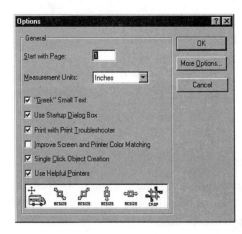

How can I measure the objects on my page?

Depending on the specifications for the project you intend your publication for, you might need to work and think in measurement units other than inches. The available measurement units are:

- Inches
- Centimeters
- Picas
- Points

 Plain English, please!

Inches and **centimeters** are, of course, standard units of measurement. But picas and points are measurements used in printing.

A **point** is a measure of height. To give you a frame of reference, think about the standard Courier type that comes out of a typical dot-matrix printer. The height of that type is 12 points.

A **pica** is also a measurement of height and represents 12 points. Because points are so small, if you choose to use them, the ruler on your screen will indicate picas (otherwise you probably wouldn't be able to see the individual markings).

Points versus CPI

Points are a measure of the height of a character, not a measure of width or the number of characters you can fit in an inch. Dot-matrix printers and other printing standards occasionally refer to **CPI** (characters per inch). In fact, the Courier typeface I referred to previously as being 12 points high is measured at 10 CPI by the printer's documentation and also in many software packages that display a printer's internal fonts for you to choose from. There is no real relationship between the two measurements, and

you should never confuse them. Other 10 CPI typefaces might not be 12 points high.

Professional printers never use CPI, they only use points or picas when they talk about size.

A typeface that has really wide characters can be 12 points in height and only fit a couple of characters in an inch. When you make a string of characters bold, you frequently fit fewer characters in the same space, but they don't get taller—the points don't change.

Greeking small text

In the printing industry, it's common to use the term **greeking** to indicate the process of filling in parts of a publication with Greek letters and words when you're looking at some sort of display of the publication instead of the real thing. That display can be your computer screen or a "mock-up" or "rough" display used to present ideas, or any other interpretation of a product not yet in its final stages. Publisher doesn't really display Greek letters, it uses meaningless, nonsense words to establish greeking.

Publisher uses the term slightly differently and offers to "greek in" small type when you're working in the software. It means that gray bars will display whenever text is smaller than seven points. Don't worry, the real characters will print—it's just faster to work and redraw the screen if all those teeny characters don't have to be displayed.

By default, greeking is turned on.

Seeing the Publisher Opening dialog box every time you start Publisher

By default, your system is set up to make sure you see the dialog box that presents choices about what you want to do every time you start Publisher. That way, you can choose to start a new publication with the help of the PageWizard, or open an existing publication, or go to a blank page. If you deselect this option, you see a blank page every time you launch the software and, if you want to use the PageWizard or work on an existing publication, you have to use the menus and toolbar buttons to get there.

Troubleshooting printing problems

You can have Publisher keep an eye on your printing and offer troubleshooting guidelines and help whenever there's a problem by selecting this option. The Print Troubleshooter makes suggestions about your printer setup and your publication to help you when there's a problem.

Matching colors

The colors on your monitor don't always exactly match the color that will print on either your own color printer or an outside printer. You can force the system to improve the match between the monitor and the final output by choosing this option.

Create an object with one click

Another extremely useful feature is the Single Click Object Creation option. By selecting this option, you can click a shape button on the Publisher toolbar (such as the rectangle) and then click a page to insert the shape. Publisher places the center of the shape at the point of your mouse pointer. If you need to resize it, just use the selection handles.

The process is much longer if you deselect this option. To draw a rectangle, you have to click the button, bring your mouse to the page, and drag the mouse horizontally and vertically to create the shape.

Change the mouse pointers to match the job they're doing

One of the cool tools Publisher provides is a device called Helpful Pointers. As you move the mouse pointer around a selected portion of your publication, the mouse pointer changes from an arrow to something designed to be helpful. If your pointer is near a corner of a frame, for example, it changes to a Resizer.

By default, Use Helpful Pointers is enabled in the Options dialog box (refer to fig. 4.6). If you have a reason to stick with a plain arrow, you can deselect this option (although I can't personally think of any reason that sounds logical or makes sense).

Click More Options to open the More Options dialog box (see fig. 4.7).

Typeover versus Insert Mode

By default, when you enter text at a point that has existing text, the new text types over and replaces the old text. In word processors, this is called Typeover Mode. If you want to enter new text and have it push existing text along in front of it, deselect this option (this is called Insert Mode).

Fig. 4.7
There are options for editing, user assistance, and other features in the More Options dialog box.

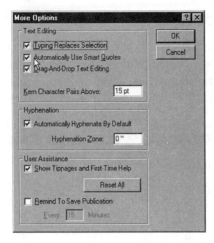

Smart quotes

By default, the option to use smart quotes automatically is selected for you.

Smart quotes are quotation marks that are smart enough to know which end is up—or, rather, which end is first and which is last. On the standard typewriter and computer keyboard, there is only one key with quotation marks. And, unless you use software that can do something to change it, the quotation marks look the same and face the same way no matter where you type them. It doesn't make any difference if the quotation mark is at the beginning of the quote or at the end. That can mean the beginning quotation mark is facing or leaning the wrong way—away from the quote.

You never see dumb quotes (what else would you call them?) in professionally published documents, so Publisher offers to change all quotation marks so there is a difference between the opening and closing quote marks. Like this:

> "The quotation marks here are leaning (facing) in different directions so they seem to enclose this sentence."

Dragging text

The Drag-And-Drop Text Editing option lets you highlight a block of text and then drag it to a new position. If you disable this choice you have to use Cut and Paste after you select the text. This is a handy feature, and there is no good reason to disable it.

Kerning makes spacing look more professional

You can specify a size (in points) above which Publisher will **kern** pairs of characters. This means that Publisher adjusts the spacing between characters. Kerning is a typographical term that means spacing between characters depends on their shapes. For example, if you type **WA**, kerning pushes the left side of the A closer to (and under) the right side of the W. When characters get larger, especially in headlines, the white space stands out; kerning makes your text look professionally typeset.

Hyphenation eliminates ugly white space

If you let Publisher hyphenate automatically, you'll find that you have fewer gaps—or white spaces—between words and at the end of lines. This feature is selected by default, and there isn't a particularly good reason to change that.

You can also set the Hyphenation Zone, which is the minimum width of a gap required to force hyphenation. If you make the zone smaller, there are fewer gaps—but more words have to be hyphenated to produce that effect. Sometimes the abundance of hyphenated words is more annoying than the gaps.

How much assistance do you want from Publisher?

Publisher performs two helpful procedures that you can enable or disable.

If you select Show Tippages and First-Time Help, the first time you use a feature, Publisher shows a Help message that gives you a head start on using that feature. And, if you do something wrong (or, at least something out of the ordinary), a Tippage appears to explain the mistake to you and suggest a solution.

You can select Reset All to configure Publisher to think you've never used any features. Publisher will then show the first-time help the next time you use each feature.

In addition, you can ask Publisher to remind you to save your work and specify the amount of time that should elapse between each reminder.

CAUTION   **The Remind To Save feature is not the same as auto-save, which is** in many software applications. Publisher merely displays a dialog box reminding you that it's time to save your work. You can choose Yes to perform the save or No to keep working without saving.

In the background...

When you were a kid, did you ever have one of those magic slates that had a sheet of plastic over a hard surface? You used a stylus to draw and write on the plastic, and when you lifted the plastic up, all your work disappeared.

What you probably didn't think about was that when you lifted the plastic, you had access to the hard surface—the background. And, if you drew on the background, that drawing would show through the plastic top sheet. In fact, no matter how many times you lifted the top sheet and put it back to change your artwork, that background drawing would continue to show.

Here's how this translates to Publisher: for every page in your publication, there's another page lurking behind it—the **background**. You can place elements on the background; they appear on every page of your publication.

What goes on the background?

The background of a publication holds the elements and objects that appear on every page of your publication, such as:

- A logo
- A color strip across the top or bottom of the page
- The grid lines that keep the layout consistent
- Headers and footers
- A page numbering system
- Anything else you think of

Getting to the background, and back again

To move to the background, choose <u>V</u>iew, G<u>o</u> to Background. To move back to your publication, choose <u>V</u>iew, G<u>o</u> to Foreground. Or, you can press Ctrl+M to toggle between the two.

Most of the time it's not very hard to tell whether you're on the foreground or the background—unless you have a blank page. Figure 4.8 shows a view of the foreground of a blank page and figure 4.9 shows a view of the background of the same page.

Fig. 4.8

The foreground of a blank page.

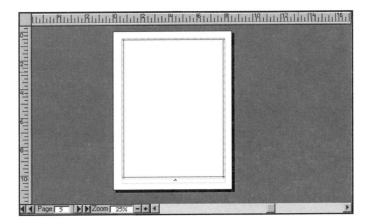

Fig. 4.9

The background of a blank page. (I promise, this is a different figure!)

Hard to tell the difference, isn't it? Look more carefully, or do this on your own screen and look carefully.

The difference is on the Status bar. When you work in the foreground, you see the page buttons and a page number indicator box—to the left of the Zoom button. When you work in the background, the page controls are replaced by the background page icon, which looks like a rectangle. In fact, in figure 4.9, two background pages appear, because the formatting for this newsletter has mirror margin setups and there's a left background page and a right background page.

Hiding the background

You can hide one or all of the elements on the background. This isn't something you do because you don't want to look at the background items; what hiding really means is **suppressing** the background object, not letting it print.

The capability to hide the background is handy in several scenarios:

- You have a template you use for all publications of a certain type (perhaps flyers) and one or more of the background elements isn't appropriate for the flyer you're preparing today.

- You don't want to put a certain background item on every page— perhaps only the left pages or only the right pages.

- Your background includes a company name and address as a header, and you don't want it to print on the first page because you already have a complete logo there.

To give a practical example, when I prepare a training manual, I like to give students plenty of space for note-taking. Most of the time, I try to use the left page for that purpose, with the text and illustrations appearing on the right. In this case, the background might have:

- A nice wide band of color down the outside edge to make each page look interesting and professional

- A company name and logo and telephone number across the bottom (Always advertise!)

- The name of the course across the top of each page

- The words "Your Notes" below the name of the course

The last item is hidden on all the odd, or recto, pages.

 Plain English, please!

In publishing jargon, the words "odd" and "even" aren't really used to explain page positions. After all, suppose the pages don't have numbers printed? For precision, the terms are **recto** and **verso**.

Recto means the page that appears on the right and also means "read first." Odd pages are always recto pages.

Verso means the page that appears on the left and also means "read second." Even pages are always verso pages.

You can hide the whole background for one page

If you want, you can eliminate all background items for one or more pages of your publication.

1 Use the Change Pages button to move to the page of which you want to eliminate the background.

2 Choose View, Ignore Background. This places a check mark next to that option.

If you want to put the background items back on that page, follow the same steps. When you choose Ignore Background again, it removes the check mark.

You can do the same thing for any additional pages you want to print without any background objects.

Note that when you are working on any other page in your publication, there is no check mark on the Ignore Background option.

Or just one background object on one page

The way to suppress the printing of one background object on a single page is to cover it with something that prints over it, but doesn't really print. Sound confusing? It really isn't. What you have to do is cover the object on the page that doesn't need it. If you eliminate the object altogether, it won't print on any pages, which isn't what you're trying to do.

1 Move to the page where you need to remove the background object.

2 Make sure you are on the foreground, not the background.

3 Create a text frame and size it so it covers the background object. Click the Text Frame button, then position the pointer in the upper-left corner of the background object you want to hide. Drag the mouse down and right until you cover the background object.

TIP You can also insert a rectangle with a white fill and no border.

You created an object (the text frame) that prints over the object under it (the background object). But, because there's no text in the text frame, you get a blank space. Empty text frames don't show up in printing.

Q&A *I created a blank text frame to cover a background object and the frame prints. What can I do?*

Your text frame has a border, and it's the border that's printing. Go to the frame and click it to select it, then click the Border button and choose None.

Or one background object on all pages

If your background has an object on it that you don't want to see when you print this particular publication, you can hide it rather than delete it. That way, it is still available for another printing of this publication or even as a template of another publication.

Use the same concept (putting a non-printing object over the object you want to hide) and the same steps used to hide a background object on one page, except *you must move to the background to create the empty text frame.* When you want the background object to print again (perhaps on the next publication), just move to the background and delete the text frame.

Adding and deleting pages

Regardless of the decisions you made when you first formatted and configured your publication, you can add and delete pages at will.

Inserting pages

Here's the plot:

You're on the third page of a four-page publication. You already formatted the back page and filled it with stuff that must be on the last page. But the article you're working on is going to be too long to fit on the third page, you need more space. You don't want to move to a smaller font. And you certainly don't want to cut any of your wonderful prose. The only solution is to add a page. But you already told the PageWizard that this is a four-page publication.

Don't worry. You can change just about everything you tell the PageWizard. And adding a page is a piece of cake.

1 Choose Insert, Page, which opens the Insert Page dialog box (see fig. 4.10).

Fig. 4.10
Use the Insert Page dialog box to add pages to your publication.

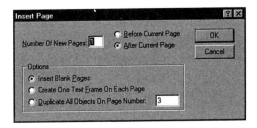

2 Specify the Number of New Pages you want to add.

3 Enter the new page(s) before the current page or after the current page.

4 In the Options area, choose one of the following:

- Insert Blank Pages

- Create One Text Frame on Each Page (the new page will have a single text frame that extends to the margins)

- Duplicate All Objects On Page Number (insert the page number you want to clone)

When you're finished, choose OK.

Adding Pages

Same plot, new twist. You're rolling along, writing, inserting graphics, and you're almost at the end of page four of a four-page publication (the last page isn't formatted for anything special). You could fill another whole page with your prolific prose.

Don't worry, this one's easy. To append a page at the end of a publication, just click the Next Page button on the Status bar. Publisher knows you're on the last page, and figures out what you're trying to do. Up pops a message asking if you want to insert a new page, just in case you clicked the button accidentally (see fig. 4.11). Just say OK.

Fig. 4.11

If you try to move to the next page when there isn't a next page, Publisher will insert a next page.

TIP   **When you create a newsletter or brochure that you'll staple or** fold, it should always have an even number of pages. If you append a fifth page to a publication that started out as a four-page publication, you should also create a sixth page to avoid the "blank page at the back" syndrome, which is pretty unprofessional looking. When this happens to me, and I've run out of things to say, I find a graphic and make it fairly large, placing an appropriate caption under it. For example, in May, I might find a piece of artwork that looks like a nice lady and then put "don't forget to send your mother greetings for Mother's Day" under it. I also make sure the header, footer, or any graphical designs print on that last page so it looks like I planned it.

Deleting a page

You can delete a page by choosing <u>E</u>dit, Delete Page. Of course, you have to confirm your action and tell Publisher you really mean to do this (see fig. 4.12).

Fig. 4.12

Just in case you didn't really mean to do it, Publisher makes sure you wanted to delete a page.

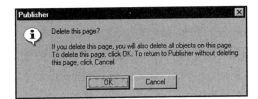

Part II: Working with Words

5

Working with Text Frames

● In this chapter:

- **How my words look is just as important as what they say**

- **Setting up text frames**

- **How do I set the text properties?**

- **Connecting and disconnecting text frames**

The writing is brilliant and sparkling, the humor so wonderful that you'll roll on the floor, the information is earth-shattering in its importance. So why is my report still in your in basket?. . . . .

The way you format and present contents is as important to the effectiveness of your publication as the words you use.

Your publication is a message. Actually, it's a lot of messages. It says what it says, meaning it imparts information. But the format and the layout also send messages—about you, your business, your level of professionalism, or even your credibility.

You need to think carefully about the text you put in your publication, considering not only the words and the message, but also the impact of the placement of text. What will the overall layout look like to readers and what subliminal messages are you sending? What's the positioning? While I can't cover all the subtleties of marketing strategies, I can go over some of the tools you have to help your audience read between the lines.

Placing text in a publication

For the purpose of demonstration, create a new publication so you can practice placing and playing around with text. I'm starting from scratch with a blank page, which I'll design myself, adding text and artwork as needed.

The look of your publication reflects your positioning

In the world of advertising, there's a concept known as **positioning**. It's separate from advertising. The look and feel of your publication contribute to your positioning.

For example, you might see ads for two furniture stores, both selling similar furniture for about the same price. One store has a headline pushing low prices and shows lots of furniture in the ad. This store is positioning itself as a discount store with plenty of stock on hand. The other store shows only a few pieces of furniture and the headline is

more subtle, referring to special prices. The positioning is to make you understand that this is an expensive store carrying high-end items that happens to be having a sale.

Both stores are sending a message beyond the price of the items on sale, they're telling their audience who they are. The first store wants customers who price-shop. The second store wants customers who will pay a premium price for better made articles (and who like the image of shopping at expensive stores). There are plenty of customers for both kinds of stores.

You can follow along with a similar project, or use a publication style from PageWizard.

The first decision is placing the text. If you have a picture to add, do you want the text above or below it? After you decide (I'm putting text above the artwork), you have to get the page ready to accept text.

Inserting a text frame

To put text in a publication, there has to be a text frame. To insert a text frame, click the Text Frame button on the Publisher toolbar, then move your pointer to the page, positioning it at the place where you want to insert the text frame.

You have two ways to insert your text frame:

- You can click the mouse pointer on the page to have a text frame appear instantly

- You can place the mouse pointer on the edge of the area where you want to place the text frame and drag across and down. When the frame is approximately the size you need, release the mouse button.

Either way, you have a text frame, it's selected (you can see the selection handles), and the cursor is blinking in the upper-left corner of the frame, waiting for you to begin typing (see fig. 5.1).

Fig. 5.1
The text frame is ready
for text entry.

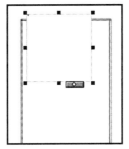

Add some text appeal

The properties of a text frame are those elements that determine the way it looks.

- Fonts

- Text size

- Margins

- Tabs

- Alignment

You can enter text immediately after you insert a frame, and then make changes to the properties, or you can set the properties immediately and enter the text after you're satisfied with the design. Or, a little of both.

Just so you can see the effects of changes in the properties, go ahead and enter some text in the frame.

Because the default font size is 10 points (which is rather small), the first keystroke produces a Publisher Tippage offering a suggestion for making the work easier (see fig. 5.2).

Fig. 5.2
Working in small type can be difficult, so Publisher offers a solution.

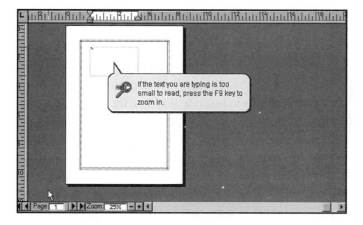

Press F9 to move in, and enter the text. You can use the F9 key to toggle in and out as you work. When you enter the text you want in the frame, it's time to create a real publication by setting properties.

Pick a font

Fonts have personalities. There are sober fonts, and fonts with a flair; there are fancy fonts, and more. There are even fonts that seem to have no personality (I personally find fonts like Courier pretty dull, although it's easy to read). Pick a font that's compatible with the text and the overall impression of your publication. For example, it wouldn't work well if you used a funky-looking font for a sober, serious subject or a font with scrolls and fancy curls for the fine print in a contract.

 Plain English, please!

A **font** is a collection of characters that have a specific look and have a name (for instance, Century Schoolbook or Courier). Each individual character in the collection looks similar in style to all the other characters in the collection. You can learn a great deal more about fonts in Chapter 7. *99*

The font Publisher automatically uses is Times New Roman, which works well for many things. But if you want something different, you can easily change it. To do this, select the text frame to show its handles. The Text Formatting toolbar appears, including the Font list box that displays all the fonts installed in your system.

Highlight all the text in the text frame, or just the part of the text you want to change, then press the arrow to the right of the Font list box (see fig. 5.3).

Fig. 5.3
Go wild—choose a font that makes people notice.

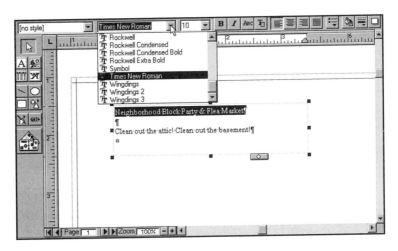

Choose a font—you see the change in your text immediately. You can keep changing fonts until you find one that pleases you.

Is this a good size?

You can also change the size of the font by using the text formatting toolbar. With text selected, click the arrow next to the Font Size list box and choose a font size. Remember that the font size is a measure of points (height). The change is made immediately.

TIP **You should always make font changes before making size changes,** because some fonts have limited sizes available.

Figure 5.4 shows text formatted differently (different fonts and different sizes) for each line. The first line is big and bold, announcing an event; the second line goes on to provide more details in a quieter, calmer voice.

Fig. 5.4
Mixing different fonts and sizes is sometimes effective.

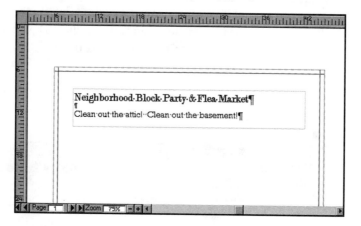

TIP **By creating a different text frame for each type of information,** you can better control the appearance and configuration. You can place details and body in one text frame, headlines in another. This makes formatting a bit easier.

The finished page has all the necessary frames inserted and fonts and sizes chosen. I even added some graphics to make it more interesting (see fig. 5.5).

Now it's time to clean up the rest of the formatting and configuration to make it perfect.

Fig. 5.5
The page is filled with all the frames needed for this publication.

Margins, tabs, and alignment

For an effective publication, you need to correctly space the text, align it properly, and generally make it readable and attractive.

Text frame margins

Start with the margins. Besides the margins you set for the page, there are also margins for each text frame. A **text frame margin** is the space between the edge of the frame and the contents of the frame. This is especially important if your frame has a border of some kind.

Now set margins for a text frame.

1 Select the frame.

2 Choose Format, Text Frame Properties to open the Text Frame Properties dialog box shown in figure 5.6.

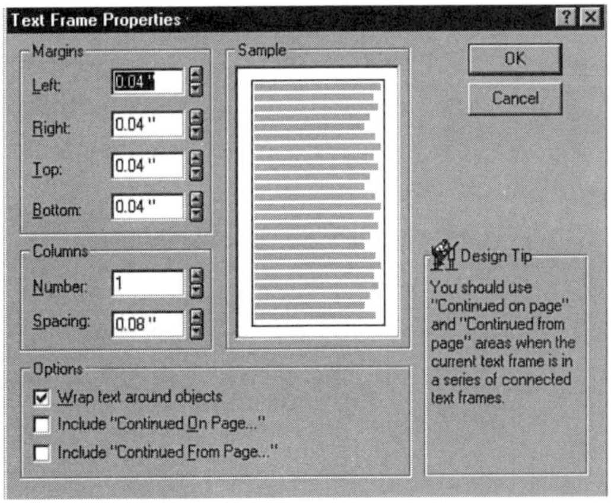

Fig. 5.6
This is the place to customize the frame you selected.

3 In the Margins area of the dialog box, specify the margins for all four sides.

Repeat the process for each text frame. It can be effective to have different margins for different frames, depending on the contents.

TIP   **The text frame margin settings you establish affect the look and** readability of your text. It isn't generally a good idea to have different margins left and right, but different margins top and bottom usually aren't troublesome.

The more white space you have, the easier it is for the reader's eye to catch the message in the frame. So don't make the margins too narrow.

Q&A   *I set my frame margins wider to get more white space and now I can't see any text. What happened?*

Your new margins probably didn't leave enough space in the frame for the text. Widen the frame or reduce the font size (or put the margins back the way they were).

Some paragraphs stand out better if you use tabs

You can set tabs for the text in a text frame the same way you set tabs in any word processor. Select the text frame and notice that the ruler highlights the area occupied by the text frame (see fig. 5.7).

Click here to change the tab type

The ruler shows you exactly where your frame is on the page, and how big it is

Fig. 5.7
The ruler highlights the width of the selected text frame.

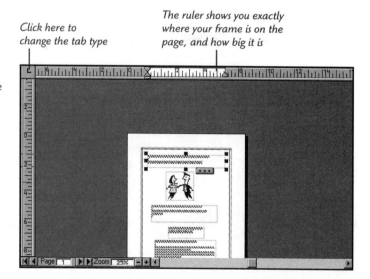

To set a left tab, click the ruler at the point you want the tab stop. When the cursor is on a line of text and you press the Tab key, everything to the right of the cursor jumps over to align with the tab you just set. You can enter as many tab settings as you need.

Of course, there are other types of tabs besides left tabs.

- **Right tabs** move the pointer to the tab setting and then push text to the left as you type. This works well if you're typing a list of numbers so that three digit numbers line up properly under two digit numbers.

- **Center tabs** move the pointer to the tab setting and then alternate moving the text left and right so the text stays centered around the tab setting. This is handy for titles or headlines over columns of text.

- **Decimal tabs** move the pointer to the tab setting and push all text entry to the left until you type a decimal point. Then all text entry is placed on the right of the decimal point. This is the only way to align columns of numbers that have varying numbers of characters after the decimal point.

To set these other tab types, move the pointer to the left side of the ruler (the mouse pointer turns into a double-headed arrow). Click the L (for left) to see the next tab type. Keep clicking until you find the tab type you want, then click the Ruler at the point you want the tab stop.

The appearance of the tab types vary so you know what kind of tab you're inserting:

- An L is a left tab

- A vertical line is a centered tab

- A vertical line with a dot next to it is a decimal tab

- A backwards L is a right tab

For more precise settings, or if you need to set a lot of tabs, you might try another approach. Select the text frame and choose F<u>o</u>rmat, <u>T</u>abs. The Tabs dialog box appears (see fig. 5.8).

Fig. 5.8

If you need real precision for a tab setting (perhaps down to an eighth of an inch), or you want to change the leading characters in front of a tab, using the Tabs dialog box is the answer.

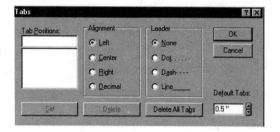

Indents: like tabs but different

You can also indent a paragraph of text. **Indenting** means that when you move the first line of the paragraph to the tab stop, the rest of the lines move with it. This is a way to make a single paragraph stand out.

To see the effect of indenting, look at figure 5.9, which shows several paragraphs of a publication in which there are no special effects to make one paragraph more important (or easier to notice) than another.

Fig. 5.9

A standard page of text with no special treatment for any of the paragraphs.

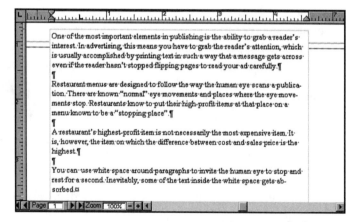

The third paragraph is an interesting tidbit of information that's not directly concerned with the information discussed in the publication. Because the writer felt it was an interesting fact, there was a feeling that if the reader could be "hooked" by glancing at this paragraph, there was a better chance the reader would go back and read the entire article.

To make the paragraph stand out a bit, and catch the eye of a casual reader, indent it.

1 Select the paragraph you want to indent.

2 Choose F<u>o</u>rmat, <u>I</u>ndents and Lists, to display the Indents and Lists dialog box (see fig. 5.10).

Fig. 5.10
To make a paragraph special, I created indentations for both sides of the text's margins.

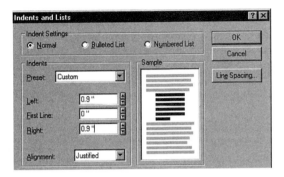

3 Specify the measurement options available in the Indents area of the dialog box. You can indent both from the left and the right, which creates white space on both sides of the paragraph.

Notice that the preview in the Sample area changes to reflect your choices. Choose OK when you finish to see the results in the publication (see fig 5.11).

Fig. 5.11
The indentation attracts attention to the paragraph.

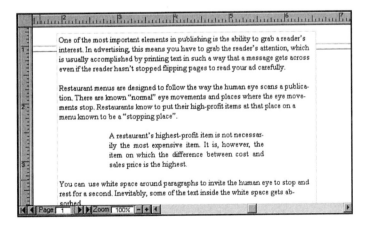

Alignment is an important tool, too

If you use headlines and titles and specially formatted paragraphs, their effectiveness lessens if you don't position them properly. Usually, the positioning problems are alignment problems.

TIP   **The process of aligning text involves a host of features, but for** now I'll talk about the position of the text relative to the margins. For more involved alignment functions, see Chapter 8.

There are four choices for aligning text:

- **Align Left**. The left side of the text lines up and the right side is uneven.

- **Align Right.** The right side of the text lines up and the left side is uneven.

- **Align Center**. Each line is centered and the left and right edges of the text are uneven depending on the length of the line.

- **Justify Text.** Both the right and left sides of the text line up.

To set the alignment of a paragraph:

1   Click anywhere in the paragraph.

2   Click the appropriate alignment button from the text formatting toolbar.

In figure 5.12, you see a text frame with paragraphs that have been formatted with Center and Justified alignment, each decision being made on the basis of what was appropriate for the paragraph.

Use 'em sparingly

You have to be careful when you choose to Center or Justify text.

Centering doesn't work very well with regular body text. It's difficult to read text when each line of the paragraph stops and ends at a different place. Reserve center alignment for titles and headlines.

Justified can create some additional problems. To reach the same spot on the right for every line in the text, there has to be some playing around with the spacing between letters. This can cause some very strange white space gaps.

Justified text is always turned off automatically for the last line of a paragraph—imagine trying to justify a line that has two or three words.

Fig. 5.12
Mixing Center and
Justified alignment
makes a text frame
easier to read.

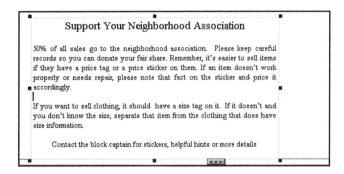

Hyphenation

Keeping text neat and clean without a lot of white spaces at the end of a line is a lot easier if you hyphenate words. Otherwise, if the last word in a line is long and won't fit, it gets pushed to the next line, and the gaping hole it leaves usually looks unprofessional.

By default, Publisher automatically hyphenates (unless you disable it in the Options dialog box). However, you can change the default option for specific text by selecting the text and choosing Tools, Hyphenate. The Hyphenate dialog box appears (see fig. 5.13).

Fig. 5.13
Sometimes you want to
change the way
hyphenation works.

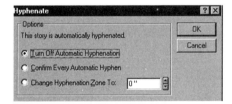

This dialog box works a little different than most. The first choice always displays the reverse of the currently selected option, and it is already selected. If automatic hyphenation is operating, the choice is to Turn Off Automatic Hyphenation. Just click OK to implement it. The next time you return to the dialog box, the pre-selected choice is Automatically Hyphenate This Story and, again, just click OK to implement it.

You can also opt to be shown every hyphen so you can approve it (or move it to another space in the word if possible).

If you want, you can change the **hyphenation zone**. This is a measurement of the amount of space you're willing to accept at the end of a line before forcing hyphenation. The larger the zone, the fewer hyphens (but more ragged edges).

For instance, if you're willing to accept up to .75" of white space before forcing a hyphen (the default is .25"), then Publisher will hyphenate fewer words. However, you will have some lines that have .75" of white space between the last word on the line and the right margin. This is bothersome to some people, but then, lots of hyphenated words can be equally bothersome.

Connect frames so text flows into another frame

You can connect text frames to each other, forming an abiding relationship between them. This is a way to begin a story in one frame and have it move automatically to another frame when you fill the first frame.

You'll find this useful if a story begins on the first page and continues to another page, and also if a graphic (or something similar) divides a story on the same page.

It's also helpful when you edit the text. You don't have to keep redoing the frames, because they automatically give and take as necessary.

After you define and size a text frame and you start to enter text, if you enter too much text to fit the frame, Publisher hides the extra text in an "overflow area."

Even though Publisher hides the text that didn't fit, it tells you what it's done. When you select a text frame, a Connect button appears at the bottom. This button is a clue to the amount of text assigned to the frame. If the Connect button has three dots on it, there's more text in the frame than is being displayed (see fig. 5.14). If the Connect button displays a diamond, what you see is what there is.

Fig. 5.14
Three dots on the Connect button give you a quick clue that there's more text in the frame than is being displayed.

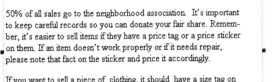

50% of all sales go to the neighborhood association. It's important to keep careful records so you can donate your fair share. Remember, it's easier to sell items if they have a price tag or a price sticker on them. If an item doesn't work properly or if it needs repair, please note that fact on the sticker and price it accordingly.

If you want to sell a piece of clothing, it should have a size tag on it. If it doesn't, and you don't know the size, separate that item from the clothing that does have size information.

Connect button—there's more to this story

Making the connection

To connect text frames, you need an overcrowded frame and a new, empty frame. Then, just click the Connect button on the overflowing frame, move to the empty frame, and click. When you click the Connect button, the shape of your mouse pointer turns into a pitcher. You're supposed to pretend the pitcher is filled with excess text, and the second click on the empty frame "pours" the text into that frame.

If the second frame is small and all the text in the pitcher doesn't fit, this frame will also display three dots on its Connect button. Repeat the process with as many connected frames as you need to accommodate the text. It's like playing "follow the dots."

Q&A *I have overflow text but I don't want to connect it to a new frame. How can I solve the problem without cutting some of my text?*

Just enlarge the frame. When you select the frame, the selection handles provide a way to stretch it. Move the mouse pointer over one of the handles (the pointer changes to a Resizer) and drag in the direction that enlarges the frame. You can make it wider or deeper, whatever fits best.

Disconnecting frames

If you connect a text frame to another one, the Connect button looks like a section of a chain-link fence (see fig. 5.15). Click it to disconnect the frame from its partner.

Fig. 5.15
Break the connection
by clicking the chain's
link.

Of course, if you disconnect, make sure you either reconnect to another text frame or enlarge the original frame to accept all the text. Or, you could edit your story so there's less text.

How Do I Put Text in My Publication?

● **In this chapter:**

- **Getting text into a publication— choose your weapon**

- **Now I want to make it perfect—tell me about editing text**

- **Can I export my text to use it in other documents?**

You can add text by typing it, copying it from another publication, or importing it. Publisher can do everything for you automatically, but it can't help you write the words. . . . . . ⊳

Now that you know how to create, manipulate, and jazz up a text frame, you have to start the hard part, writing the text. To make you more comfortable when you face this daunting task, Publisher offers several different methods for getting your text into your publication. Unfortunately, there's no help for the words themselves. That's your job.

Type it in

When your text frame is sitting in front of you, blank, waiting for you to enter the words that will inspire all the readers of your publication, you can just type stuff. Put your fingers on the keyboard and start typing.

As you learned in Chapter 5, you have plenty of formatting help on the Formatting toolbar: you can change the alignment, the font, the size, whatever you need.

Different people work different ways. It might be easier for you to type, letting the words flow, and then go back and create paragraphs and formatting. Or you can format as you go, which might make it easier for you to move to each section of writing, or from topic to topic.

 TIP   As your fingers fly on the keyboard (or your finger hunts and pecks), remember, safety first! Save early and often.

Copy it from other documents

Suppose you wrote some text a few months ago that would work nicely in the publication you're working on now. Does that mean you have to retype it? Of course not. You can grab stuff you've already written, and save yourself a lot of time and energy. There's a number of ways to go about it, depending on where you're starting from.

Get text from other Publisher publications

You might have another publication in Publisher that has material that goes with the topic of the current publication. Or, the current publication might be a short version of a larger, more complex publication. Or, the other way around.

Unfortunately, you can't just open the other publication and grab the text you need. Publisher only permits you to work on one publication at a time.

Of course, there's a workaround. (You didn't really think I'd leave you hanging, did you?)

I only need one section of text

The easiest way to grab one chunk of text from another publication is to close the current publication and open the publication that has the text you want to use.

1 Save the current publication.

2 Choose File, Close Publication.

3 Choose File, Open Existing Publication. This opens the Microsoft Publisher opening window with the Existing Publication page displayed (see fig. 6.1). You can choose a file from the Most Recently Used Files list or from the list of files in the directory that holds your publications.

or

If you only want to choose from Publisher files, click the Open button and use the Open Publication dialog box (see fig. 6.2). Double-click the publication you want.

Q&A **The difference between the two file lists is that the files displayed** in the Most Recently Used Files list might not be Publisher files. For example, if you imported a file from Microsoft Word so you could use it in a publication, that file would be considered recently used. It's not a Publisher file, however.

4 When the publication is open, move to the text frame that has the text you need and zoom in so you can read it.

5 Use your mouse to drag across all the text you need, highlighting it (see fig. 6.3).

Fig. 6.1
Your existing publications display so you can open a publication that has text you like so much you want to use it again.

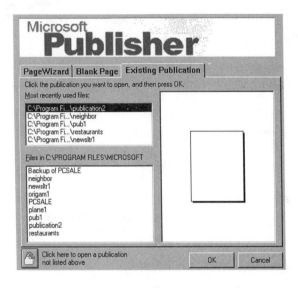

Fig. 6.2
The Open Publication dialog box lets you limit the file names you see to those files created in Publisher.

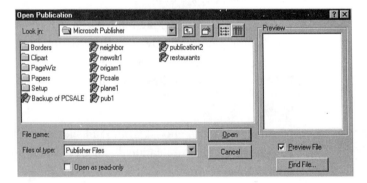

6 Click the right mouse button and choose Copy Text from the shortcut menu (or just click the Copy button). This places the selected text on the Clipboard.

7 Now, just close the publication and open the publication that needs this text. The selection is on the Clipboard and will stay there until you cut or copy another selection of text.

8 When the publication is loaded, move to the text frame that will receive the text and click it to select it, then right-click and choose Paste from the shortcut menu (or just click the Paste button).

Fig. 6.3

It's easy to select text when all you have to do is drag the mouse.

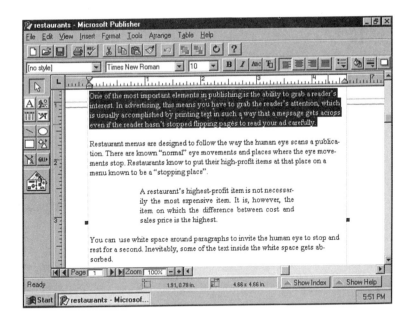

I need selections from a couple of places

It gets a little more complicated when you need several different text selections from another publication. Because the Clipboard won't let you add the second selection to the first, you have to get the text one selection at a time, opening and closing publications.

No, you don't—I'm kidding. There's a much easier way to do this.

1 Open the publication that has the text you need and create a new text frame in it.

2 Move through the publication and grab each section of text you want, copying it to the Clipboard and pasting it into the new frame.

3 Eventually, all the text you need will be in one text frame. Copy the entire contents of that frame onto the Clipboard.

4 Close the publication.

CAUTION   **Be careful—Publisher will ask you if you want to save the**
publication before closing it because you made changes. Answer No. After
all, when you open this publication again, you want it back the way it was.

5 Open the receiving publication and paste the contents of the Clipboard
into it.

Of course, if you need all that text in one text frame, you're finished. If you
need that text in various places around the new publication, just use Cut and
Paste to move each section out of the text frame you originally pasted it in.

You can copy text from other programs, too

You can take advantage of multitasking by opening another Windows'
program (usually a word processor) that has the text you need and copying
from it to your open publication. The only warning is that it must be a
program that can interact with the Clipboard.

Import it from a word processor

The text you need might already exist in your favorite word processor. Or,
you might have found it easier to write and manipulate text in a word processor that you've been using for a long time. That's just fine, because you can
import the text into Publisher.

Better yet, try it this way

Instead of going through the procedures listed
above to move multiple sections of text from one
publication into another, you could run another
copy of Publisher. After all, Windows 95 is a
multitasking operating system. This technique
might or might not work, depending on how your
computer is set up, but if it does, it's a faster,
easier way to do it.

Load the sending publication in one session of
Publisher and the receiving publication in the
other. You cannot load the same document in
two sessions of Publisher.

Then, just highlight, copy, and paste to your
heart's content.

Publisher can convert files of the following types:

- Microsoft Word for Windows

- Microsoft Works for Windows (files with a WPS extension)

- Microsoft Write for Windows

- WordPerfect versions 5.0 and later

- Plain text

If you don't use any of the programs listed, there's no problem. All word processors provide an opportunity to save a file as plain text, which might be called "ASCII" or "DOS Text," depending on the language used by the word processor.

To import a file from another program:

1 In Publisher, create a text frame or select an existing text frame to hold the new text.

2 Choose Insert, Text File. The Insert Text File dialog box appears (see fig. 6.4).

Fig. 6.4
Rather than enter text again, you can import a file from another program that has the text you need.

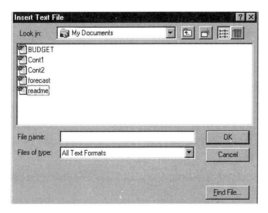

3 Type the file path and file name in the File Name box, or use the buttons to open folders and get to the file.

4 If you're not exactly sure where that file is hiding, choose Find File. The Find File dialog box opens (see fig. 6.5).

Fig. 6.5

The Find File dialog box can help you locate any file in your system.

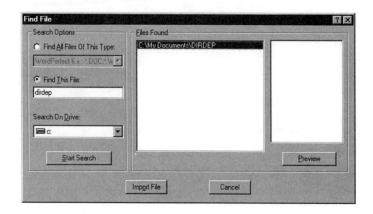

TIP **The more information you can provide, the faster the search is.** Sometimes it's faster to look for groups of files instead of a specific file name, because frequently you don't really remember the file name accurately. Coming close to the file name and getting a list to choose from is faster than typing the wrong name again and again.

Search for the type of file and use wild cards to narrow the search and let the system do the grunt work.

Now you can edit it

There's always a point at which you need to clean up your text, to edit it—to make things clearer, more concise, or even to make the words prettier and more literate. Frequently, you just need to make everything shorter so it all fits in your publication and leaves room for the necessary white space.

Moving, copying, and deleting text

After you highlight the text, it's quite easy to move, copy, or delete it.

Moving text means taking it from its original location and placing it somewhere else. This is an easy, four-step process.

1 Select the text, then click the right mouse button to see the context menu.

2 Choose Cut Text to put the selection on the Clipboard.

3 Click the new location and click the right mouse button.

4 Choose Paste Text.

Copying text means that it stays where it is and another, duplicate copy of the text is placed somewhere else.

1 Select the text, then click the right mouse button to see the context menu.

2 Choose Copy Text to put the selection on the Clipboard.

3 Move to the new location and click the right mouse button.

4 Choose Paste Text.

Use Copy Text to save keystrokes

Sometimes the Copy Text command can be a quick way to do more than make an exact duplicate of the selected text. You can also use Copy Text to save keystrokes when you need text that's merely similar to the original text. For example, look at the two sections of numbered steps above. They are very much alike, except that one talked about cutting and the other copying. Do you think I typed out the second section? Nooo, I'm much too lazy for that. I copied it, then edited the few words that needed to be changed.

Another useful shortcut is to use the Copy Text command to add repetitive elements all over your publication. Suppose you have a title at the beginning of every frame. It has certain formatting; perhaps it also has asterisks or other characters that make it stand out. Copy it and change the text that needs to be changed, but the rest of the formatting and configuration is already done for you.

Or, maybe you use a short graphic line between paragraphs or some other interesting element. Copy that.

Remember that once you copy to the Clipboard, the text or object you copied stays on the Clipboard until you cut or copy something else. That means you can take a repeating selection, copy it once, and paste it all over the place as many times as you want.

Deleting text means you get rid of it. It is not placed on the Clipboard. If you want it back, immediately choose Edit, Undo Delete Text. If you don't act right away, and perform another action, the option won't be available on the menu. Undo puts the text back where it was, regardless of where your pointer is when you choose it.

Don't forget to check your spelling!

There's nothing more embarrassing than having a publication go out to the world with a word spelled incorrectly. You can avoid this humiliation (and keep your job) by using the spell check feature available in Publisher.

1 Select the frame you want to spell check.

2 Choose Tools, Check Spelling.

3 When a word appears in your text that is not in the Publisher dictionary, the Check Spelling dialog box appears (see fig. 6.6).

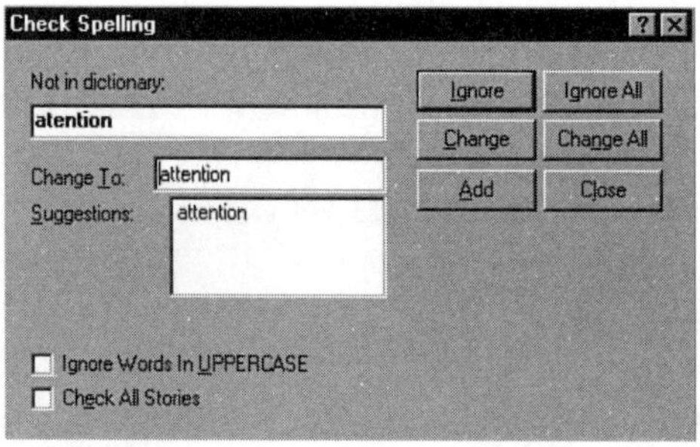

Fig. 6.6
The Check Spelling
dialog box helps you
correct your mistakes.

If there are no errors, nothing happens. You're just back in your text frame (you'd think the spell checker would flash a message saying "Good job!" or something, but it doesn't).

There are a number of options in the Check Spelling dialog box:

- If the dialog box offers suggestions, highlight the correct one and choose Change. If you know the same word is in the frame more than once and want to correct every instance of it, choose Change All.

- If you know a word is correct but the spell checker questions it (usually this happens with proper names or technical jargon), choose Ignore. To make sure the spell checker doesn't stop at the next instance of that word, choose Ignore All.

- If the spell checker stopped at some terminology or phrase or proper name that you know you'll be using frequently, choose Add. This puts that text into the dictionary and it will not longer be considered a mistake.

- To tell the spell checker to ignore text that is in uppercase, select the Ignore Words in UPPERCASE check box. This is useful if you tend to use uppercase for proper names or product names, and especially if you use acronyms.

- To have the spell checker move throughout your document and check all the text, instead of just the selected text frame, select the Check All Stories check box.

 CAUTION   **The spell checker only looks at text frames and table frames. If** you spelled something wrong in a frame that has WordArt, it won't see it.

Seek out changes with Replace

If there's a word or phrase you want to change, you can use the Replace command, which also finds the text for you. There are several useful applications for this feature.

- You sent a publication to Mr. Jones about JONES' WIDGETS and have that text all over it. Now you want to send the same publication to Mr. Brown about BROWN'S WIDGETS.

- Your publication, which is an instruction book, has a zillion subheadings or opening paragraphs with the word "Then" starting a phrase. You've decided it should be "Next."

To replace text:

1 Select the frame you want to search.

2 Choose Edit, Replace to open the Replace dialog box (see fig. 6.7).

Fig. 6.7

Using the Replace dialog box, you can make wholesale changes to words or phrases.

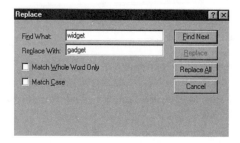

3 Enter the current word or phrase that needs changing in the Fi<u>n</u>d What text box.

4 Press Tab to move to the Re<u>p</u>lace With text box and enter the new word or phrase.

5 Click <u>F</u>ind Next to locate the next occurrence of the current word or phrase. Publisher highlights it and you can choose <u>R</u>eplace to change it.

Using the options available in the Replace dialog box can make your changes easier and more accurate.

- If you don't want to stop at each occurrence of the text to confirm the change, choose Replace <u>A</u>ll.

- If you only want to replace a word if it's a whole word instead of a part of another word, select Match <u>W</u>hole Word Only.

Don't have an itchy trigger finger!

As powerful as the Replace function is, it can be dangerous if you don't use it correctly. Always save your publication before replacing. If things get messed up, you can close the publication and open it again with everything the way it was before you ran the Replace command.

The big danger is not thinking out all the possible ramifications. Usually, you can avoid the danger if you remember to select the Match <u>W</u>hole Word Only check box when applicable. For example, suppose you decide it would be better, or more elegant, to replace the word "other" with "else." (You remember that you frequently used the phrase "try something other" and now it doesn't sound right.) You could end up with a document full of strange words, like "melse," "brelse," or "belse."

- If you want to replace the word or phrase with the exact upper- and lowercase characters you entered in the Replace With text box, select Match Case. This is handy for correcting phrases, when the text in the Find What text box matches the text in the Replace With text box, but the capitalization is different.

Can I use Microsoft Word to edit my stories?

If you have Microsoft Word version 6.0 or later on your computer, you can edit your Publisher text there.

1 Select the frame you want to edit.

2 Click the right mouse button to see the shortcut menu and choose Edit Story in Microsoft Word. This launches Word, which appears on your screen with your text loaded and ready to work on.

3 Edit your text as necessary.

4 To close the Word document and move the edited text back to your Publisher text frame, choose File, Close and Return from the Word menu bar. Word remains open.

5 To exit Word, choose File, Exit. Word closes, you return to Publisher, and the edits have been transferred.

Exporting: I like this text so much I want to use it in other programs

Just like you can import text from another program, you also can send all the text in your publication to another software application.

1 Click outside the page to deselect anything that might have been selected.

2 Choose File, Save As to open the Save As dialog box (see fig. 6.8).

Fig. 6.8

You can send Publisher text to a different software application.

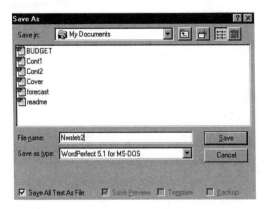

3 Enter a name for the text in the File Name text box.

4 Open the Save as Type drop-down list and select a file type that's appropriate for the software receiving the file.

5 Select the Save All Text As File check box.

6 Choose Save.

When you open the software application you sent your file to, you can load the file using the appropriate commands for that software.

7

More About Fonts

● In this chapter:

- Please explain fonts in plain English

- I don't know which font to use!

- I want to change this font

- How do I add characters that aren't on my keyboard?

Mood-altering fonts? Fonts are powerful stuff—choose them carefully and you can hook your readers . . . . ●▶

You can't do desktop publishing—you can't even use a word processor—without running across the term "font." You might think the term is just another piece of the techno-jargon that clings to computers like lichen to a rock, like RAM, ROM, and VESA local bus. But that's not true. Even though computers make it easy to change fonts, fonts themselves predate the computer age by several centuries.

Okay, so what is a font exactly?

A **font** is simply a complete set of characters drawn in the same style. You think of letters in terms of the alphabet—A, B, C, D, and so on—and you know what each letter looks like. But if you write out the alphabet, have a friend write out the alphabet, and then compare the two, you'll see that no two people actually *form* the letters in exactly the same way. They're similar enough to be recognizable and readable, but quite different in the details.

That's the way it is with fonts. Someone designed each letter of the typeface in which the main text of this book is set. Someone else designed each letter of the text used on the cover. Like the alphabets written by you and your friend, they're different, but equally legible. Each design is given a name, such as "Stone Serif" or "MCPDigital."

You can also distinguish fonts by their size, which you measure in points.

 Plain English, please!

A **point** is a basic unit of measurement used by printers. A point is equal to 0.013837 of an inch, which is kind of an awkward number to work with mentally. ("Let's see, so 12-point type would be how tall? That's 12 times 0.013837...two times seven is 14...carry the one...times three is...umm, I'll get back to you on that.") It's easier to think of it as about 1/72 of an inch. (72 times 0.013837 is technically 0.996264, but it's close enough for all practical purposes.)

Point size refers to the height of the capital letters, so if you choose 36-point Bodoni, you're choosing a particular style of font, Bodoni, whose tallest letters are one-half inch high.

When printing was done using cast metal (the word "font" is from the French word *fonte*, which means "casting,") most printers made do with a rather limited selection. The desktop publisher doesn't have that problem: her problem is more likely having too many fonts to choose from than too few.

Computers add another level of complexity to the discussion of fonts by introducing new divisions of fonts: screen fonts, printer fonts, and TrueType fonts. The following sections explain these divisions.

Screen fonts

Screen fonts are fonts that display on your computer screen. Most of the time, information on how to print screen fonts is stored in the computer, so you can print the fonts you see on the screen. Some fonts, however, are *only* intended to be seen on the screen. The fonts used by programs in dialog boxes and menus are good examples. They aren't intended to be printed and, in Publisher, they don't even show up as options.

Printer fonts

Printer fonts are the fonts installed in your printer. Most printers come with a number of these fonts—some might have screen fonts to accompany them.

 CAUTION　**If you use a printer font in a Publisher document that doesn't** have an accompanying screen font, Publisher chooses a similar font for the screen display: however, your printed document might look quite different due to differences in letter size and spacing between the printer font and the screen font. This can cause serious layout problems, so be careful.

TrueType: Two! Two! Two fonts in one!

To avoid these problems, Publisher recommends that you only use **TrueType fonts** in your documents. TrueType fonts contain both screen and printer information, so they look exactly the same on the computer screen as they do on paper.

Your computer probably already has several TrueType fonts installed, especially if you've used a word processor. Publisher comes with several new TrueType fonts, some of which are shown in figure 7.1.

Fig. 7.1

The new fonts supplied with Publisher can help you set the ideal mood for your publication.

> This is Comic Sans MS. 123
> THIS IS COPPERPLATE GOTHIC BOLD. 123
> THIS IS COPPERPLATE GOTHIC LIGHT. 123
> This is Flexure. 123
> This is Goudy Old Style. 123
> **THIS IS GOUDY STOUT. 123**
> This is Harrington. 123
> **This is Imprint MT Shadow. 123**
> *This is Lucida Calligraphy. 123*
> *This is Lucida Handwriting. 123*
> This is Modern No. 20. 123
> This is Rockwell. 123
> This is Rockwell Condensed. 123
> **This is Rockwell Condensed Bold. 123**
> **This is Rockwell Extra Bold. 123**
> This is Maiandra GD. 123
> ⊠↝⊙⊕ ⊙⊕ ⊙⊙⊛↝⟪⊠⊙⊙↝⊗⊠ ⛫⊡⛊
> ^↑↓▽ ↓▽ ↵↦→⟲↦→▽↾↘ ↦↑▉

Q&A   ***What's the difference between a font and a typeface?***

As printers use the two terms, a "typeface" includes all sizes of letters and numbers drawn in the same style, whereas a "font" is all the letters and numbers *in one size* within the typeface. But that's a throwback to when typefaces were cast in metal and you only had so many fonts, or sizes, of a particular typeface to work with; computers make it so easy to change sizes that "font" and "typeface" have become synonymous.

Choose your weapon, er, font

So you have all the fonts supplied with Publisher, and maybe hundreds more already on your computer. Choosing the right font can be a paralyzing decision. How do you decide which font to use where?

Personality contest

Every font has its own personality. Using a font gives your document that same personality. The goal, then, is to find the font that has the personality you want your document to have.

Take another look at the Publisher fonts in figure 7.1. Harrington has a light, frothy, 1890s feel to it. It might be perfect if you're preparing a brochure about your company's new brand of sarsaparilla ice cream, and you want to conjure up images of small-town Fourth of July celebrations, band shells, parasols, and tandem bicycles. But it would give your document a very odd flavor if you were creating a brochure about your company's new line of road-building equipment: for that you might want something heavier, solid, no-nonsense—like Rockwell Extra Bold.

TIP   **Some fonts, like Goudy Stout, don't have lowercase letters.** Stay away from these fonts for extended sections of text. Although they're great for headlines and titles (which is why they're sometimes called **display fonts**), they're difficult and tiring to read after more than a few words (see fig. 7.2).

Fig. 7.2
With Goudy Stout, and other fonts in all capital letters, it's hard to tell where words and sentences begin and end.

> TEXT SET IN ALL
> CAPITAL LETTERS IS
> DIFFICULT TO READ IF
> THERE'S TOO MUCH OF
> IT. USE THESE FONTS
> SPARINGLY.

Size matters

Point size is like the volume control on a public address system: crank it up too much and the reader feels like you're shouting at him; turn it too low and your voice becomes a whisper that is easily ignored.

Text that's too small looks dull and uninviting and is as fatiguing to read as text in all caps. Publisher lets you set the size of fonts at anything from 0.5 to 999.5 points. You have a lot of leeway, but the main text of your document will probably be in the 9- to 12-point range.

I don't like this font. How do I change it?

So how do you actually apply fonts to text in Publisher?

As discussed in Chapter 5, when you first draw a text frame, Publisher asks you to select a font and a font size. But maybe, after you've typed a bit of text into the frame (see Chapter 6), you find the font you chose just isn't working. Maybe it's the wrong style, maybe it's the wrong size. How do you go about changing it?

Changing the font

The first step is to select, or **highlight**, the text whose font you want to change. Just point the mouse to the part of the text where you want the change to begin, click and hold the left mouse button, and drag the cursor straight down until you reach the place where you want the change to end.

Release the mouse button. The text between those two locations will be highlighted (see fig. 7.3).

Fig. 7.3
Any font and size changes you make will only affect the highlighted text.

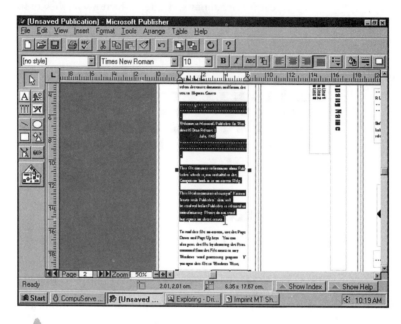

 TIP **If you want to highlight the entire story, make sure you select** the text frame, then choose Edit, Highlight Entire Story (or right-click and choose Highlight Entire Story from the shortcut menu). This is often easier and faster than dragging your mouse through a long text frame—or several frames.

When you select the text frame, a whole new toolbar full of buttons appears. Some of these are formatting buttons that the next chapter covers. For now, you need to know about the Font and Size list boxes (see fig. 7.4).

Fig. 7.4
The Font and Size boxes appear when you select a text frame.

Font list box *Size list box*

Font drop down list

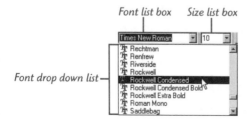

The Font list box displays the name of the font currently applied to the highlighted text. If you click the down-arrow button at the right, you see a long drop-down list of fonts. Moving your mouse arrow down the list highlights each in turn; you can see more fonts by using the scroll bar at the right of this little window.

Highlight the font you want to apply to your text and click the left mouse button once. Your text immediately changes to the new font. The highlighted text remains highlighted: you can preview it and decide if you want to keep the new font, revert to the original font, or try another font.

TIP **You can also type a font name directly in the Font list box.** Simply highlight the font name that first appears (without displaying the drop-down list), type in the name of the font you want, and press Enter. This can be faster than scrolling through the menu if you have several dozen fonts installed—if you know the exact spelling of the one you want.

Changing point size

Changing point size is exactly the same as changing fonts, except, of course, you use the Size list box. Select your text, highlight the point size you want from the Size drop-down list, click once, and *voila*! Your text changes size.

Q&A *When I open the Size drop-down list, only certain numbers appear. There's no 20-point option, for instance. Why not?*

The point sizes displayed are the most commonly used sizes in traditional printing. When type was made of cast metal, a printer might have complete sets of a typeface in, say, 5-, 6-, 7-, 8-, 9-, 10-, 12-, 14-, 18-, 30-, 36-, and 60-point sizes. It would have been enormously expensive and bulky to maintain a complete set of type in every single point size, but a series like this gave adequate flexibility. Computers have made it possible to print text in any point size at all, but the convention of listing only the most common sizes continues. (It shortens the list of sizes Publisher has to display, too.)

If the point-size you want is not displayed, simply click in the Size list box and type the size you want. Press Enter when you're finished.

Basic formatting

When you settle on a font style and size, there are still many formatting options available to help you achieve exactly the look you want. The three available to you right off the text-frame formatting toolbar are bold, italic, and small caps.

Be bold!

Making a font **bold** thickens and darkens characters, which can help them stand out from surrounding non-bold text. To make text bold in Publisher, highlight the text you want to change and click the Bold button on the formatting toolbar.

> **This is an example of bold text.**

To return bold text to normal, highlight the text and click the Bold button again.

Italicizing text

Italic text slants to the right and takes on a cursive look—more like handwriting and less like printing. (Italic also means "relating to ancient Italy," and that's no coincidence: italic text is called that because italics began with an Italian Renaissance script in which all the letters slanted to the right.) Italics are often used to set off the titles of books and magazines, for foreign words, to add emphasis, and so on.

> *This is an example of italic text.*

You can use the Italics button the same way you use the Bold button: highlight the text you want italicized, and simply click the Italics button. To return italic text to normal, highlight it and click the Italics button again.

You can activate both formatting buttons at the same time, resulting in bold italic text (or italic bold text, depending on how you want to look at it).

> ***This text is both bold and italic.***

What the heck's a "small cap"?

Take a look at the font in figure 7.5. This is Copperplate Gothic Light, and you'll notice that it only comes in capital letters—but some of those capital letters are smaller than the others.

Fig. 7.5
Not all fonts have both capital letters and small letters; some make do with just capitals.

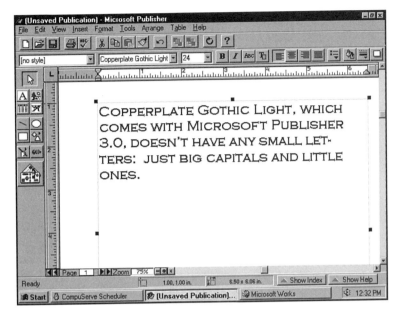

A font like this allows you to use all capital letters for effect, while still maintaining the distinction between capital and lowercase letters in, for example, a proper name.

THIS IS AN EXAMPLE OF SMALL CAPS. NUMERALS LIKE 1, 2, 3 LOOK THE SAME.

You don't have to use a special font like Copperplate Gothic Light to achieve this look. Publisher lets you apply this **small capitals** style (known as just **small caps**) to any font.

Just highlight the text you want to appear in small-capitals style and click the Small Caps button. Capital letters in the text you highlighted don't change, but lowercase letters become smaller capital letters. Numerals and other symbols don't change.

Today's special on the Character menu

There are several other ways to format your text that aren't available at just the click of a button, but aren't that far away, either.

To access them, highlight the text you want to format, then choose Format, Character (or right-click and choose Format from the shortcut menu). The Character dialog box appears (see fig. 7.6).

Fig. 7.6
You have detailed control over the look of individual characters or groups of characters in your text.

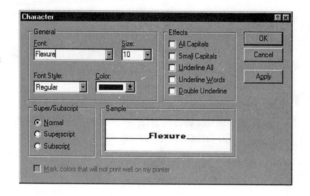

There are several options to choose from, some of which you have access to without opening this dialog box: font, size, style, and small capitals. There are other options here, however, which you can't access anywhere else. Notice the Sample box, which shows you the effects of the options you chose so you can see what they look like before applying them to your document.

A few exotic options

To the right of the General options is another set of options called Effects. Small Capitals shows up again. With it are several other effects: All Capitals, Underline All, Underline Words, and Double Underline. In the bottom-left corner of the dialog box are the Super/Subscript options. Figure 7.7 shows what these formatting options look like when applied to text.

Fig. 7.7
You can apply all of these formatting options and more to your text.

ALL CAPITALS HAS BEEN TURNED ON FOR THIS TEXT.

Underline All has been turned on for this text.

Underline Words has been turned on for this text.

Double Underline has been turned on for this text.

This text is normal. $^{This\ is\ superscripted.}$ $E=mc^2$

This text is normal. $_{This\ is\ subscripted.}$ H_2O

- **All Capitals** turns all lowercase letters into capital letters. Numerals and other symbols don't change.

- **Underline All** does just what you'd expect—it underlines the entire selection.

- **Underline Words** is a variation of Underline All that only underlines text; it doesn't underline the spaces between words.

- **Double Underline** puts two fine lines under the highlighted text instead of just one. Unfortunately, you can't select it with Underline Words; if you choose this one, you're stuck with underlined spaces as well.

- **Superscript** makes the highlighted text appear slightly above and quite a bit smaller than normal text. You might use this option to indicate footnotes in a term paper, or to reproduce a mathematical formula, such as the famous example in the figure.

- **Subscript** makes the highlighted text appear slightly below and quite a bit smaller than normal text. Chemical formulas make frequent use of subscripts.

This dialog box also lets you change the color of a font. And yes, there are still *more* special formatting options available to you in Publisher…but you explore those in the next chapter.

 Q&A   *Is there any limit to how many different fonts and effects I can use in a single text frame?*

Nope. You can make every character a different font if you want to. It might slow down your computer and your printer quite a bit, depending on your system, but the main hazard is producing a document that will be mistaken for a ransom note.

I ñeed to üse some other çhαracters

Almost all fonts contain certain basic characters—the letters of the alphabet, numerals, punctuation marks—but many of them also contain special characters you don't ordinarily see—and which you can't easily access through your keyboard. Where, for example, can you find the acute accent é common in French words?

Publisher gives you easy access to these special hidden characters through the Insert menu. Just place your cursor where you want to insert the special symbol and choose Insert, Symbol. You see the Insert Symbol dialog box, which displays all the characters available (see fig 7.8). The dialog box opens showing the characters in the same font as the text where you placed your cursor, but you can access all the fonts through the Font list box.

Point at the symbol you want, click it with the mouse, then click OK. The symbol appears where you had your cursor.

Fig. 7.8

Here you can access characters you might not even have realized are available in your selected font.

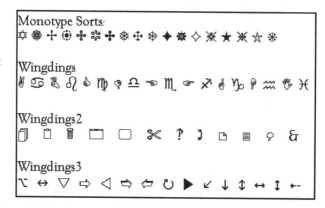

Fig. 7.9

A picture might be worth a thousand words, but a single font can contain dozens of pictures.

Modern Hieroglyphics

Among the fonts Publisher supplies are three picture fonts: Wingdings, Wingdings2, and Wingdings3. Another, Monotype Sorts, comes with Windows 95. Picture fonts are the exception to the statement that almost all fonts contain the alphabet and numbers. Picture fonts consist entirely of special symbols, everything from bullets and arrows to the symbols used on playing cards to tiny images of telephones and airplanes.

Figure 7.9 shows a few examples from each of these picture fonts. You can make some of these images very large and use them as clip art; others work best to highlight ordinary text. Instead of using ordinary black dots to set off each number in a list of phone numbers, for example, you could use a tiny image of a telephone.

Choose the Insert menu to see what symbols are available in Monotype Sorts and the three Wingdings fonts and familiarize yourself with them. That way, when you need something a little special to spice up your publication, you'll know where to look.

8

Making Text Stand Out: Special Formatting

In this chapter:

- **Writing purple (or any other color) prose**

- **I need more space between lines and characters**

- **Heading up my to-do list: make some lists!**

- **Doing it with style-sheets**

From color to fancy first letters, text–formatting options in Publisher go far beyond just changing font styles and sizes. . . . .

or decades, "purple prose" has been a pejorative term among writers, implying an overabundance of flowery adjectives at the expense of readability. But with Publisher, even a lawnmower-repair manual can be written in purple prose—on a bright green background, if you want.

Writing purple (or any other color) prose

One of the ways Publisher 3.0 has been improved is in its handling of color. If you have a printer that can take advantage of it, colored text can be another way to make your publication stand out from the crowd.

How do I change the text color?

In Chapter 7, you looked at the Character dialog box. One of the options in that dialog box allows you to choose a font color. However, you can access the same option directly from the workspace. First, highlight the text you want to color, then click the Font Color button.

The color palette opens, with several colored boxes (see fig. 8.1). Click the box that contains the color you want for your text—the color of the text changes.

Fig. 8.1
Choose from this offering of 35 colors for your text—but if that isn't enough...

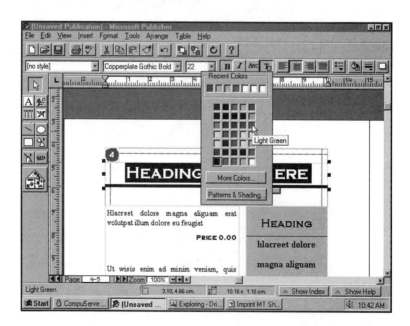

If these aren't enough colors for you, click the More Colors button to open the Colors dialog box (see fig. 8.2). As the Design Tip in the dialog box says, the colors were placed in each column because they work well together. If you confine your choices to one column, you can avoid any horrible color *faux pas*.

Fig. 8.2
...choose from 84 coordinated colors in the Basic Colors Color Model. If you still aren't happy...

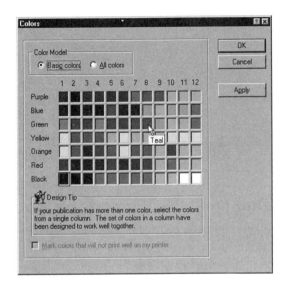

In the Colors dialog box, you can choose between Basi<u>c</u> Colors—the ones presented in the coordinated columns—or <u>A</u>ll Colors. If you choose <u>A</u>ll Colors, you open a different color palette (see fig. 8.3). Click the palette and cross-hairs appear; move the cross-hairs around the palette with your mouse until you see a color you like in the Solid box below. You can adjust the brightness using the sliding control on the skinny rectangle to the right of the palette, or you can enter numbers in the text boxes. (See Chapter 11 for a more detailed description of this dialog box.)

 Q&A ***I don't want to use the color in the Solid box in the All Colors Color Model. I want to use the color in the Color box. Why can't I use it?***

Most of the colors you create using the palette are represented on the screen by a mixture of pixels of many different colors. In Publisher, text generally cannot be a "mixed" color like this; instead Publisher matches it with a solid color as best it can, and that's the color you see in the box on the right.

Fig. 8.3

...create your own color using the color palette and brightness control.

What other kind of color controls can I use?

In the color palette that appears when you click the Font Color button, you can also choose the Patterns & Shading button. This opens the Fill Patterns and Shading dialog box, which has three options: Tints/Shades, Patterns, and Gradients. You can only apply Tints/Shades to text, which is why you can't access the other two options. (The Patterns and Gradients options are covered in the next section, which talks about background color.)

Tints/Shades presents you with a series of rectangles, showing the text color with a range of tints and shades applied (see fig. 8.4). Essentially, this is the brightness control. When you choose a rectangle, the color appears in the Sample area so you can better judge what it looks like before you apply it to your text.

Color my world—or at least my background

You're not limited to changing the color of your text; you can also change the color of the text frame's background. Just select the frame whose background color you want to set and click the Background Color button in the toolbar. The same color palette you saw when you clicked the Font Color button appears. This time, though, if you make your way to the All Colors palette, you *can* apply any mixed shade you create using the palette and brightness slider.

Fig. 8.4
Like the brightness
control on your TV,
Tints/Shades allows you
to fine-tune the color
you choose.

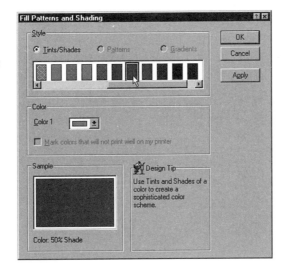

 TIP **If you're working with a black-and-white printer, the most com-**
mon text/background color combination to use, outside of black-on-white,
is white-on-black (also called **reverse text**). Simply make your text white
and your background black.

Patterned backgrounds

In the pop-up color selection dialog box, click Patterns & Shading. This time,
when the Fill Patterns and Shading dialog box opens, the P̲atterns and
G̲radients options are available.

Choose P̲atterns and a new series of rectangles appears, showing a variety of
patterns you can apply to your background. You can choose crosshatching,
brickwork, thatching, and more. You also have more color options: you have
to choose both a Base C̲olor and a C̲olor 2.

The Base C̲olor, by default, is the current background color; Publisher uses it
to draw the pattern. C̲olor 2 defaults to white. So your initial choice here is a
pattern drawn in the color you first chose on a white background. Click the
C̲olor 2 drop-down arrow, which displays the color palette (see fig. 8.5).
C̲olor 2, in other words, is the true background color, while the Base C̲olor
draws patterns on Color 2—your text color is on top of both of them.

Fig. 8.5
Tired of a plain color background? Choose a pattern to spice it up, and apply a second color.

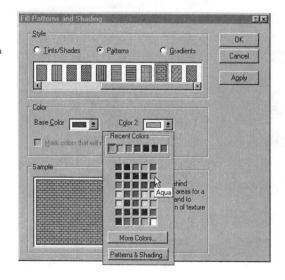

What's a gradient?

Choose the Gradients option. You now have a selection of background options that look like an airbrush artist applied carefully graduated shades (see fig. 8.6). The Base Color continues to be the color with which the effect is applied; Color 2 is still the background color. The best way to understand gradients is to try them; you can't truly appreciate them until you do. Check out the examples in figure 8.7.

Fig. 8.6
Gradients are the most exotic background options Publisher has to offer. Used appropriately, they can make your text leap off the page.

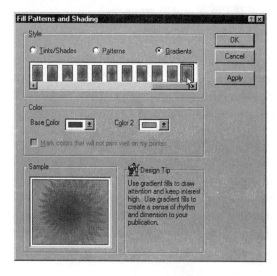

Fig. 8.7
Patterns and gradients
have really different
effects. Choose one
that works well with
your message and it
will add that special
touch.

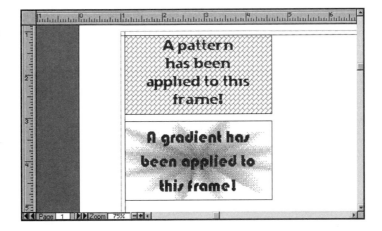

 TIP **Whenever you use colors, patterns, and shading to perk up your**
publication, keep one thing in mind: the purpose of text is to be read.
Mauve letters on a background of orange bursting in a star-shaped gradient
over green might appeal to your aesthetic sense, but the text will be almost
impossible to read. Colors don't convey any information, and conveying
information is the goal of any publication. Use colors to draw the reader's
eye to important text, but be careful not to overwhelm your message.

I need more space between lines and characters...

Whether your text appears in multiple colors with fancy backgrounds or in
plain old black-and-white, sometimes it just won't fit in the space you allot
for it. Maybe there's just a little space left over at the bottom of that story, or
maybe this headline is just a little too wide.

 Plain English, please!

Desktop publishers often talk about **white space**. That's the part of the
publication that's intentionally left blank—and it's an important element
of design. White space allows the other elements of your publication to
"breathe," making them stand out and catch the eye of your reader even
more. Too much, however, can make your page look starkly empty. As is
true of most elements of page design, using white space correctly is a
balancing act. **99**

Publisher deals with these common layout problems by allowing you to adjust the space between lines and between letters.

Add some space between lines

To adjust the space between lines

1 Highlight the text whose spacing you want to adjust.

2 Choose F**o**rmat, **L**ine Spacing. The Line Spacing dialog box appears as shown in figure 8.8.

Fig. 8.8
To avoid extra white space, or sometimes to create some, use these controls to decrease or increase the space between lines of text and paragraphs.

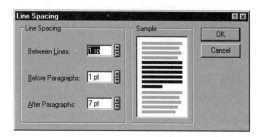

3 Adjust the controls as necessary. The Sample area gives you a clear idea of how your changes will affect your text.

- **Between Lines**. This adjusts the white space between lines of text. The default is one space: the size of a space depends on the size of the font, but basically it's just a little bit taller than the tallest letters of the font. This ensures there's enough white space between lines of text to make them easily readable.

  To increase or decrease this spacing, click the up or down arrows of the Between **L**ines text box. Each click raises or lowers the value by a quarter of a space. You can enter precise values (0.9 space, for instance, or 1.1) by typing them directly in the text box.

- **Before Paragraphs**. This adjusts the space inserted before each new paragraph. This control measures the inserted space in points, not spaces. Remember that a point is 1/72 of an inch.

- **After Paragraphs**. Every time you hit Enter to start a new paragraph, Publisher inserts the amount of space you specify in this text box. This control, too, measures the inserted space in points.

4 After you make your changes, click OK to implement them and return to your publication. Figure 8.9 shows the effects of various line spacing.

Fig. 8.9
In the paragraph on the left, I increased the space between lines to 1.25; on the right, I decreased the space between lines to .75. The paragraph in the middle has the default line spacing.

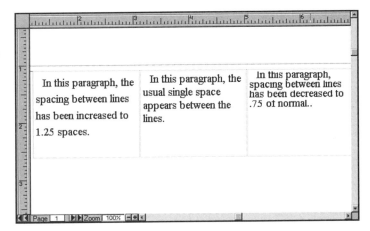

Spaces? Points? I'm confused...

The fact the space between lines is measured in spaces and the space between paragraphs is measured in points can be confusing. However, you can use either measurement system in any of the boxes. Generally, changing Between Lines to measure in points is more helpful. That's what printers normally use in measuring the space between lines, called **leading** (pronounced *ledding*). If you're preparing your publication to send to an outside printer, it helps you and the printer understand each other if you're both using the same measurement system. For a printer, normal leading isn't "one space," it's 120 percent of the text's point size.

To change the Between Lines measurement to points instead of spaces, simply highlight the number in the box and type in the number of points you want your text "leaded," replacing the sp with pt (for example, you might type **11 pt** over the original 1 sp). If you later return to the Line Spacing dialog box to change the leading again, the measurement is still in points. You can change the measurement back to spaces at any time by replacing the pt with sp.

You can also change the measurements of the Before Paragraphs or After Paragraphs text boxes from points to spaces. But when you return to the Line Spacing dialog box later, they again measure in points. They simply converted your command to their preferred measurement system.

Q&A *I decreased the space between lines in my paragraph; now the tops of all the characters are cut off on the screen. What's going on?*

Publisher lets you decrease space between lines or between letters to the point where letters print on top of each other. If the tops of letters are cut off, first print a test page. Sometimes the text will print fine, nicely squashed together, despite what it looks like on-screen. If your letters print on top of each other, however, you have to increase the line spacing again.

Can I put more space between letters?

Printers also have a name for the space between consecutive letters. They call it **kerning**, which originally referred to the non-printing metal that surrounded the raised letter itself on a single character, or *slug* of metal type. It's also called **tracking**.

Whatever you want to call it, you can adjust this spacing as easily as you adjusted the space between lines. To change the tracking of one or more paragraphs

1 Highlight at least some of the text in all of the paragraphs you want to adjust.

2 Choose F̲ormat, Spacing B̲etween Characters. The Spacing Between Characters dialog box appears (see fig. 8.10).

Fig. 8.10
Shrinking or expanding space between characters can help you fit more text into less space or, with some fonts, improve legibility.

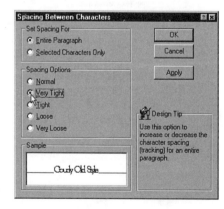

3 Choose E̲ntire Paragraph (the default setting).

4 In the Spacing Options area you can choose N̲ormal, V̲ery Tight, T̲ight, L̲oose, or Ver̲y Loose.

Tight means the letters move closer together than normal, while **loose** means they move further apart. The option you choose will be applied to all the paragraphs that contain highlighted text. (Even if you highlighted less than a whole paragraph, the entire paragraph will be affected.)

5 Look at the Sample area to see what your text will look like with the new spacing in place. Figure 8.11 shows examples.

Fig. 8.11
Altering the spacing between characters can help long text fit in tight spaces. On the left, the spacing between characters is Very Tight; on the right it's Very Loose, in the middle it's Normal.

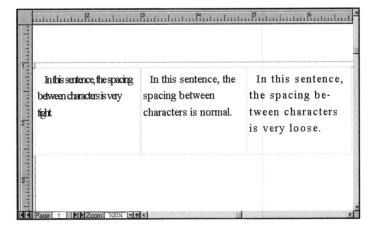

To change the spacing only between specific characters

1 Highlight the characters you want to adjust, and choose Format, Spacing Between Characters. The Spacing Between Characters dialog box appears.

2 Choose Selected Characters Only. The dialog box changes the available options (see fig. 8.12).

3 You can add or subtract a precise amount of space (measured in points) between the letters you highlighted. First, select Squeeze Letters Together or Move Letters Apart. Then choose the number of points you want added or subtracted from the spacing in the By This Amount text box. You can return to normal spacing at any time by choosing Normal.

4 Look in the Sample area to see what your text will look like with the new spacing applied.

5 Click Apply to change your text's spacing while keeping the dialog box open—you can double-check the results before making them official. Or, click OK if you're sure you have the spacing right. The dialog box closes and your text adjusts to the new spacing.

Fig. 8.12

You can alter the spacing between as few as two individual characters—sometimes all it takes to make an over-long headline fit in its assigned space.

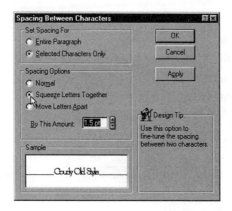

Heading up my to-do list: make some lists!

The Lord High Executioner in Gilbert & Sullivan's *The Mikado* sings a song about the "little list" he made up of all the annoying people he hopes to eliminate. Whether you're a Lord High Executioner or just very organized in your shopping plans, the time will come when you, too, will need to make a little list.

You can do it the hard way, using tabs and indents and so forth, or you can let Publisher create a **bulleted list** (in which each item is set off by a graphic symbol) or a **numbered list** for you.

To create a list, first draw a text frame or select an existing one. Then choose the Bullet or Number List button on the formatting toolbar.

You are immediately presented with six possible bullets and an option to see more. If you choose one of these bullets, you can start creating your list immediately. Every time you press Enter, Publisher inserts a bullet at the beginning of the line and your text automatically indents. If your list item continues past the end of the line, the next line of text automatically indents to match the first line.

If this list isn't what you had in mind, you can modify it by clicking the Bullet or Number List button again and choosing More. The Indents and Lists dialog box appears, offering a plethora of possibilities (see fig. 8.13).

Fig. 8.13
Whether you have
a little list or a big
one, customize it to
meet your precise
requirements.

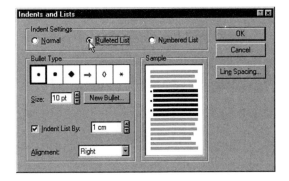

Number one, with a bullet

At the top of the Indents and Lists dialog box, you first have to choose an
indent setting: Normal, Bulleted List, or Numbered List. The default is
Bulleted List, so choose that for now.

The Bullet Type area shows the same bullets you see when you first click the
Indents & Lists button. Now, using the Size text box, you can make them
larger or smaller.

If all of these bullets are shooting blanks as far as you're concerned, click
New Bullet. This opens the New Bullet dialog box. Identical to the Insert
Symbol dialog box, the New Bullet dialog box displays all the characters
available for a font. It defaults to the Symbol font, but you can use the Show
Symbols From list box to see all the characters in any font installed on your
computer. Choose any character you want to use as a bullet; it appears in the
Bullet Type area of the Indents and Lists dialog box.

 TIP **Most fonts contain an ordinary bullet or two, but those might not**
be what you want. The best places to look for a more exotic bullet are the
special fonts that come with Windows 95 (Symbol and Monotype Sorts),
and the three that come with Publisher (Wingdings, Wingdings2, and
Wingdings3). From Greek letters to arrows to tiny telephones, these special
character sets can provide you with bullets for every occasion.

Next, enter the amount of indentation you want in the Indent List By text
box. This determines how far from the left edge of the text frame the text of
each bulleted item will appear (the bullets line up on the left edge). As noted

earlier, if the text is long enough to wrap to a second line, that line will begin directly under the start of the top line.

Finally, in the Alignment list box, choose how you want the text to align. The default is Left Alignment, where the left edge of all text aligns with the invisible line of the specified indentation. Center Alignment centers the text between the indent line and the right margin of the text frame. Right Alignment aligns all text against the right margin. Justified aligns text evenly on both the left and right margin, with extra space added between words to make that possible.

Number one, with a number

If you choose Numbered List in the Indent Settings area, the dialog box options change (see fig. 8.14).

Fig. 8.14
Use these options to set up a numbered list, useful for an agenda or a sequentially arranged publication.

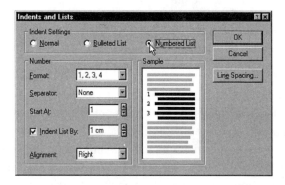

The indent and alignment options are the same as before, but the bullet boxes are gone. Instead you have three new options:

- The Format list box lets you choose numbers or letters to distinguish the elements of your list.

- The Separator list box gives you various elements to use to separate the number from the list: colon, parentheses, and so on.

- Start At lets you select which number or letter you want to begin the list. It doesn't have to be 1 or A.

TIP **A bulleted list is more graphically interesting than a numbered list,** but a numbered list is better if you want to easily refer your readers to a specific item within the list, such as "If you'll take a look at item number three on tonight's agenda..."

Indentation

The final option in the Indents and Lists dialog box, in the Indent Settings area, is <u>N</u>ormal. (It's actually the first option, but I'm discussing it last.) If you select the <u>N</u>ormal button, the dialog box changes so you can fine-tune paragraph indenting (see fig. 8.15).

Fig. 8.15

There are a lot more ways to indent a paragraph than just moving the first line over a few spaces.

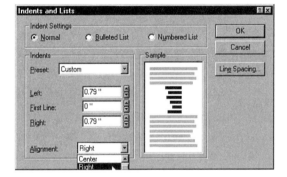

In the Indents area, you can choose a <u>P</u>reset mode, which includes Flush Left (no indent), 1st Line Indent (standard paragraph indentation), Hanging Indent (first line flush left, subsequent lines indented—the way your bulleted and numbered lists indent), and Quotation (the whole paragraph indented from the left and the right sides).

You can also create your own indentation scheme. Use the <u>L</u>eft, <u>F</u>irst Line, and <u>R</u>ight options to set how far, in inches, the left side of the paragraph should indent from the left margin, how far the first line should indent, and how far the right side of the paragraph should indent from the right margin.

With the list and indent options, you can position your paragraphs with perfect precision! Look at figure 8.16 to see a few examples.

Fig. 8.16
The way you indent a paragraph can have a large impact on how easy it is to read and on how it looks next to other text.

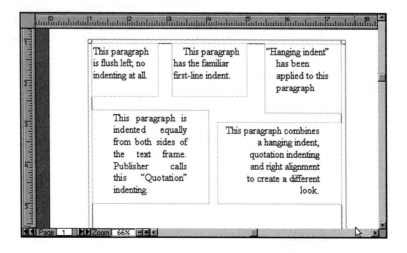

Getting fancy with first letters

Here's another way to set off paragraphs that's a new feature in Publisher 3.0: fancy first letters.

Drop caps, as they're sometimes called, add flair to a publication. They remove a publication from the realm of the gray and ordinary. In previous versions of Publisher, you had to laboriously create drop caps manually. In Publisher 3.0, they're just a couple of mouse clicks away.

1 Select the paragraph where you want to apply the letter. You don't have to highlight the whole paragraph; placing your cursor anywhere in it does the trick.

2 Choose Format, Fancy First Letter. The Fancy First Letter dialog box opens (see fig. 8.17).

Fig. 8.17
Medieval monks labored for days over fancy first letters in their illuminated manuscripts. You can have one in seconds!

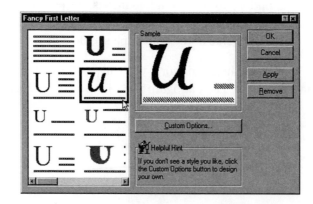

3 You have several possibilities. The gray lines represent lines of text, so you can see exactly how each of these suggestions will fit in your publication. Choose one to get a better look at it in the Sample area.

4 Click Apply, and you can check the results in your actual publication without closing the Fancy First Letter dialog box. Try others until you find the one you like.

5 If you decide you don't like any of them, click Remove and your text reverts to normal and the dialog box closes. If you decide you *do* like one, click OK. The format is applied to your text and the dialog box closes.

If you don't like any of Publisher's suggestions and would rather create your own fancy first letter, click the Custom Options button in the Fancy First Letter dialog box to open the Create Custom First Letter dialog box (see fig. 8.18).

Fig. 8.18
Used appropriately, fancy first letters add instant class to a publication.

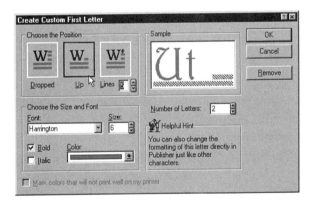

Designing your own fancy first letter

To create your own fancy first letter:

1 Choose the position. Choose Dropped to drop the first letter down into the body of the text; choose Lines to change the number of lines the letter drops into. Choose Up to raise the letter above the top of the text.

2 Choose the font from the Font list box. It can be any font; it doesn't have to be the same as the main body of the text.

3 Choose the size from the Size box. The number in the Size box doesn't represent the first letter's size in points, but its height in lines of text.

The number of lines you can drop the letter into the text is always equal to this number: you can drop a 10-line-tall letter 10 lines into the body of the text, whereas you can only drop a three-line-tall letter three lines into the text.

4 If you want to make the first letter bold or italic, select the Bold or Italic check boxes—or select both.

5 Choose the color of the letter in the Color list box. This opens the pop-up color selection dialog box you saw earlier in this chapter.

6 You probably noticed some of Publisher's pre-set fancy first letters were actually fancy first and second letters. Select how many letters at the beginning of the paragraph you want in the Fancy First Letter format from the Number of Letters text box. To set the whole first word in the fancy format, for example, enter the number of letters in that word.

7 Click OK to return to the Fancy First Letter dialog box. Notice that the design you just created has been added to the pre-set selections. This saves you from having to recreate it each time you want to apply it; from now on, while you're working on this publication, it will be readily available.

8 Click Apply to preview the letter in your publication while keeping this dialog box open, or choose OK to add the letter to your publication and close the window.

Do it with style

You finally have your text looking just the way you want it: it's the right size, the right font, the right color, the right spacing, *and* it has that fabulous Fancy First Letter. It was a lot of work, but it's perfect.

But now you move to a new text frame. You want all the same formatting elements, but you don't want to go through all that work again. How can you avoid it?

There are several ways, one of which is brand-new with this version of Publisher: the Format Painter.

Format painting

In the formatting toolbar, there's a button with a paintbrush on it. That's the Format Painter, and it's a huge new time saver for Publisher users.

Using it is simplicity itself. Suppose you want the same indents and color schemes in two text frames. Just select the one that has the formatting you want, click the Format Painter—the pointer changes to a paintbrush—and click the second text frame. The indents and color scheme from the first text frame are instantly applied to the next.

CAUTION **The Format Painter is a help, but it's not perfect. Not all format-ting transfers. If there are two styles of text, for example, only one might make it to the new box. Fancy first letters don't transfer, either. Check the newly formatted text frame carefully to make sure it looks the way you want it to.**

Pick Up & Apply Formatting

The Format Painter is good for transferring formatting from a single object to a single object; but if you need to transfer formatting from one text frame to many other text frames, all at once or one after the other, Publisher offers an alternative that involves much less mouse clicking:

1 Select the text frame with the formatting you want to transfer.

2 Right-click the text frame and select Pick Up Formatting, or choose Format, Pick Up Formatting.

3 Select the objects you want to format either by "lassoing" them or clicking them one after the other while holding down the Shift key.

4 Right-click the selected objects and select Apply Formatting, or choose Format, Apply Formatting.

5 The format from the first object transfers to all the selected objects.

Styles

Creating a **style** is another useful way to use the same text and paragraph settings over and over without having to recreate it each time. And unlike using the Format Painter or the Pick Up Formatting and Apply Formatting commands, it allows you to save a format on disk and apply it to other publications—even publications in other applications. In addition, Styles saves all the attributes you apply to text. The others—as noted in connection with the Format Painter—don't.

Here's how to create a style:

1 Choose Format, Text Style. The Text Styles dialog box appears (see fig. 8.19).

Fig. 8.19
Creating a style saves you the trouble of having to recreate complicated formatting instructions every time you start a new text frame.

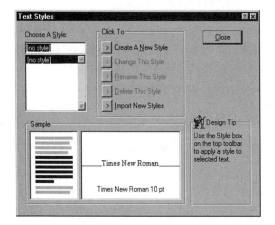

2 Click Create a New Style. The Create New Style dialog box appears (see fig. 8.20).

Fig. 8.20
Most text formatting options are in this one dialog box for the purpose of creating a style.

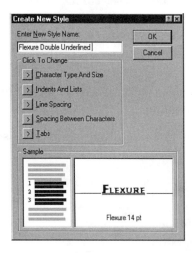

3 You can name your style right away in the Enter New Style Name text box, or you can create it first. The current settings will be identical to those of the text frame you are working in, so if its format is the one you want to use in other locations, simply name it and click OK.

4 If you want to make changes to the style before saving it, or create a new style sheet from scratch, click a button to open the dialog boxes you worked with in this chapter.

5 When the style is the way you want it, click OK. This takes you back to the Text Styles dialog box.

6 Name your style by typing text into the Choose A Style text box, then click Close. You saved your style and can now apply it to other text frames in your publication.

Editing, renaming, or deleting styles

To edit, rename, or delete an existing style, choose Format, Text Style, highlight the style you want to edit, rename, or delete in the Choose A Style list box, and click the appropriate buttons. Choosing Change This Style opens the Create New Style dialog box—simply make your changes and click OK. Choosing Rename This Style shows you the current name of the style sheet and prompts you for a new name. Choose Delete This Style to delete a style. Publisher asks you to confirm your decision, then removes the style from the list.

Imported or domestic?

Imported styles, as you find when you shop for clothes, are usually expensive. But Publisher allows you to import styles for free: not from Europe, but from another Publisher publication or even from certain other programs. To see a list of programs from which Publisher can import style sheets, choose Format, Text Style, Import New Style. Click the Files of Type list box in the resulting Import Styles dialog box. Choose the type of file you're looking for—such as a Microsoft Works 3.0 file—and click once to select it. The dialog box now displays only files of that type as you browse through the folders and files on your disk drives. When you find the file whose style you want to import, select it and click OK. You return to the Text Styles dialog box, where all the styles contained in the file you selected are now listed in the Choose a Style list box. Click Close to add the new style to those available in the publication you're currently working on.

Applying styles

To apply a style, select a text frame and choose a style from the Style drop-down list in the toolbar. Styles apply to the whole text frame; even if you highlight only a word or two in a frame before applying a style, all the text in the frame will be affected.

TIP **If you know exactly how you want to format the types of text in** your publication, design styles before you even draw your first text frame. The Create A New Style dialog box brings together in one place almost all of the formatting elements you've seen in this chapter. Rather than choosing menus here and clicking buttons there, you can do the same work in this one dialog box. Then just draw your text frames, apply the appropriate style sheet to each one, input your text, and you're on your way to a finished publication in far less time, with far less effort.

Part III:

Graphics

9

Adding Graphics

● In this chapter:

- **Enough words! I want to add pictures!**

- **Where can I find the perfect graphic?**

- **A nip here, a tuck there: making the picture fit the frame (and vice versa)**

- **How can I add artwork that's not in my computer?**

Add the right graphic, and your mundane text becomes marvelously memorable! . . . . ▶

Text is a great way to convey information, and has been ever since the Sumerians invented writing. But if text alone were enough for your purposes, you'd have been content with your word processor and wouldn't have bought Microsoft Publisher in the first place. The whole point of desktop publishing software is to combine text and graphics into a seamless whole.

Publisher makes it easy for you to add pictures to your prose. Illustrations break up blocks of gray text, draw the eye of the reader, highlight information in the text or sometimes provide new information. A particularly apt picture can even obviate the need for any text at all. Look at *Life* magazine.

Where should my graphics go?

After you decide to add artwork to your Publisher project, you have to decide where to place it.

If you're creating a publication from scratch, that choice is left entirely up to you; if you're working with a template, or one of Publisher's PageWizards, graphic elements will be pre-placed, but don't worry: it's easy to move the graphic around if you decide you don't like it where it is.

The process is a lot like hanging a painting in your house; you put it where you think it'll look good. But after you move the furniture around, you might decide it doesn't look so great there after all, so you try it somewhere else. The only difference is, moving a graphic around inside Publisher doesn't leave nail holes behind.

Preparing to add images

No matter what sort of graphic you plan to place in your publication, the first step is to click the Picture button on the Publisher toolbar. You can't miss it; the icon is a miniature picture of a desert scene, complete with cactus. Then just follow these steps.

Drawing a picture frame

1 Click the Picture button. The pointer arrow changes to cross-hairs.

2 Place the cross-hairs on your page where you want to anchor the upper-left corner of your image.

3 Hold down the left mouse button.

4 Move the cross-hairs to the bottom-right corner of the space where you want your graphic.

5 Release the mouse button. The completed frame should look similar to the one in figure 9.1.

Fig. 9.1
Drawing a picture frame is the first step in inserting any type of graphic element in a Publisher publication.

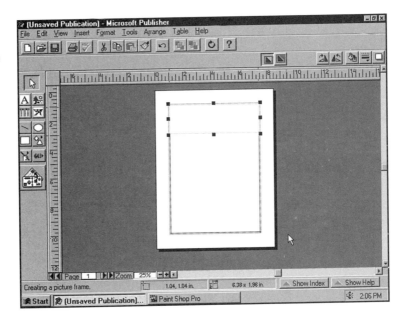

So I have an empty frame. Now what?

You now have a rectangular square framed by eight little black **handles**, one on each corner and one in the middle of each side. If you don't see those little black handles, just point your arrow at the frame and click. This selects the frame. Remember, you must select a frame before you can put a picture in it.

Now you've hung a frame, but a frame is no good without a picture. How do you get one to appear in that empty box?

Like many designers before you, you need to make a trip to the gallery.

Q&A *My picture frame is inside a text frame, but when I click it, all I select is the text frame. What gives?*

 Sometimes when you're working with several text and picture frames together, a picture frame can end up "underneath" a text frame. If you click a frame that's been buried that way, even though it's still visible, you can't select it. To get at it, select the text frame covering it and push it "underneath" the picture frame by clicking the Send to Back button. If you have several frames overlapping, keep doing that until you're able to select your picture frame. See Chapter 16, "When Elements Overlap," for more detail.

Your own personal art gallery, free with Publisher!

After you select a picture frame, choose Insert, ClipArt, or right-click the frame and choose Insert ClipArt from the shortcut menu. You suddenly find a veritable smorgasbord of images at your fingertips, clip art that's provided with Publisher.

66 *Plain English, please!*

Clip art is art that you didn't draw specifically for a publication, and instead found somewhere else (already drawn). Before computer layout was common, you literally clipped such art, with scissors, from the pages of another publication or from a special book full of clip art (many newspapers and magazines subscribe to such books, which arrive monthly). Then you had to paste the clip art onto the new publication. Although using clip art on the computer requires no scissors, the name has stuck. 99

What all's in the ClipArt Gallery?

As you can see in figure 9.2, at the center of the Gallery is the Pictures box containing several small images. At the left is a list of categories. Browsing the ClipArt Gallery is just like visiting a real art gallery; you can either walk through it from beginning to end or head straight to the room set aside for the particular kind of art you're most interested in. Just click one of the categories, and you see only the images related to that category.

You can also search for a particular file by choosing Find. Like the friendly guard at the real art gallery, Find can help you locate a particular picture based on a descriptive word, a portion of its name, or the graphics format it's saved in. When the Find dialog box appears, just fill in the information you have in the blanks provided and choose Find Now.

Fig 9.2
Publisher makes it easy for you to find the artwork you need with this virtual art gallery, which also works with other Microsoft applications.

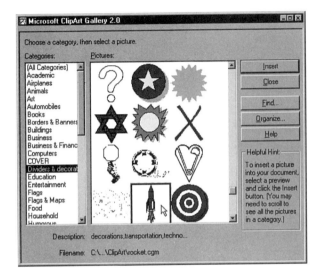

Importing Gallery artwork

When you find the picture you want, you can either double-click it or choose Insert.

The ClipArt Gallery vanishes, you find yourself back in your publication, and presto! The clip art you chose is now inside the selected picture frame.

Fit the picture to the frame, or fit the frame to the picture?

The Import Picture dialog box immediately appears, offering you two choices: Change The Frame To Fit The Picture or Change The Picture To Fit The Frame (see fig. 9.3). If you choose to change the frame, your frame adjusts to fit the picture; if you choose to change the picture, your picture stretches in one dimension or another. This can have unfortunate effects, as you can see in figure 9.4.

Fig. 9.3
The Import Picture dialog box comes up every time you import artwork into a picture frame.

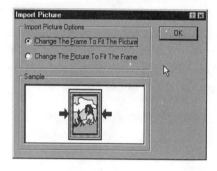

Fig. 9.4
Changing the picture to fit the frame can be very effective with decorative, abstract patterns. But take care not to distort more realistic artwork, like this rocket, in unacceptable ways.

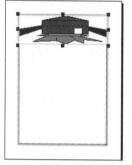

You can add artwork from almost anywhere

Of course, just as sometimes you hate everything the curator chooses to hang on the walls of an art gallery, you might find nothing in ClipArt Gallery you can use. Perhaps you absolutely have to have a picture of a cow and, inexplicably, the ClipArt Gallery doesn't have one. But maybe you have a disk full of clip art that contains an absolutely fabulous cow, or you know of another publication on your disk that contains the perfect cow, or you took a great photo of a cow on your last vacation. Maybe you're even talented enough to draw a cow. Publisher makes it possible to add any of these possible cows to your publication.

Making Changes to the Gallery

Microsoft ClipArt Gallery is actually a separate program that works not only with Microsoft Publisher but with other Microsoft programs. If you have PowerPoint or Word installed, you've probably already seen the ClipArt Gallery and already have lots of clip art in it.

As you've seen, Publisher provides several useful images with ClipArt Gallery. You can also add pieces of your own clip art collection to it.

To insert your own clip art into ClipArt gallery, open the gallery and click <u>O</u>rganize. You're given four choices:

- **<u>A</u>dd Pictures** allows you to add a specific image or images—say, images from a floppy disk—to the ClipArt Gallery.

- **<u>U</u>pdate Pictures** causes ClipArt Gallery to search your computer's drive(s) for picture types it recognizes, and add thumbnails of them to the Gallery while removing any thumbnails already in the Gallery for which it can no longer find corresponding files (after querying you first so you can point it to where the file might be).

- **<u>P</u>icture Properties** allows you to associate descriptive keywords with any picture and choose what category to place it in, like choosing what room of a gallery to hang a new painting in (see fig. 9.5).

Carefully organizing your collection becomes more and more important as you add clip art to the gallery—at least if you're planning to find it again. You can also access the Picture Properties dialog box by right-clicking the picture that interests you in the ClipArt Gallery.

- **<u>E</u>dit Category List** allows you to add, rename, or delete a category from the ClipArt Gallery list. You can also open the Edit Category List dialog box by right-clicking a category from the ClipArt Gallery.

The ClipArt Gallery helps you keep track of all the computer clip art you collect, and makes it easily accessible to you.

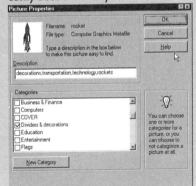

Fig. 9.5
The Picture Properties dialog box makes organizing your clip art a breeze, and provides more detailed information about each picture.

Inserting a picture file that's not in ClipArt Gallery

You can add a picture to your publication from anywhere on your hard drive, floppy drive, or CD-ROM drive. Here's how.

1 Draw or select a picture frame.

2 Choose Insert, Picture File or right-click the frame and choose Insert Picture File from the shortcut menu.

3 You see the Insert Picture File dialog box, which asks you to select a file (see fig. 9.6). Publisher lists, by default, all the formats for storing computer graphics it recognizes. You can also search for files in a particular format by choosing from the Files of Type list.

4 Locate the file you want (select Preview File if you want to see what an image looks like before you import it), and double-click it or choose OK.

5 In the Import Picture dialog box again; decide whether to change the frame or the picture as you did previously and click OK. Your imported file appears in the picture frame.

Fig. 9.6

Publisher recognizes clip art in a variety of graphics formats. Choose the detailed file listing to see which format each graphic is in—and how many bytes it will add to the size of your finished publication.

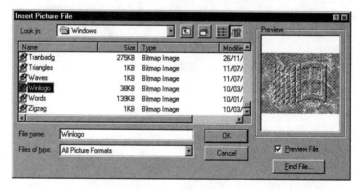

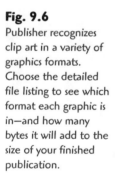 **Plain English, please!**

When you're importing a picture, Publisher looks for files that have any one of a variety of strange identifiers, including **PCX**, **CGM**, and **BMP**. The letters specify the way in which graphic information is stored in that file: CGM, for instance, stands for **Computer Graphics Metafile**. But you don't have to know what any of those strings of letters stand for: Publisher automatically converts the picture types it recognizes into images it can use.

Copying artwork from another publication

You might remember seeing an image in another publication that would be perfect for your publication. Publisher lets you go get it.

1 Open the publication that contains the graphic you want, using whatever application it requires.

2 Using the tools provided with that application, select the graphic and copy it to the Clipboard.

3 Return to Publisher. Go to the page of your publication where you want to place the copied image, click once on the page where you want the copied image to appear, then click the Paste button.

The copied object appears in a new picture frame which you can then adjust to the size you want (see Chapter 10, "Adjusting Graphics," for more information).

Adding a scanned image

Scanners allow you to turn photographs and other images into files your computer can use and manipulate. Using a scanned image is exactly the same as using any other image, if it's already stored on your drive. However, you might want to scan an image directly into a Publisher publication. Publisher lets you do that—provided, of course, you have a scanner. If you don't, the scanner options are not available.

1 Draw or select a picture frame.

2 Choose Insert, Scanner Image or right-click the frame and choose Insert Scanner Image from the shortcut menu.

3 If you have more than one scanner, you have to choose which one to use; then click Acquire Scanned Image.

4 Start the scanning process, using the software provided with your scanner and whatever settings you want to apply to the final picture.

5 When you finish scanning, exit the scanning software. The Import Picture dialog box appears. Make your choice, and the scanned image is added to your publication, as the picture of the Earth was added to the publication in figure 9.7.

Fig. 9.7
Publisher's capability to
use scanned images
opens up many design
possibilities for you—it
lets you include
photographs, hand-
writing, freehand
drawings, and more.

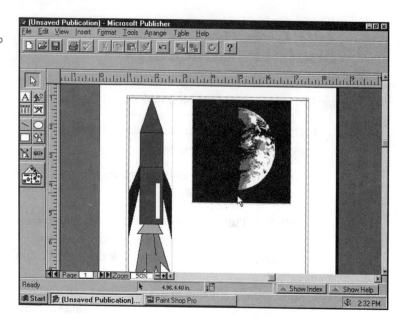

Fig. 9.7
Publisher's capability to
use scanned images
opens up many design
possibilities for you—it
lets you include
photographs, hand-
writing, freehand
drawings, and more.

Drawing your own artwork

It's not an option for everyone, but some people can draw their own artwork
and actually come up with something usable. If you have the talent, Publisher
makes it easy for you to create your own illustrations.

1 Draw or select a picture frame.

2 Choose Insert, Object or right-click the frame and choose Insert Object.

3 You see the Insert Object dialog box, which includes a list of the types
of programs that allow you to create objects to embed in Publisher
publications. (See Chapter 15, "OLE: Objects Created in Other Applications," for details.) Choose the graphics program you want to use, such
as Microsoft Draw or Paintbrush.

4 The graphics program appears, either as it usually does or on top of
Publisher, with a work window occupying the picture frame, as in
figure 9.8. (If the window is too small to work in, you can resize it by
dragging the handles.) Draw your artwork, then save it or close the
program. Publisher automatically places the artwork you created in the
selected picture frame.

Fig. 9.8

You can create graphics using other programs and place them directly in your publication. Here, I used Paint Shop Pro to create an image in a pre-selected picture frame.

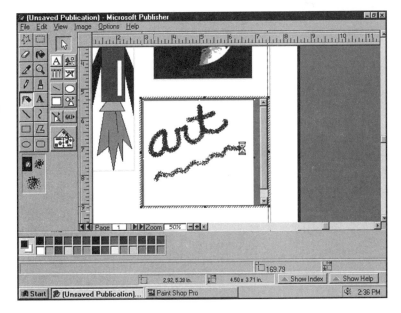

 TIP **You can draw crude images using the line, rectangle, circle, and** shape tools provided with Publisher, but it's much easier to use a dedicated graphics program such as Paintbrush or Microsoft Draw. The greater flexibility they give you will reflect in the quality of the graphics you produce.

I want a different picture here instead

Sometimes you hang a picture in a room and immediately realize you've made the wrong choice (that rugged wildlife scene just doesn't work with the frilly purple couch). The same thing can happen when you add artwork to a publication: the image that looked perfect in the ClipArt Gallery suddenly looks ludicrous in the context of the publication.

Not to worry: replacing one graphic with another is a simple matter of selecting the picture frame whose contents you want to change and using any of the previous methods to add a new image to it. The new graphic automatically replaces the old.

10

Adjusting Graphics

● **In this chapter:**

- ● **Can I move pictures around?**

- ● **This picture needs to be bigger!**

- ● **Rotation: when right-side-up just isn't good enough**

- ● **Are there any cool colors, tints, and shades?**

Get maximum impact from your graphics by changing pictures from "almost right" to "absolutely right" with Publisher's graphics tools. . . . .

How many times have you bought a new piece of artwork and hung it in what you thought was the perfect place in your home or office, only to discover that it clashes with the couch or makes the room look lopsided? How many more times have you hung it before you're perfectly satisfied?

Finding the perfect place for artwork is sometimes as much a process of trial and error as good planning. It can be the same with putting graphics in a Publisher publication. It might look fine in your rough sketch, but when you actually insert the artwork, it overpowers the text it's supposed to complement and ruins the balance of the page.

Be flexible, and be prepared to experiment. Maybe all you need to do is move it an inch or two. It's easy to do.

Moving a picture frame

1 Select the graphic and move the mouse pointer over it. The arrow changes to a set of crossed arrows and an image of a moving van (see fig. 10.1).

2 Hold down the left mouse button and "drive" (meaning drag) the moving van to the new location for the graphic. During the move, a light-gray rectangle the same size as the picture frame represents the graphic.

3 When the frame is where you want it, release the mouse button to "hang" the picture in its new location.

Can I put it on a different page?

You might decide an image would work better on an entirely different page of your publication. Because you can't see that page, you can't just load up the moving van and drive your artwork to it—so how do you get it there?

Select the object. This time, drag it right off the page, onto the **scratch area**—the gray area surrounding your pages. It remains visible there even after you change pages (see fig. 10.2). When you can see the new page, you can drag the graphic off the scratch area and move it wherever you like.

Fig. 10.1

Just as you might rent a moving van to transport artwork from one place to another, use Publisher's moving van to relocate graphics.

Fig. 10.2

The scratch area is like a virtual desktop where you can set clip art and other items from one page while you flip to another page where you want to use them.

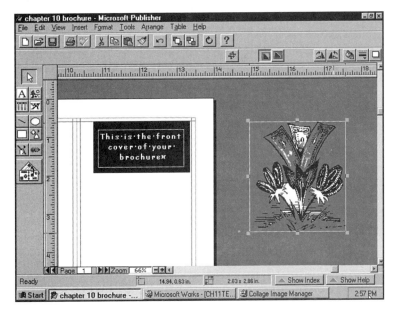

TIP **An alternative method for moving objects, graphics,** and text from page to page is to cut and paste. This can be faster than dragging, especially if you use the keyboard shortcuts. Just select the graphic you want to move and click the Cut button. The graphic disappears. Move to the page you want it on and click the Paste button. The image reappears in the same place on the new page as it was on the original page. Now you can select it and drag it wherever you want.

Q&A *I cut a graphic from one page and without thinking copied something from another page without ever pasting the first graphic. Can I get it back?*

Unfortunately, no. If you use cut, it's important to immediately go to the page you want the graphic on and paste it in place, or you run the risk of losing it. Another option is to use the Copy button instead of the Cut button—that way the original is still in your publication where you originally put it, no matter what happens to the copy. If you use Copy, though, you eventually have to go back to the original page and delete the graphic, making the whole process rather complicated and time-consuming.

I pasted the graphic I cut from another page onto a new page that already had several elements on it. Before I dragged it into place, I selected something else. Now my graphic is hard to separate from all the other elements on the page. How do I select it again?

Again, it's important to finish the cut-and-paste operation before you do something else. To select your graphic again, click it. This selects the top element of all the overlapping elements. Click the Send to Back button, then click your graphic again. If it still isn't selected, click Send to Back again. Keep doing this until the graphic you want is the one selected. Drag it into place, then check the page carefully to make sure you didn't accidentally change its appearance.

Changing the size of a graphic

Sometimes, after you placed your artwork, you're perfectly happy with the location, but you're not happy with the size. Maybe you're trying to cram a very large picture into a very small frame, and important elements have shrunk so much they're invisible; or maybe you've chosen an image too small to have the impact you want it to have.

With the artwork you hang in your home you can't do much about the size, short of making a photocopy or hiring a forger. You don't have to do that in Publisher.

Handles: get a grip on it

Just like any other frame in Publisher, you can resize picture frames. First, select the frame you want to resize. Then point the arrow at a selection handle surrounding the frame, and the arrow changes to a box labeled RESIZE, with two arrows extending horizontally, vertically, or diagonally from it. The arrows indicate the directions in which you can alter the size of the frame using that handle.

Hold down the left mouse button and move the mouse in the direction of one of the arrows, and the frame (visible as a light-gray rectangle) alters size accordingly. As soon as you release the mouse button, the picture refills the frame (see fig. 10.3).

Fig. 10.3
If you use the frame handles to change the size of your picture, you have to be careful it doesn't end up looking like this.

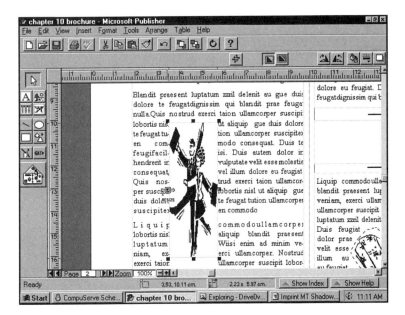

Using the scale option

But wait a minute. Take a look at figure 10.3 again. The picture's not only a different size, it's a different shape. And it's become distorted, either elongated or squashed.

Sometimes, this might be exactly the way you want it to look, but more often you'll want it to look exactly the same as it did before, only bigger (or smaller). How can you resize a picture without running the risk of distorting it?

You can eyeball it, adjusting the frame until the picture looks about right, and sometimes that's good enough—but sometimes it isn't. When it isn't, you can use the Scale Picture command instead.

With the graphic selected, choose Format, Scale Object (or Scale Picture; the name changes depending on where the image came from), or right-click the graphic and choose Scale Object from the shortcut menu. The Scale Object dialog box appears, in which you can set the Scale Height and Scale Width as percentages of the original size (see fig. 10.4). You can also reset the picture to its Original Size. Click OK and the graphic instantly changes.

Fig. 10.4
If you set Scale Height and Scale Width at exactly the same amount in the Scale Object dialog box, your picture resizes without distortion.

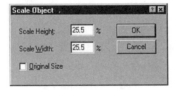

TIP **When you're resizing a picture, you're usually more concerned** about one dimension, height or width, than the other. Maybe the picture can only be two inches tall, and width doesn't matter, or maybe it has to fit into one column, and can be any height at all. Hold down Shift while you use the handles to adjust the picture to the exact size it needs to be in the dimension that's most important to you; this ensures that the proportion of height to width remains the same.

Cropping = chopping

Sometimes the problem with a picture isn't the size, it's the content. Specifically, there's too much of it. For example, say you scan in a photo of yourself taken last summer and you think it's a great picture of your face, but you really don't want the hot dog in your hand appearing in your business report.

Publisher allows you to eliminate unwanted portions of any graphic by **cropping**.

1 Select the graphic. This automatically activates the graphic formatting toolbar.

2 Click the Crop Picture button.

3 Move the pointer to a frame handle. The arrow changes to two pairs of crossed arrows with the word CROP.

4 Hold down the left mouse button and move the handle to the middle of the picture. Part of the picture will disappear, as though you were covering it with paper. Don't worry; it's still there, and you can get it back just by moving the handle back to where it started.

5 Adjust the various handles until the picture displays only what you want. In figure 10.5, much of the original figure has been cropped.

Fig. 10.5
If you only want to see part of the picture, use the Crop Picture button to isolate it.

TIP **Graphics you import often include empty space around the image.**
Use the Crop Picture button as soon as you import the image to remove
that space, so the edges of the frame exactly match the edges of the image.
This makes it easier to resize the image; you won't have to allow for any
space surrounding the image when you're trying to make it fit perfectly into
your publication.

If possible, tightly crop the image in another program even before you
import it. Lots of large images in a publication can really bog down
Publisher's performance.

Q&A *What happens if I crop a picture, cut and paste it, then*
change my mind about the cropping? Can I uncrop the
pasted version?

Yes. Cropping does not destroy any data contained in the picture file. It just
keeps some of it out of sight. When you cut or copy a cropped image, even
the invisible part of the picture is copied. You can uncover that invisible
part again by using the Crop Picture button.

Round and round and round she goes!

A new, powerful feature in Publisher 3.0 is the capability to rotate any object
in any direction you want. You'll be surprised how many times you'll take
advantage of this feature.

Publisher 2.0 only allowed you to rotate objects 90 degrees at a time. That
capability has been retained in Publisher 3.0. Simply select the graphic you
want to rotate and click the Rotate Left or Rotate Right button on the formatting toolbar.

Breaking out of right angles

If you want to rotate a graphic in anything other than multiples of 90 degrees,
click the Rotate button on the Standard toolbar to open the Rotate Objects
dialog box (see fig. 10.6). Use the clockwise or counterclockwise arrows to
rotate the image a little at a time, or enter the specific number of degrees you
want the image rotated in the Angle control box. You can cancel rotation at
any time by selecting No Rotation.

Fig. 10.6
The Rotate Object
dialog box lets you
rotate an image (or
text) frame to the left
or right by a specific
number of degrees.

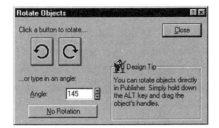

Fig. 10.6
The Rotate Object
dialog box lets you
rotate an image (or
text) frame to the left
or right by a specific
number of degrees.

The keyboard-mouse option

An even easier way to rotate an object is to press and hold the Alt key, while pointing the mouse at the corner handle of any frame. The arrow changes to two arrows chasing each other in a circle, above the word ROTATE.

Click and hold the left mouse button and move around the graphic. A line-drawing of the frame rotates as you move the mouse (see fig. 10.7). You can also flip the frame quickly by dragging your mouse directly across the middle of the graphic. When you have the picture aligned the way you want it, release the mouse button.

Fig. 10.7
The capability to rotate
graphics and text
frames frees you from
the tyranny of right
angles, and offers many
fresh opportunities for
eye-catching designs.

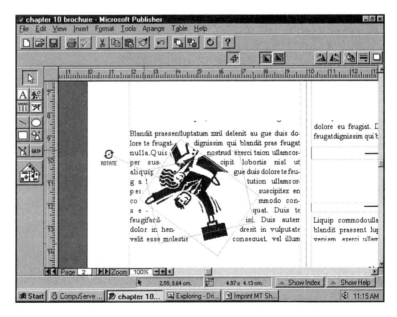

TIP **When you rotate an image using the mouse, your pointer is** connected to the center of the object by a line. You can stretch this line out as far as you like. Use it to align your rotating object with the corners of the paper, other objects, or diagonal lines. It also helps you remember which way is up! That's easy to forget because only an outline of the selected picture frame rotates at first.

Recoloring

With a desktop publishing package, you expect to be able to change a graphic's size and shape or to crop a graphic. Changing the colors of a graphic sounds more like something you'd do in a special graphics pro-gram—but all you need is Microsoft Publisher. (If you already read Chapter 6, this section will look a little familiar, except you're working with graphics now instead of text.)

Why recolor?

If you have the capability to print in color, you have another powerful weapon in your desktop-publishing arsenal to use in the ongoing battle for the reader's attention. And if you can change that color at will, you can precisely target your tactical efforts.

Publisher allows you to choose from a broad palette of basic colors or create your own colors and then lets you fine-tune those colors until they're pre-cisely what you need.

Basic colors

The first step in recoloring a graphic is, as always, to select the graphic. Then choose Format, Recolor (or right-click the graphic and choose Recolor Picture from the shortcut menu).

The Recolor Object dialog box appears (see fig. 10.8). It contains a Preview box that shows the selected graphic and has a palette of basic colors on the left.

Fig. 10.8

The Recolor Object dialog box lets you preview what your graphic will look like with a color you select. This dialog box can also be named Recolor Picture, depending on where the selected graphic originated.

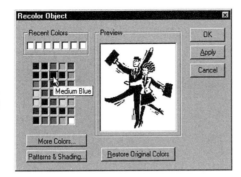

The colors cover the whole spectrum. As you move the mouse over the boxes, the name assigned to each color appears. You'll not only find `Orange` and `Blue`, but `Pumpkin`, `Peach`, `Saffron`, and `Cobalt`. Click any color and the Preview box shows what the graphic looks like with that color applied. Click Apply and the graphic in the publication takes on the hue you selected, but the Recolor Object dialog box remains open so you can experiment with other colors. Click OK to accept the color change and return to your publication.

If you decide to change color again, the next time you return to the Recolor Object dialog box, you see the last color you selected in the leftmost box of the Recent Colors area. This keeps you from repeating yourself as you experiment.

If even `Teal` and `Sienna` aren't enough variety for you, click the More Colors button.

More colors

In the Colors dialog box, you have even more colors to choose from (see fig. 10.9). The Design Tip points out that the colors in each column (1, 2, 3, and so on) are designed to work well together. Choosing colors from the same column can give your publication a more unified look.

If you look at the names of the colors in the Colors dialog box, you see that, in addition to `Coral` and `Maroon` and the like, there are boxes cryptically labeled with names like `RGB(204,51,102)`. Select All Colors at the top of the dialog box instead of Basic Colors, and you'll see why.

Fig. 10.9
Double your colors,
double your fun. With
more colors, you have
more design options.

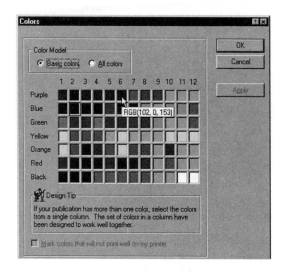

Take a look at figure 10.10. Instead of discrete boxes of colors, you see a palette where the colors flow from one to the other—like someone spilled several cans of paint across the screen. A set of cross-hairs in the palette responds to the movements of your mouse; by moving the cross-hairs around the palette, you can come up with all the hues that Publisher doesn't include in its basic color menus.

Fig. 10.10
If the 84 choices
Publisher gives for basic
colors isn't enough,
you can create your
own using the All
Colors palette.

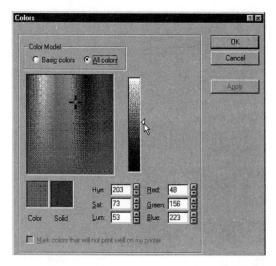

In Color and Solid boxes, you see the color you created (Color) and the solid color most like it (Solid). Publisher applies your custom color if possible, but some things (like text and objects filled with a pattern) only allow solid colors.

To the right of the color palette is a tall, skinny rectangle with the color you chose in it. It's very dark at the bottom and very light at the top. This is like the brightness control on your TV: slide the mouse pointer up the rectangle, and your color gets lighter; slide it down, and the color darkens.

The six text boxes at the lower-right corner contain numbers that change as you maneuver the cross-hairs and slide the mouse pointer. If you want, you can very precisely set all the parameters of the color using these boxes. But you're more likely to simply create something you like using the palette and brightness slider.

After you choose the color you want, click OK and you return to the Recolor Object dialog box.

Tints & shading

There's one more button to try in the Recolor Object dialog box: Patterns & Shading. Clicking it opens up another way to fine-tune your colors, presented in the Fill Patterns & Shading dialog box you see in figure 10.11.

HUE, SAT, LUM, & RGB

Hue, Sat, and Lum might sound like the names of Donald Duck's lesser-known nephews, but they're not. They're the three elements that make up the colors you see on the screen.

Hue is the pure color, with numbers assigned from 0 (red) to 120 (green) to 240 (blue) back to almost-red at 359. **Sat** is short for Saturation and represents the intensity of the color, from 0 (gray) to 100 percent (the pure color). Finally, **Lum**, or luminescence, is the color's brightness. It's what you control in the skinny rectangle next to the color palette in the All Colors Color Model. As noted earlier, this works like the brightness control on your TV set.

For even finer tuning of color than Hue can give you, you can adjust the **RGB** settings. All the colors on your computer are composed of mixtures of red, green, and blue. Increasing the setting of each color alters the mix of all three. If you play with the Red, Green, and Blue boxes in the All Colors Color Model, you'll notice that, as you increase or decrease the value of one of the colors, the value of Hue also changes, but more slowly.

Most users never need to touch these boxes, but if you want to precisely match a color someone else has used, these boxes allow you to do so.

Fig. 10.11

Here you can apply tints and shades to your chosen color. Basically, this controls your color's brightness.

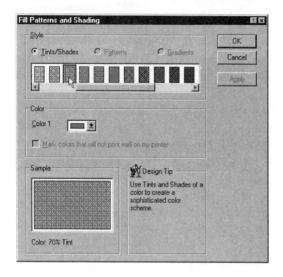

This dialog box features three areas: Style, Color, and Sample.

You only have one Style option during recoloring: Tints/Shades. At the bottom of the Style area, you can see what your selected color will look like with the application of tints (from 0 to 100 percent, shown on the left) or shades (in the same range, shown on the right).

In the Color area, the color you selected is displayed. Clicking it opens the Recent Colors area and the More Colors button from the Recolor Object dialog box, in case you've changed your mind.

Finally, at the bottom, a sample of your color with the current tints and shades is displayed.

Tints are essentially lighter versions of the pure color, while shades are darker versions: this is just another way to adjust your color's brightness.

Choose the tint or shade you like here, and the sample changes. Click OK in the Fill Patterns and Shading dialog box and again in the Recolor Object dialog box. Publisher applies the tint or shade to your sample.

I think I was better off with the original

If you make lots of changes to the color of your graphic then decide you've made a big mistake, there's a button to undo all your damage. In the Recolor Object dialog box, click the Restore Original Colors button. And you're back where you began!

11

Let's Table That

● In this chapter:

- First, how do I make a table?

- Now, how do I put information in my table?

- I want to make my table look really professional

- Can I add graphics to my table?

Tables are the perfect, eye-catching way to present lots of information in a small space...and Publisher makes them easy to create. . . . .

Sentences and paragraphs are a great way to impart information. But sometimes you don't need that many words—all you need is to present data with a few identifying labels, like the tear-out card in this book. That's where a table comes in. A table is a space-efficient and graphically interesting way to present information. In Publisher, tables are sort of a cross between a text frame and a graphic.

First you create the table...

Creating a table is as easy as creating any sort of frame in Publisher. First, click the Table button on the Publisher toolbar. The pointer arrow changes to cross-hairs.

Decide where you want your table to appear in the publication and how much space you want it to fill. Holding down the left mouse button, place the cross-hairs where you want to anchor the upper-left corner of the table, and move the mouse down and to the right to draw a box. Release the button, and your table appears—followed immediately by the Create Table dialog box (see fig. 11.1).

Fig. 11.1
Choose a pre-set table style and then polish it to your specifications.

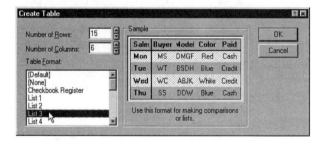

Rows and columns

In the upper-left corner of the Create Table dialog box, you see two controls for setting the number of rows and columns. The default numbers were chosen based on how big a space you drew for your table, based on average sized cells. Changing these numbers changes the size of your cells to a width and thickness that will fit in the space you outlined.

Plain English, please!

A **cell** is a room where a prisoner is kept, the basic unit from which living things are made—and the little rectangle formed by the intersection of a row and a column in a table. You enter data in it—something like a tiny text frame.

Preset styles

If you want, you can shop for Publisher tables in the Create Table dialog box much as you might shop for a kitchen table in a furniture store window. Publisher offers a number of styles of tables; view one by clicking a format in the Table Format list. A small example appears in the Sample area. If you see one you like, just click OK, and Publisher applies that format to the table frame you drew. If you just want a very basic table to build your own design on, choose (None) in the Table Format list.

Fine-Tuning a Format

If you see a format that has some elements you like and others you don't, you can choose to apply only portions of it to your table...but not when you first draw the table. Instead, choose (None) from the Table Format list when you first draw the table and click OK. Now open the Auto Format dialog box by choosing Table, Auto Format. This time, the dialog box includes an Options button. Choose the format you want to partially apply to your table from the Table Format list, then click Options. This adds the Formats to Apply area to the Auto Format dialog box. The Formats to Apply area contains four options.

- Select **Include Text Formatting** to retain text style selections such as Bold and Italic. If you don't select this check box, all text will be normal style.

- Select **Include Patterns & Shading** to retain the shaded and colored cells you see in some of the pre-set styles. If you don't select this check box, all the cells will be white.

- Select **Include Text Alignment** to retain the text's positioning in each cell. In many of the pre-set styles, the text is centered in each cell; in others it is aligned to the right margin. If you don't select this check box, all text will be set flush left in each cell.

- Select **Include Borders** to retain any lines delineating cells, rows, or columns, or surrounding the whole frame. If you don't select this check box, no lines appear.

Plugging stuff in

The sample tables in the Create Table dialog box also include sample text. That text doesn't appear in your newly created table (see fig. 11.2). Just like a brand-new kitchen table, it's bare. Your kitchen table isn't any use until you start putting place settings and maybe a nice vase of flowers on it, and your Publisher table isn't any use without text…maybe it could use a nice vase of flowers, too.

Fig. 11.2
Although the table frame is different from those created for graphics and text, it has the same handles, and you can move or resize it the same way. It strongly resembles an Excel spreadsheet!

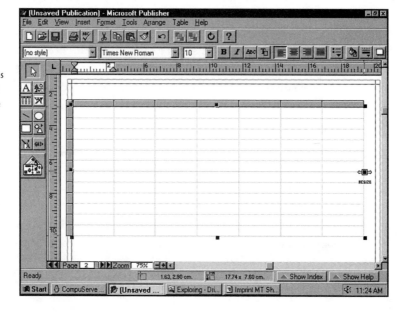

Just start typing

You can type text in each cell of the table just as though it were a miniature text frame—which is essentially what it is.

Simply click a cell to move the cursor there. You can also press Tab to move from one cell to the next, or Shift+Tab to move from one cell to the previous one. You can also navigate from cell to cell using your keyboard cursor keys.

TIP **If you type in more text than the cell can hold, the cell** automatically grows larger. This can cause the table to grow longer, with dire consequences for the rest of your layout. To avoid this, lock the table size by choosing T_able, _Grow to Fit Text (which is active by default; choosing it again deactivates it). You can still type as much information as you want in any cell, but the extra text isn't visible and the table doesn't expand to hold it.

Use Fill for the tedious work

If you have a lot of repeating elements in a table, you don't have to type each one separately. For elements that repeat randomly throughout the table, use Cut and Paste. For elements that repeat over and over again in the same row or column, however, you'll appreciate the Fill Down and Fill Right commands.

To use the Fill Down command, highlight the cell in which the repeating element begins, then drag your mouse down until you reach the last continuous cell in which you want it to appear. (Make sure no cells are included in the highlighted section in which you don't want the repeating element to appear!) Choose T_able, _Fill Down, and every cell you highlighted fills with the text you typed in the topmost cell.

CAUTION **Be careful when using Fill Down or Fill Right: the repeating text** will overwrite any text you might already have in the highlighted cells.

You can highlight cells from the bottom up, too, but you can't Fill Up. Whether you started highlighting from top or bottom, it's the text in the topmost cell that is inserted in all the cells.

Repeating elements can likewise be easily inserted across a row by highlighting them and choosing T_able, Fill _Right. All the cells fill with the text that appears in the leftmost cell of the highlighted series.

Can I use data from another program?

If the data you want to insert in your Publisher table has already been entered in another program, you don't have to type it in. You can't import it like you do graphics or text, but you can easily copy it and paste it into place. Here's how.

1 Open the program in which you originally entered the table data.

2 If the data is already in the form of a table, simply select it and copy it to the clipboard.

3 If the data isn't in table format—which probably means it's straight text—you need to insert a tab between the elements of what will form a row and press Enter at the end of the row. Each tab-separated element will appear in a different column in the row. After you apply tabs and returns to the whole publication, select it and copy it to the Clipboard.

4 Return to Publisher.

5 Place the cursor in the cell where you want the new data to begin appearing.

6 Choose Edit, Paste Special, and you see the Paste Special dialog box in figure 11.3. You have four options:

- **Table Cells with Cell Formatting.** Choose this if you want to insert the material from the other program into an existing table, and you're sure it's formatted properly.

- **New table.** This inserts table-formatted information from another program into Publisher as a brand-new table, which Publisher draws automatically. This option can save you several steps.

- **New text frame.** If you're importing text that hasn't been pre-formatted to fit in a table, this might be your best choice. Publisher inserts the text in your publication in a new text frame it draws automatically. After it's in a text frame, you can format it and add tabs and returns, then copy it to your table.

- **Formatted text.** Choose this one, and all the selected text copies to a single cell of your table. Generally, this is not what you want!

  Depending on what program you copied the data from, this list of options might expand. Copying data from some programs, such as Excel, even allows you the option of linking your Publisher publication to the other program. So when the data changes in the other program, your table in Publisher is automatically updated. (See Chapter 15 for more information on links.)

Fig. 11.3
Paste Special is just that: a special way to paste information into Publisher that offers you more options than just clicking the Paste button.

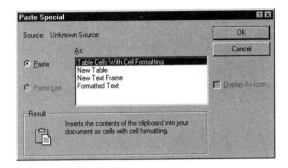

Working with Excel spreadsheets

If you work with Microsoft Excel and want to import a spreadsheet from that application into Publisher as a table, the procedure is even easier. Just open Excel, copy the cells from the spreadsheet you want to import as a table, return to Publisher, select the cell where you want the data to begin appearing, and choose Edit, Paste or press CTRL+V.

Nothing dresses up a table more than a floral centerpiece...

When you're setting your kitchen table for a special dinner party, you might change your mind about what plates to use, what flatware really suits the mood, and what candlesticks look best. The same thing can happen when you set your Publisher table. Maybe you used a pre-set design and it's just not quite right, or maybe you designed your own and you want to give it that final layer of polish that distinguishes good desktop publishing from average desktop publishing.

Most of the formatting options available to you with regard to text and graphics frames are also available for your use with tables. See Chapter 8 for a complete description of color, patterns, gradients, small caps, lists and indents, and more.

The primary difference between using these tools with a text frame and using them with a table is the way in which you highlight the text you want to format.

How do I select things in a table?

You can highlight one or several cells in a table by dragging the mouse across them while holding down the left mouse button. However, often when you're working on a table, a single change in format will apply not only to a single cell or small group of cells, but to all the cells in a row or column. For example, you might want to put all the text in a row or column into bold italics.

To select an entire row or column, first select the table frame, then click the selector on the left side or across the top that corresponds to the row or column you're interested in. This highlights the entire row or column. You can select more than one row or column at a time by holding down the left mouse button and dragging the pointer across several selectors.

You can format the highlighted text just as you would the text in a text frame. Choose foreground and background colors, patterns and shades, fonts and sizes, line spacing and spacing between characters (see fig. 11.4). About the only formatting option that isn't available is Fancy First Letter.

Fig. 11.4

Careful formatting of the text in a table helps distinguish column headers and other labeling elements from data elements.

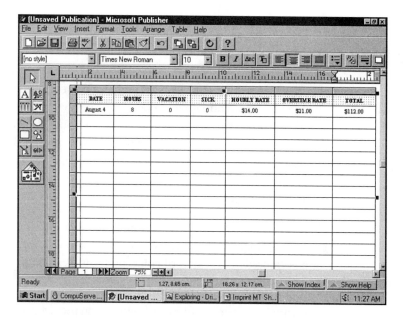

Resizing rows and columns

As noted previously, if Table, Grow to Fit Text is selected, text that is too long for the space provided automatically starts a new line, swelling the depth of its own cell and the table as a whole.

You might want to alter the size of the cell to avoid that, perhaps lengthening it so the text inside it still fits on one line. Increasing and decreasing the size of cells is easy in Publisher.

First, select the table you want to adjust. Move the mouse pointer over the column or row selectors. When the arrow passes over the intersection between two rows or two columns, it changes to an image of two parallel lines attached to arrows going in opposite directions and is labeled ADJUST.

Now hold down the left mouse button and drag the line in the direction you want to expand or shrink the row or column. It alters accordingly.

The external frame of the table also changes. A dotted line appears to show you what its dimensions will be (see fig. 11.5).

Fig. 11.5

As you resize a row or column, you can judge the impact on the dimensions of the table as a whole by watching the dotted lines that appear.

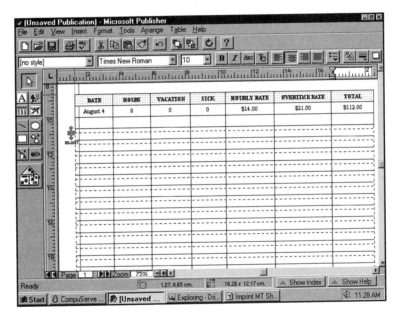

I need to add a row (or column) here

If someone arrives unexpectedly for dinner, you have to find room for another place setting at your kitchen table. Sometimes data arrives late to your Publisher table and you discover you need additional rows and columns.

1 Place the cursor in the row or column closest to where you want the new one to appear, or select the whole row or column.

2 Choose T<u>a</u>ble, <u>I</u>nsert Rows or Columns, or right-click the table and choose Insert Rows or Columns from the shortcut menu. The Insert dialog box appears (see fig. 11.6).

3 Choose <u>R</u>ows or <u>C</u>olumns, then choose the number of rows or columns you want to insert.

4 Choose whether you want the row or column to appear <u>B</u>efore Selected Cells or <u>A</u>fter Selected Cells.

5 Click OK. The new row or column, empty of data, is added to your table (see fig. 11.7).

Fig. 11.6

Insert as many additional rows or columns as you need in an existing table. Make sure you know where your cursor is first, though!

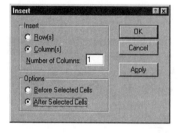

Fig. 11.7

Don't worry if you misjudged the number of rows or columns you need; you can always add more.

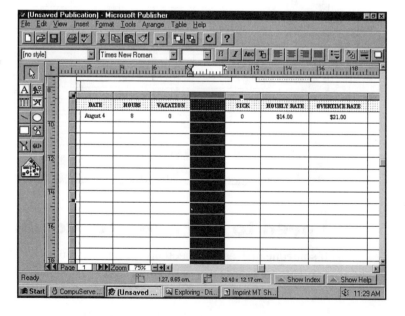

Don't need that one? Get rid of it

You might want to remove a row or column entirely. If so, just select the row or column you want to get rid of and choose T<u>a</u>ble, <u>D</u>elete Rows or <u>D</u>elete Columns (the command visible depends on whether you selected a row or a column).

Copying, cutting, and pasting cells

You can't cut or copy a column or row as such, but you can cut or copy the data in it. Simply select the column or row and choose <u>E</u>dit, Cu<u>t</u> Cells, or <u>E</u>dit, <u>C</u>opy Cells. You can then paste the data from that row or column into another column or row.

CAUTION **When you paste data from one column or row into another, any** data currently in the column or row you're pasting to will be overwritten.

TIP **To create a cell larger than normal, perhaps for a title bar running** across the top of the table, you can **merge** two or more cells together. Just highlight the cells you want to merge and choose T<u>a</u>ble, <u>M</u>erge Cells, or right-click the table and choose Merge Cells from the shortcut menu.

Give those cells some elbow room

Like a text frame, each cell has its own internal margins—which, also like a text frame, default to .04 inch. To change these margins, place your cursor in a cell without selecting any of the text it contains, then right-click the table and select Table Cell Properties, or choose F<u>o</u>rmat, Table Cell <u>P</u>roperties. The Table Cell Properties dialog box appears (see fig. 11.8). Adjust the margins using the four controls.

TIP **Remember that all of the formatting tools available to you in a** text frame are available to you in a table, too. That means if you're having trouble fitting text in a table, you can reduce the font size, tighten up the spacing between characters or lines, or change to a narrower font. The number of formatting tools available in Publisher means there's always more than one solution to a problem.

Fig. 11.8

If text almost-but-not-quite fits in a cell, you can sometimes squeeze it in by reducing the cell margins to zero.

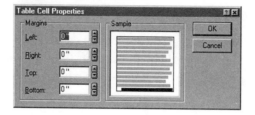

Lines and borders

In the next chapter, you look at adding borders to all kinds of frames. But with tables, there's a particular kind of border that's an important element inside the frame: borders around individual cells or groups of cells.

1 Highlight the cells you want to work with.

2 Choose F̲ormat, B̲order. The Border dialog box appears (see fig. 11.9).

Fig. 11.9

Lines between cells in a table can make the table as a whole easier to read and individual cells easier to pick out from the others.

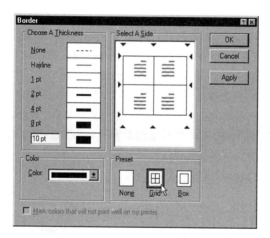

3 From the Preset options at the bottom of the dialog box, choose Non̲e (to remove lines already in the selection), G̲rid (to put lines between rows and columns, therefore putting borders around all cells in the selection), or B̲ox (to put a border around the outside of the selection only).

4 If you want lines only between rows, or only between columns, or only along one, two, or three sides of the entire selection, or even a combination of these, begin by choosing Non<u>e</u> from the Preset options. Now you can add just the lines you want.

5 In the Select A <u>S</u>ide area, you see a simple grid of four cells, surrounded with gray lines. To switch any of those gray lines from printing to non-printing, simply click it. This marks it with two black triangles, one at either end.

6 To add more than one line, press Shift and click each line in turn, as shown in figure 11.10.

Fig. 11.10
How lines flow around the cells in your table is completely under your control in Publisher.

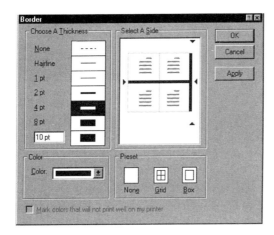

7 Set the thickness to any point size you want with the Choose A <u>T</u>hickness options. You can also choose a color you like from the <u>C</u>olor drop-down list for the lines you install.

8 When you complete your selections, choose A<u>p</u>ply to see what they look like in your publication without closing the dialog box, or choose OK to accept the lines you installed and close the dialog box. Figure 11.11 shows a table with lines installed.

Fig. 11.11
Adding lines gives your
table an organized,
business-like look.

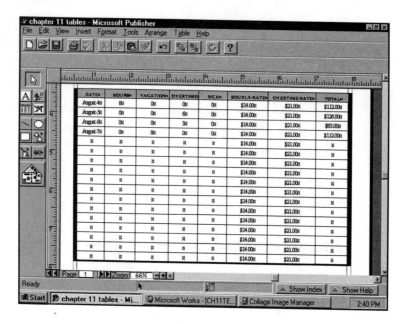

Adding a picture to a table

When you finalize your table, you can spruce it up by adding graphics to it.
Simply draw the graphic frame on top of the table and import graphics as you
would anywhere else (see fig. 11.12). And you thought I was joking about
adding a vase of flowers. Notice, however, that the text in the table doesn't
flow around the graphic the way text in a text frame does, so be careful to
place the graphic where it won't render text illegible.

TIP   **The borders briefly discussed in this chapter are just one of the**
special effects available for text frames, picture frames, and tables alike. See
Chapter 12 for a closer look at how you can use some of these more
"exotic" tools to polish your table—and all the other elements of your
publication.

Fig. 11.12
A touch of artwork can lift a table from the ordinary to the extraordinary, and make the reader look twice at its contents.

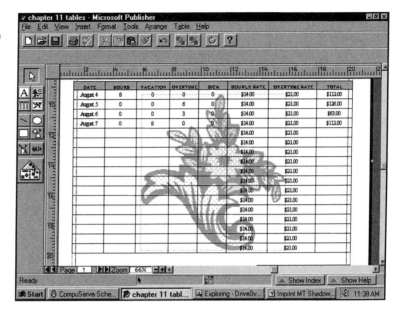

Part IV:

Special Effects

12

Borders and Shadows and Fills, Oh My!

● In this chapter:

- I'd like my art in a frame!

- What are my options?

- Not all borders have four sides

- How can I add even fancier borders?

Borders enhance text, graphics, and tables—and Publisher offers you plenty of borders to choose from. Wrap your publication in lightning bolts or hearts! . . . . >

Most towns have at least one store devoted simply to framing things. It's not just artwork that's being framed, either; you're just as likely to find framed movie posters, framed needlework, or even framed and pressed flowers.

People frame things because those things are special to them. They want to highlight them, make them stand out in a crowded room. They frame them so they can enjoy them better and visitors can admire them, too.

That's the same reason you put a border around objects in Publisher: to make them stand out from a crowded page and catch the interest of visitors—in this case, the readers of your publication.

And just like real life, you don't have to limit yourself to framing artwork, although you certainly can. In Publisher, you can put distinctive, decorative borders around text and tables, too.

Add a simple border

The simplest border is a line, and Publisher makes it easy to put one around any object.

1 Select the text, graphic, or table frame you want the border to surround.

 2 Click the Border button in the Formatting toolbar. This pops up a menu just below the button with several options on it.

3 Click one of the four lines that matches the thickness you want. That line instantly is applied to your object.

4 If you want to remove a border you previously added, choose None. Whether it's a simple line border or one of the fancy borders you'll see later in the chapter, it disappears.

5 If you don't like any of these choices, choose More. The Border dialog box appears (see fig. 12.1). You can also open this dialog box by choosing Format, Border.

Fig. 12.1
You have complete control over the thickness, color, and positioning of lines around any text, graphic, or table in Publisher.

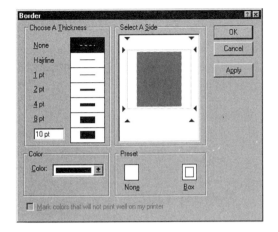

TIP **If the Border dialog box—or any other dialog box you open—** blocks your view of the object you're working on, you can move the dialog box out of the way by grabbing its title bar and dragging it somewhere else on your screen.

Through thick or thin

The first choice you have to make is what thickness of line you want around your object. The preset options range from None to Hairline (0.5 points) to 10 points (remember, a point is 1/72 of an inch); but if that's still not thick enough, you can type your own amount in the text box at the bottom of the Choose A Thickness list (see fig. 12.2). Your choice appears in the Select A Side box so you can get some idea of what it will look like around the object you're framing.

Fig. 12.2
Make a border of whatever thickness you want, and preview it in the sample box.

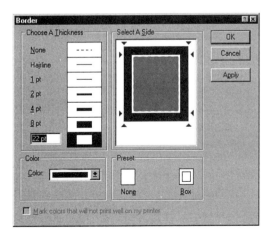

Light or dark, red or green?

You're not limited to just a solid, boring black line around your object. You can make a shaded line or a colored line, using this same dialog box.

Just open the Color drop-down list, and you see the color palette you've used with text, graphics, and tables in earlier chapters. (Chapter 10 discusses selecting color in detail in the "Recoloring Graphics" section.) Pick a color from this basic selection or choose More Colors or Patterns & Shading to see more possible colors or fine-tune the brightness of your selected color, respectively (see fig. 12.3).

Fig. 12.3
If you want to set off your text frame, graphic, or table with a colorful border, you can create it here.

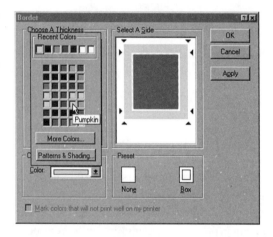

A border doesn't have to have four sides!

You know from everyday life that a border doesn't necessarily have to have four sides. After all, the border between Canada and the U.S. is really just a single line that mostly follows the 49th parallel.

Borders in Publisher don't have to have four sides, either. They can have three, two, or just one.

Take a look at the Select A Side box in the Border dialog box. It looks similar to the Sample area you've used in many other Publisher dialog boxes. There's a triangle at each end of the four lines that make up the border.

Aim your mouse pointer at any side of the light gray rectangle inside the box and click the left mouse button. All the triangles disappear except the two marking the line you clicked (see fig. 12.4).

Now choose the thickness of line you want to appear on that side of your object from the list at left, and that thickness is applied to the line you selected. You can select or deselect all four lines at once by choosing Box or None in the Preset area. None removes all lines, while Box replaces all lines with lines of the default thickness. To choose two or three lines at once, hold down the Shift key while clicking the lines you want to edit one after another.

In figure 12.4, all lines were removed by choosing None, then the bottom line was selected and a custom 22-point line applied.

Fig. 12.4
Click the sides of this box to choose which parts of your border you want to print.

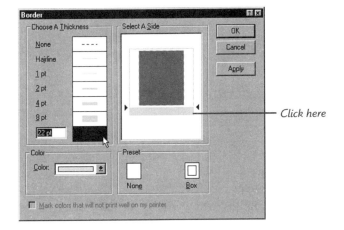

Click here

If you click OK and return to your publication now, you see that only the line on the bottom of the border chosen in figure 12.4 was applied (see fig. 12.5). Or, if you want to continue experimenting, click Apply; the changes you made to the border apply to the object you selected, but the Border dialog box remains open so you can make more changes.

TIP   **Be creative with your borders. Make two sides thick and two sides** thin, or all four of a different weight. Use a different color on each side. A simple border outlining all four sides of your text, graphic, or table might be the best choice—but then again, it might not. Take advantage of Publisher's flexibility to experiment with fresh designs.

Fig. 12.5
This is what the border looks like applied to a graphic in a brochure.

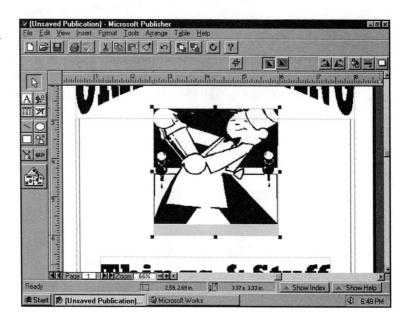

Getting fancy

You can do all the playing around with line thickness and color you want, but sometimes the border you create just won't do the object justice. Just as in your home, a simple metal frame might work best for a quiet watercolor, while a richly hued Renaissance oil painting cries out for an ornate frame of gilded wood.

The Publisher equivalent of gilded wood frames is BorderArt.

Choosing your border

To access BorderArt, select the object you want to apply BorderArt to, and choose Format, BorderArt. The BorderArt dialog box appears (see fig. 12.6).

To browse the borders, simply scroll down through the Available Borders list. Highlight a border to see it in the Preview box; you can check out how it looks in your publication by choosing Apply. If you do this, the BorderArt dialog box remains open for further experimentation in case you don't like the result.

Even if you like the border you choose, you might not like how thick or thin the program makes it by default. It might completely overwhelm your text, graphic, or table like the ornate frame of the Renaissance oil would over-whelm the pastel delicacy of a watercolor. Or it might disappear around the object like the metal frame of the watercolor would around the oil.

Fig. 12.6
Abstract designs, fancy lines, ice cream cones and flowers: BorderArt offers all kinds of borders to spice up your text, graphics, or tables.

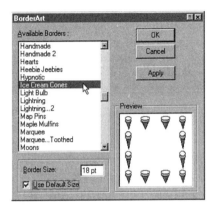

Adjust the thickness of your BorderArt using the <u>B</u>order Size option in the BorderArt dialog box. Enter how thick you want the border to be in points. If you check the effect and decide you like the original, recommended size, you can return to it by selecting <u>U</u>se Default Size.

I chose Ice Cream Cones in figure 12.6 because the graphic I'm putting the border around is of a guy making a milkshake. In figure 12.7, you can see what this border looks like, thickened up to 24 points and applied to the graphic.

Q&A *Can I modify BorderArt to print on only some sides of my object, the way I could modify an ordinary border?*

No. BorderArt is not affected by changes in the regular border window. However, you *can* click the Border button and choose None to remove BorderArt; you don't have to return to the BorderArt dialog box.

Q&A *Won't a thick frame of BorderArt make the framed object take up more room?*

No. The amount of space taken up remains the same; the object itself shrinks to fit inside the BorderArt. This can cause problems with text frames and tables, so check your publication carefully if you add BorderArt.

Fig. 12.7
BorderArt that relates visually to the subject of the text frame, graphic, or table it's surrounding adds extra impact to the topic at hand, like an exclamation mark at the end of a sentence!

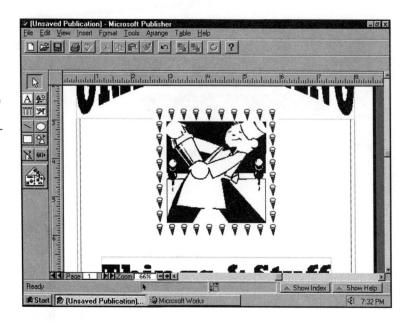

Adding a drop shadow

An effect similar to a border that's also available for use with any text frame, graphic, or table—as well as some of the more unusual shapes discussed in Chapter 15—is a **drop shadow**.

 Plain English, please!

A **drop shadow** is a dark line that outlines the right and lower edges of the frame. It's called a "drop shadow" because it makes the frame appear to cast a shadow. Drop shadows add an intriguing three-dimensional look to publications.

 Simply select the text frame, graphic, or table you want to apply the shadow to and click the Add/Remove Shadow button on the formatting toolbar.

In figure 12.8, I applied a lightweight regular border and a drop shadow to a text frame.

 Q&A *Can I add a drop shadow to a frame that's already got BorderArt around it?*

Yes. Remember, BorderArt actually takes up space inside the frame you drew; the drop shadow will appear outside the original frame. No matter what kind of BorderArt you've applied, the drop shadow will be rectangular: it won't outline each individual drawing that makes up the BorderArt.

Is a drop shadow always rectangular?

No. When it's applied to the fancy shapes discussed in Chapter 14, it follows the outline of the shape.

Fig. 12.8
Drop shadows add a three-dimensional effect to your publication that can visually lift important information off the page.

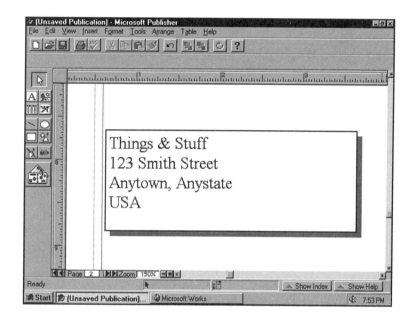

Me And My Shadow

Publisher's drop shadow is always the same thickness and always the same color: gray. You can also create your own drop shadow, which can be any thickness and color you want.

Just draw a box exactly the same size as the frame you want to add the drop shadow to. Use the Color Object button to fill the box with whatever color you want the drop shadow to be, then

position the box where you want the shadow to appear. Select the object you want shadowed and click Bring to Front. Presto! A drop shadow designed to your specifications.

Using this method, you can also create a shadow filled with a pattern or a gradient, for an even more unusual effect.

13

Getting Creative with Shapes

● In this chapter:

- How can I draw a line, a rectangle, or an oval?

- I'm looking for a fancy, eye-catching shape. How can I create one?

- Is there any way to draw shapes without so much mouse-work?

- I want to make my shapes look sharper

You don't have to be Rembrandt to create beautiful and useful designs with Publisher's built-in drawing tools. . . . .

Why do I need drawing tools?

Sometimes clip art is overkill. You don't need a scanned, full-color image of the Earth from space; all you need is a circle. You don't need a festive drawing of a Christmas gift; all you need is a box.

Similarly, sometimes BorderArt offers both too much and too little: graphics that are too fancy, in a shape that's too simple. The only way you can use BorderArt is to surround a text, graphic, or table frame, and that means it's limited to a rectangular shape (or a diamond shape if you rotate it).

If you need a simpler border around a more complex shape, you need Publisher's drawing tools.

The shortest distance between two points...

You can't get much more basic than drawing a straight line. And even people who flunked high school art because they couldn't draw a line *can*, with Publisher.

 Publisher's four drawing tools are grouped together in the Publisher toolbar. To draw a line, click the Line button.

When you click this button, the pointer arrow changes to cross-hairs. Simply position the cross-hairs on the page where you want your line to begin, click, and move the cross-hairs to where you want the line to end. In figure 13.1, you can see the line being drawn. It stretches and shrinks like a rubber band as you move the cursor around. When you release the button, Publisher plants the line, in the default thickness (one point) and color (black) right where you drew it.

You don't have to draw just a plain-vanilla line, either. You can add arrow-heads to one or both ends even before you begin, or add them after it's in place. You can even alter the size and color of the line.

Fig. 13.1

Indicate the shortest distance between two points with Publisher's line-drawing tool.

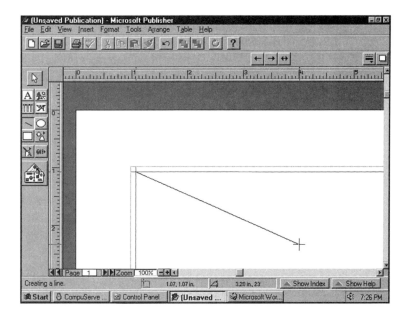

I want an arrow, not just a line

To add arrow tips to one or both ends of your line, click one of the arrow-buttons in the formatting toolbar. The Add/Remove Left Arrow button adds an arrow tip to the left end of your line (or the top, if it's vertical); The Add/Remove Right Arrow button adds an arrow tip to the right end of your line (or the bottom); and the Add/Remove Both Arrows button adds arrow tips to both ends of the line. Clicking any of these buttons again removes arrow tips you already added. You can also click any of these buttons before you draw your line, and the line will be drawn with an arrow tip already added to it (see fig. 13.2).

Thick or thin?

You can also pre-select the thickness of your line before you begin drawing, by clicking the Line button, then clicking the Border button in the Formatting toolbar before you begin drawing.

This opens a drop-down list with four preset values to choose from. Pick the weight of line you want to use and click it. The drop down list closes, and the next line you draw is the thickness you chose. Until you change the thickness again, this is the default value for lines, and every line you draw will be this thickness.

Fig. 13.2

Arrow tips on one or both ends of your line can be useful for creating flow charts or other publications where you need a sense of direction.

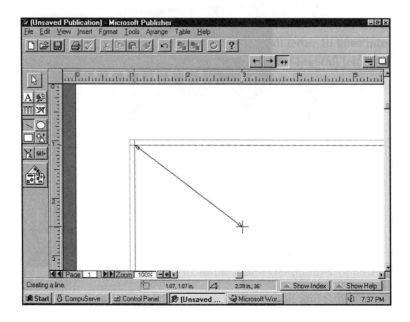

How do I change a line after I draw it?

There are a lot more line drawing options available than just the default arrow tips and four preset thicknesses. After you position your line, select it and click the Border drop-down list again. You can apply one of the thicknesses you didn't use the first time, or you can click More. Clicking More opens the Line dialog box shown in figure 13.3 and a host of new formatting possibilities for your line.

Fig. 13.3

When is a line more than the shortest distance between two points? When it's been formatted from this dialog box.

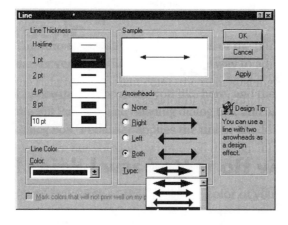

You can choose the thickness of line from those offered at the left or enter your own. What's more, you can choose a color from the color palette—just click the Color drop-down list, and take your pick from a large selection of arrow tips available by clicking the Type drop-down list.

A few clicks in this dialog box and the arrow drawn in figure 13.2 becomes the far more interesting arrow you see in figure 13.4. Choose Apply to see your changes without closing the Line dialog box, or choose OK if you're sure your arrow is now exactly what you want.

Fig. 13.4

Applying a new thickness, new arrow tips, and a new color to a line can change both its appearance and usefulness in your publication. This line is more forceful than the thin one in figure 13.2.

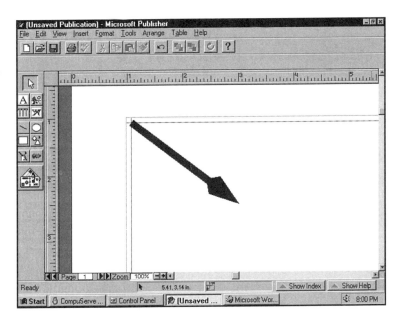

Boxing Helena: drawing squares and rectangles

Drawing a box in Publisher is exactly the same as drawing a frame, except there's no text or image to add afterward.

Simply click the Box button in the Publisher toolbar, and the mouse arrow changes to cross-hairs. Place the cross-hairs where you want to anchor one corner of the box, click the left mouse button, and move the mouse to where the opposite corner of the box should be (see fig. 13.5). Release the mouse, and the box takes its place in your publication.

If you want to ensure that your box is a perfect square, hold down the Shift key while drawing. This keeps all four sides equal.

Fig. 13.5
Draw a box of any dimension using Publisher's Box button.

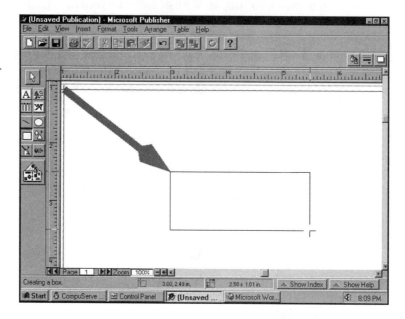

You can choose the thickness and color of the box's lines ahead of time, just as you did when drawing a line, or you can select the box after you draw it and change the line thickness and color.

TIP **The formatting commands available to you when you draw a box** are exactly the same as those available when you add a border to a text frame, graphic, or table (discussed in Chapter 12). That means you can draw a box with only three sides, for instance, or replace its edge with BorderArt. If you need a fancy border around something other than a text frame, graphic, or table, draw a box around it and then apply BorderArt to the box.

Circles and ovals

Click the Circle button to begin drawing ovals. Again, the mouse arrow changes to cross-hairs. This time, though, it's harder to position the object. You can't position the cross-hairs where you want the corner of the oval to be, because ovals don't have corners.

Instead, you have to picture the oval you want to draw inside a box whose sides it just touches. Position the cross-hairs where one corner of that imaginary box would be to start your drawing, then click and hold the left mouse button as you move the mouse toward where the opposite corner of that imaginary box would be. It's sort of like fitting a round peg into a square hole.

After you start, you can see the oval you're drawing (see fig. 13.6). When the oval looks the way you want it to, release the mouse button.

If you need a perfect circle, you can ensure you're getting one by holding down the Shift key while you draw. It's a much easier way to draw a circle than digging out that old high school geometry set!

Fig. 13.6
Drawing an oval can feel a little strange because the cross-hairs indicating your mouse position aren't act-ually in contact with the oval.

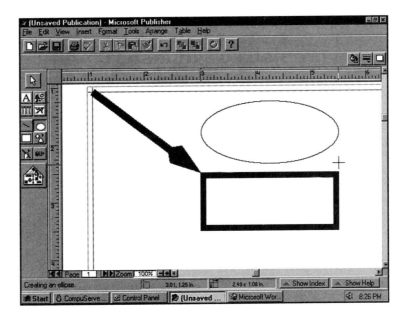

TIP   **Thinking of your oval being drawn in an imaginary box helps you** position it precisely, because you can line up the edges of that imaginary box with the rulers.

You can edit the oval you drew exactly as you did the box, except BorderArt is not available, and you can't print just half an oval, or a quarter of an oval, as you can with a box. You have to print the whole thing.

Starbursts and more

There's one more tool in the Publisher toolbar whose function is nowhere near as immediately apparent as the Line, Box, and Circle buttons are. It's the Custom Shapes button.

 Click this button and the small pop-up window shown in figure 13.7 appears.

Fig. 13.7
If the basic shape buttons are too simple for what you need, chances are you can find something more to your liking here.

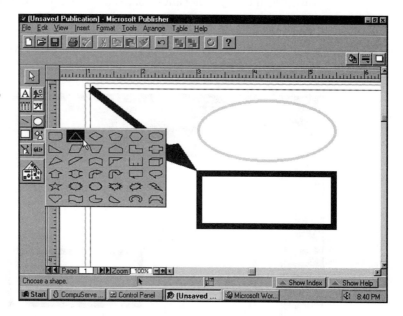

Choose any shape you like from here, and draw it just like you did the oval. Remember, the best way to position these non-traditional shapes is to picture them, as you did the oval, inside a box that completely encloses the shape. Its furthestmost points will touch that box. The result can be like the lightning bolt in figure 13.8.

Again, you can edit the line thickness and color of any of these shapes by clicking the Border button and choosing More. You get the same limited window as you did for the oval; unlike with boxes, you don't have the option to print only some of the object's sides.

Fig. 13.8
You can nicely match even the oddest shape to the dimensions of another if you picture each of them inside an imaginary box and use the rulers to ensure that the edges of those boxes align.

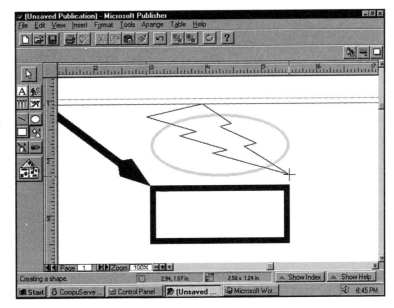

Resizing and moving objects

If you click any of the objects you just drew using Publisher's drawing tools, you'll see the familiar black handles appear around them. Resizing and moving objects is the same as resizing and moving any of the frames you looked at in earlier chapters.

Working with basic objects

To resize a basic object, select it, then place your mouse arrow over one of the handles. The pointer takes on a new shape and shows the word RESIZE. Click and hold the left mouse button while you move the handle to where it should appear in the resized object (see fig. 13.9). Release the mouse button, and the object appears in its new size.

One-Click Drawing

There's an even easier way to draw objects in Publisher than the method described above, but you have to go looking for it.

Choose <u>T</u>ools, <u>O</u>ptions, and you'll see, among other choices for customizing Publisher, one called Single <u>C</u>lick Object Creation. Choose this command if it's not already selected and return to your workspace.

Now, to draw an object, all you have to do is choose the tool you want, point your arrow at the place where you want the object to appear, and click the left mouse button.

Like magic, the object you selected appears in that spot. Of course, it might not be the right size, and it probably won't be in quite the right place, which means you have to resize it and adjust its place-ment (see the next section of this chapter). You

might not even save mouse-clicks or time with this option, but there's still a certain enjoyable feeling of wizard-like power inherent in being able to just point at a spot and zap! make an object appear.

As well, because every object initially appears with exactly the same dimensions, this method can also be useful for creating complex objects that consist of several simpler objects layered on top of each other: for example, a star inside a pentagon inside a cross.

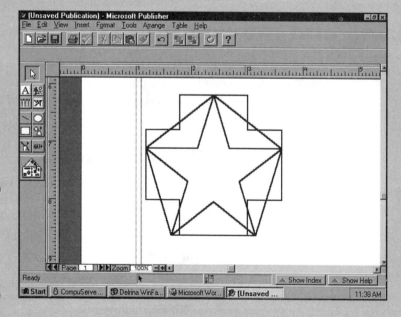

Fig. 13.9
Publisher provides a
light gray outline of
the object as you resize
it, so you can see
exactly what effect
your efforts will have.

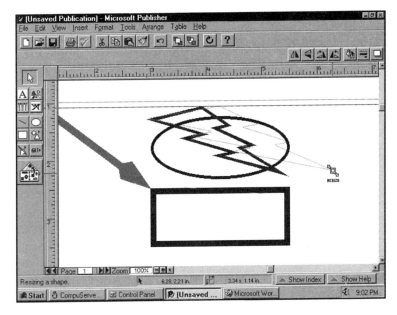

Do I have to do something different with more ornate objects?

If you draw certain objects and then select them (such as a cube), you see a new handle—a gray diamond—in addition to the usual black rectangular handles. This indicates that there is another dimension in which you can adjust the graphic in addition to the usual height and width. If you place your arrow over this gray handle, the pointer arrow changes to two parallel lines with arrows attached to them at right angles, labeled ADJUST. Click your left mouse button and hold it while you move the mouse back and forth; light gray lines show you how that movement changes the shape of the object.

Take a look at figure 13.10. The cube at left is the object as originally drawn. I moved the Adjust handle down to produce the shape in the middle; moving it up produced the shape at right. Note that although the shape changes, the object isn't really being resized; its height and width remain unchanged as long as the black handles aren't touched.

Adjust handles only appear on some of the custom shapes, and their effect varies from shape to shape. If you see an adjust handle on a custom shape, experiment with it to see what effects you can achieve.

Fig. 13.10
The Adjust handle that appears on certain custom shapes means you effectively have a far greater number of shapes to play with.

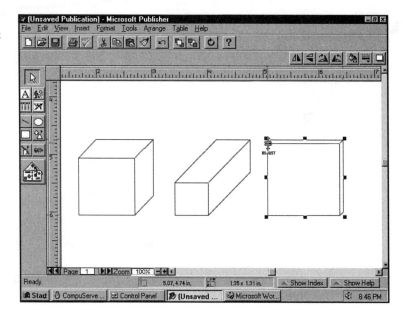

This shape would look better over there

You can reposition all of the shapes you draw with Publisher in the same way you can reposition any other Publisher object: simply select the object and move the arrow over it until the arrow changes to the "moving van" symbol. Then just hold down the left mouse button and "drive" the object wherever you want it go on the page. See Chapter 9, "Adding Graphics" for more details on relocating graphics.

Rotates, flips, and other shapely twists

There's something else you can do with all of the shapes you draw with Publisher. You have the option of rotating them, flipping them, or both.

Flipping shapes

Although some shapes, such as boxes and ovals, are symmetrical, some aren't. The lightning bolt in figure 13.9, for example, has a very definite orientation.

You might like a shape, but not like the way it's facing—maybe it leads the reader's gaze off the page. All it needs is a good flip, and Publisher makes it easy. Just select the graphic and click one of the Flipping buttons on the formatting toolbar, or choose A_rrange, _Rotate/Flip to open a drop-down list of options.

The Flip Horizontal button flips objects horizontally, while the Flip Vertical button flips them vertically. Figure 13.11 shows the lightning bolt the way it was originally drawn on the left, flipped horizontally in the center, and flipped vertically at right.

Fig. 13.11
If you don't like the way an object is oriented, you can flip it with a single click.

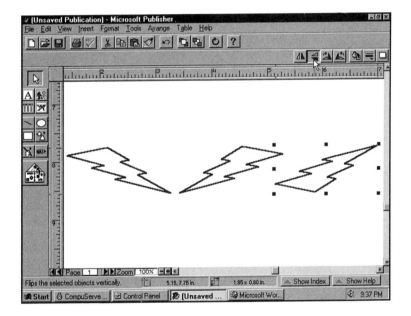

Rotating shapes

 You can also rotate shapes 90 degrees at a time by clicking one of the Rotate buttons. The Rotate Right button rotates objects 90 degrees clockwise; the Rotate Left button rotates them 90 degrees counterclockwise.

You can also rotate an object any number of degrees, from one to 365, by selecting it and choosing A_rrange, _Rotate/Flip, _Custom Rotate. This brings up the Rotate Object dialog box, in which you can rotate the object left or right by clicking a button or set a specific number of degrees you want to rotate the object. You can also press and hold the Alt key and grab one of the object's black handles. The pointer arrow changes to say ROTATE and lets you rotate the object by hand.

For a more detailed discussion of rotating objects, see Chapter 9.

You can add color to shapes, too

You've already seen how you can select the color of an object's lines, but you have another color option with most of these objects; you get to choose a color to fill them with.

 To do that, select an object, then click the Object Color button in the Formatting toolbar.

You see a drop-down box of several basic colors to choose from; you can see more colors by clicking More Colors. This opens the Colors dialog box, from which you can see even more colors by choosing All Colors. For more details on choosing a color from this dialog box, see Chapter 9.

Whatever color you choose fills the shape you select. You can also adjust the tint and shade (brightness) of the color you choose by going back to the initial color selection dialog box and choosing Patterns & Shading.

Select Patterns from the Patterns & Shading dialog box, and you see several background patterns to choose from. You can also choose a second color, which is the background color against which your initial background color will draw the pattern.

Select Gradients from the Patterns & Shading dialog box. You have several designs to choose from in which one of your background colors shades into another.

For a more detailed discussion of Patterns & Shading, see Chapter 8.

Shadowing

 There's one final effect you can apply to your object: you can add a drop shadow by selecting the object and clicking the Shadow button on the formatting toolbar. The shadow forms by default along the right and bottom sides of the object. But after you apply it, you can rotate and flip it with the object (see fig. 13.12).

For a more detailed discussion of drop shadows, see Chapter 12.

Fig. 13.12
A drop shadow adds a 3-D effect to any object, no matter how strangely shaped.

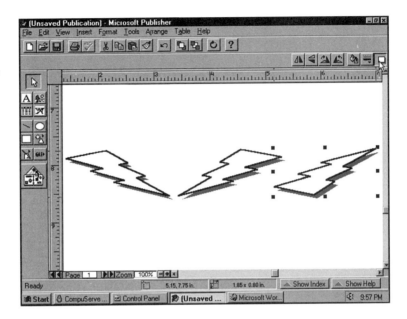

14

WordArt, for Characters with Character

● In this chapter:

- **What is WordArt?**

- **More stretches and pulls than an aerobic workout**

- **Can I add shadows to letters and make words odd shapes?**

- **How can I change colors, add a border, and use the rest of Publisher's graphics tools on WordArt?**

WordArt makes plain old text as malleable as graphics. Shape it and shadow it—make your publication shine! . . . . ➤

Most people think of text and graphics as two very different things. In fact, a lot of page designers don't much like text. They see it as dull and gray, a real drag, always cluttering up the white space that would otherwise help their artwork sparkle. That's one reason why the amount of text in many magazines and newspapers has dwindled over the past few decades. It's a long way from the political speeches printed verbatim of the 19th century to the style of *USA Today*.

But the differences between text and graphics are more perceptual than actual. Text, after all, is made up of letters, and letters are nothing but little drawings—drawings that come in a wide variety of styles, as you saw in Chapter 7 when you looked at fonts.

What if you could play with those drawings the way Publisher lets you play with other graphics—stretch them out, change their shapes, add shadows and colors and other special effects? No one could find that dull!

WordArt lets you do exactly that. It removes the artificial distinction between text and graphics and, in the process, opens up a whole new world of design possibilities.

Creating WordArt

 As is the case when you want to add most new elements to a Publisher publication, creating WordArt begins with drawing a frame—and drawing a WordArt frame is exactly the same as drawing any other frame in Publisher. Just click the WordArt button on the Publisher toolbar, position the cross-hairs where you want one corner of the frame to be, and drag the mouse to draw the frame.

 Q&A *When I drew my WordArt frame, my regular toolbar disappeared! Did I do something wrong?*

No. WordArt, like ClipArt Gallery, is a separate program you can access in other Microsoft programs in addition to Publisher (such as Word for Windows). When you draw a WordArt frame in Publisher, WordArt "takes over" the workspace, and its own menu bar and toolbar replace Publisher's menu, standard toolbar, and formatting toolbar.

Programs like this—that aren't part of Publisher but you can open in Publisher to create objects—are called OLE programs. You can find out all about them in the next chapter.

Fig. 14.1
The first step to
creating WordArt is to
draw a frame like this
one. Notice the new
formatting toolbar that
appeared. This is what
you always see first
when you draw a
WordArt frame.

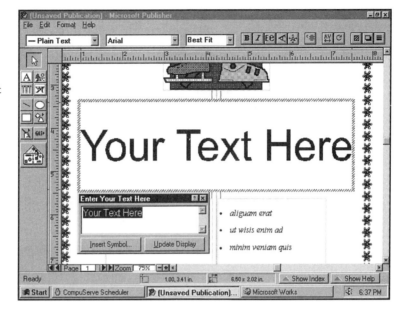

Fig. 14.1
The first step to creating WordArt is to draw a frame like this one. Notice the new formatting toolbar that appeared. This is what you always see first when you draw a WordArt frame.

First, enter the text

The first thing you notice about your new WordArt frame is that it's urging you to type your own text. It shouts `Your Text Here`. The text in the Enter Your Text Here dialog box underneath the WordArt frame is already high-lighted; just type the words you want to appear in the WordArt frame and they automatically replace `Your Text Here` in the dialog box. The text you type doesn't replace the text in the WordArt frame until you choose Update Display.

Can I use special symbols in WordArt?

Sure! If ordinary letters and numbers aren't quite what you're looking for, choose Insert Symbol. This updates the display with the text you already entered, and opens the Insert Symbol dialog box (see fig. 14.2). Just click the symbol you want to insert (in this case, an upside-down question mark) and click OK to return to the Enter Your Text Here dialog box. The symbol you chose immediately appears in your WordArt frame.

The Enter Your Text Here dialog box remains open as long as you work in WordArt—unless you deliberately close it—so you can always update your text.

You're not limited to a single line of text in WordArt, either; you can hit Enter after typing your first line to add a second line of text underneath it (see fig. 14.3). And more underneath that, if you want.

Fig. 14.2

You have access to all the characters a font contains through the Insert Symbol dialog box.

Fig. 14.3

You can add as many lines to headlines as you want in WordArt.

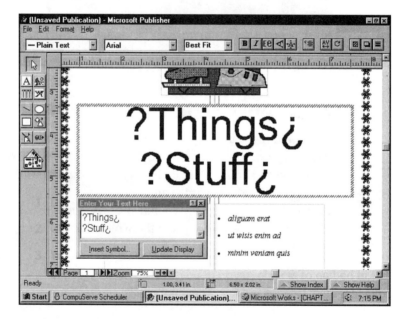

Then, choose the font

Just like an ordinary text frame, WordArt allows you to set all the standard parameters for text: font, size, style, alignment, and color—with a couple of interesting twists.

Select the font and size the same way you do in an ordinary text frame. Click an option in either list box, and your choice is applied to the text in the WordArt frame.

Notice, however, that the Size list box has a new option: Best Fit (see fig. 14.4).

Fig. 14.4

Best Fit is the default selection when you're choosing the size of your WordArt text.

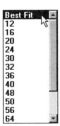

You've already seen Best Fit in action. When you typed your text, it appeared in the WordArt frame in a much larger size than it was in the Enter Your Text Here dialog box. If you added a second line, the characters automatically shrank to enable both lines of text to fit in the frame.

Best Fit makes your characters the largest point size they can be and still fit inside your text frame.

Give that text some style!

You can make WordArt text bold or italic (or both) by clicking the Bold or Italic buttons (or both). This is another way WordArt frames are like text frames. But WordArt offers another style choice that text frames don't: the Same Size button.

On the Even Height button, the uppercase E and the lowercase e are exactly the same height. That's because when you click this button, all characters in your WordArt frame become the same height, whether they're uppercase letters, lowercase letters, or punctuation marks. See figure 14.5 to get a better idea of what this effect looks like.

Fig. 14.5
That odd-looking
character after Things
is a comma blown up
to capital-letter size.

Fig. 14.5
That odd-looking
character after Things
is a comma blown up
to capital-letter size.

Making your text flip out

Look at any picture of New York's theater district (or take a stroll through it, if you happen to live close by) and you see that a lot of theaters run the letters in their names vertically down narrow signs. This "marquee" look is hard to achieve in an ordinary text frame—you have to add a return after every letter. But Publisher makes it easy in WordArt—all you have to do is click the Vertical Text button. The result looks something like figure 14.6.

One size fits all

"One size fits all" is a phrase to be wary of when buying clothes, but it really does apply to WordArt frames. No matter how much or how little you put in your WordArt frame, you can make it fit snugly—filling the whole frame—by simply clicking the Stretch button or choosing Format, Stretch to Frame. The result looks something like figure 14.7.

Fig. 14.6
You wouldn't want to read a lot of text set this way, but it's another interesting effect you can add to your publication.

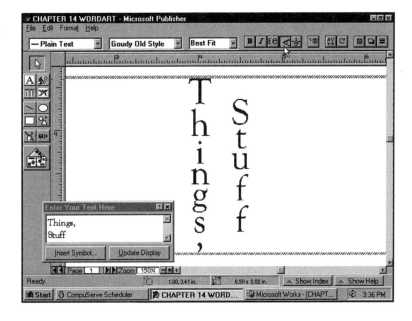

Fig. 14.7
Choosing Best Fit for your font size ensures that your text fits snugly from top to bottom in the WordArt frame; choosing Stretch to Frame stretches the letters out to fill the frame from side to side, as well.

How do I align WordArt text?

You have the usual assortment of text alignments available to you for WordArt text. There's also a couple you haven't seen yet. Find out what's new by clicking the Alignment button—it's the button with the letter C in the upper-left corner.

When you click this button, you see a list of six alignments: Center, Left, Right, Stretch Justify, Letter Justify, and Word Justify. Click the one you want, and it applies to your WordArt text.

You can probably guess what the first three options do.

- Center centers the text in the WordArt frame.

- Left places all the text in the WordArt frame flush against the frame's left margin.

- Right places all the text in the WordArt frame against the frame's right margin.

Justified text is text that's flush against both the left and right margins. WordArt has three versions of justified text:

- Stretch Justify justifies the text by horizontally stretching the letters.

- Letter Justify justifies the text by adding spaces between letters, regardless of their position in a word.

- Word Justify justifies text by adding spaces between words, without affecting the spacing of letters in words.

You can see samples of all three kinds of justification in figure 14.8.

Fig. 14.8
Each type of justified text WordArt offers has a unique look; choose the one that best suits your publication's design.

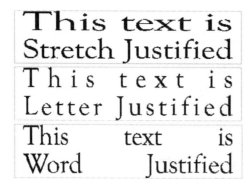

TIP **Although you can spread text in a WordArt frame over several** lines, you cannot apply formatting to those lines separately: you can't, for example, center the text in the top line and align the text against the left margin in the second line. Whatever formatting choices you make apply to all text in the WordArt frame, indiscriminately.

If your design needs a series of lines of text in different formats and only WordArt gives you the tools you need to make them look the way you want, draw a series of WordArt frames, stacked one above another. It's a bit clumsy, but it works; and if you group them together you can resize them all at once (see Chapter 16 for more information).

Rotating and "sliding"

You can rotate an entire WordArt frame just as you can rotate other frames in Publisher (I talk more about using Publisher's standard tools on WordArt later in the chapter), but you also have access to an entirely different rotation tool within the frame itself.

 Click the Special Effects button on the toolbar, or choose Format, Rotation And Effects. The Special Effects dialog box appears (see fig. 14.9). Figures 14.9 through 14.11 show you the effects of using the Rotation and Slider options.

Use the Rotation control to set how many degrees you want to rotate the entire body of text. Click the down or up arrow buttons to change the number of degrees, or type in a specific value. Positive numbers rotate the text counter-clockwise, while negative numbers rotate it clockwise, so applying a value of 45 degrees makes the text slope up.

Use the Slider control to set the angle at which characters tilt, based on a percentage between two preset extremes. Straight up and down is 50 percent (the default setting); 100 percent tilts the characters back; and 0 percent tilts them forward.

By setting both controls, you can create a variety of effects. For example, combining the 45-degree rotation of figure 14.9 with the 100-percent slide of figure 14.10 gives you the oddly off-kilter text in figure 14.11.

Fig. 14.9
Text doesn't have to
be horizontal in
WordArt! Use the
Rotation control to
slant it up or down.

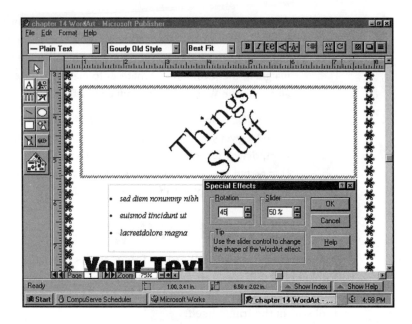

Fig. 14.10
The Slider control can
make your text lean
left or right faster than
an opportunistic
politician.

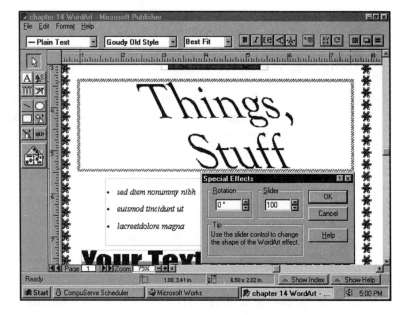

Fig. 14.11
Use both the Rotation and Slider controls to create new effects that aren't possible using just one.

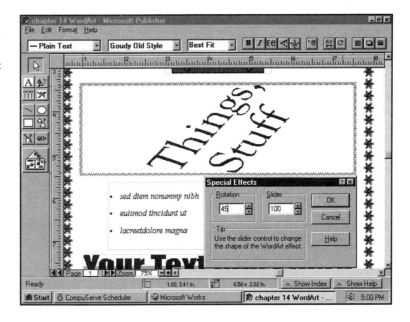

Character spacing

Making text fit in just the right amount of space is always a challenge. Of course, in WordArt, you could just click the Stretch button and fill the entire frame by altering the shape of the letters, but sometimes you don't want to alter the look of the font you've chosen that much.

1 Click the Character Spacing button. The Spacing Between Characters dialog box appears.

2 You have five options for changing the space between characters in your WordArt text: Very Tight, T̲ight, N̲ormal, L̲oose, or V̲ery Loose. Choose the tracking you want. (Tracking is the spacing between all the letters in a block of text.) Figure 14.12 shows the Very Tight tracking.

3 When you select a tracking option, the C̲ustom box shows you the percentage of normal spacing the preset spacing selections represent. If you don't like any of the preset spacing, enter a number in the C̲ustom box.

Fig. 14.12
You can adjust the spacing between letters in your WordArt from zero percent of normal (all letters print over top of each other) to 500 percent of normal.

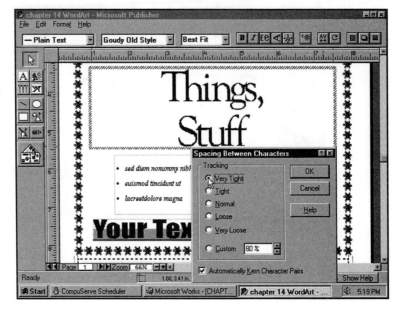

4 You must also decide if you want to Automatically Kern Character Pairs. Certain pairs of letters look better if they're moved closer together than other characters. A and V are one such pair, which is why they're on the Character Spacing button. If you select this check box, WordArt automatically kerns those awkward pairs; WordArt adjusts the spacing between them so they look their best. If you're trying for a particular effect with your WordArt that automatic kerning messes up, then don't select this check box.

5 After you make your choice, click OK; the dialog box closes and you're back in business editing your WordArt text.

Fine-tuning the text: color, shadows, and borders

You've already looked at a long list of formatting options for your WordArt text—but there's a lot more to come, starting with color.

Add a dash of color

The Shading dialog box for WordArt offers options similar to those that come up when you click the Object Color button for other Publisher frames. In fact, it's a throwback: in Publisher 2.0, this dialog box was the standard for all the other frames, too.

Click the Shading button. The Shading dialog box appears (see fig. 14.13).

Fig. 14.13
The Shading dialog box lets you specify colors and patterns for your WordArt characters. Burgundy bricks with saffron "cement," for example.

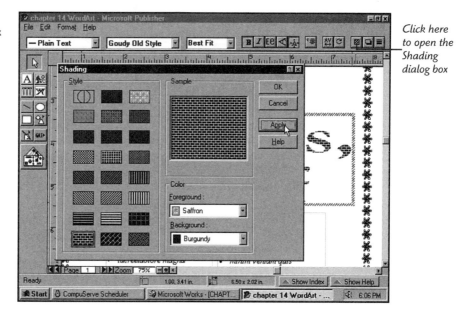

Click here to open the Shading dialog box

There are a lot of patterns to choose from, plus foreground and background color. These choices are similar to those offered with other frames. The biggest difference here is that the patterns are applied to your text.

The foreground color is the color with which the selected pattern is drawn on the background color.

Use outlines to make your text more legible

The bricks pattern in figure 14.13 is an interesting thought, but it makes the characters a little hard to read—they don't have definite edges. If you experiment with some of the other patterns in the Shading dialog box, you'll find they can make the characters even harder to read.

Placing an outline around the outside of the characters alleviates that problem. Click the Line Thickness button at the far right of the formatting toolbar, or choose Forma<u>t</u>, Bor<u>d</u>er, to access a selection of lines. The Border dialog box appears (see fig. 14.14).

Fig. 14.14
You can choose the thickness and color of the line you want to outline your WordArt characters.

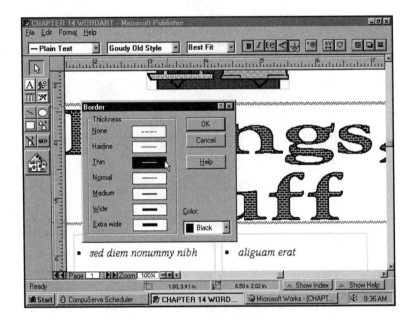

Simply choose the thickness of line you want to outline your WordArt characters, from <u>N</u>one to Hair<u>l</u>ine to <u>E</u>xtra Wide. As soon as you click an option, you can see it added to your WordArt in the background; click OK when you're satisfied.

TIP **Although you might have some fonts in your collection in which** the characters appear as empty outlines, Publisher does not support an "Outline" format that can be applied to any font.

However, you can achieve that effect using WordArt. Just click the Color button on the toolbar and choose solid white, then click the Thickness button and choose an outline. The result: your chosen font in outline.

The Shadow knows...

The Shadow button is available when you select any frame in Publisher, but its function is different here. Instead of putting a drop shadow around the WordArt frame, it lets you add a variety of shadows to the WordArt text.

When you click the Shadow button, the Shadow dialog box appears (see fig. 14.15).

Fig. 14.15
The Choose a Shadow boxes give you an idea of how each shadow will look applied to your text, but the only way to tell for sure is to try each one.

In addition to choosing from various shadow options, you can choose a color for the shadow.

Some shadows take up quite a bit of space and, as a result, your WordArt text will shrink to allow the shadow enough room in the frame. Fortunately, previewing the effects is easy; your WordArt text automatically changes as soon as you click any of the Shadow controls.

Now for the really cool effects: shape shifting

So far, although you've changed the width and height of your WordArt text and even added a shadow, you haven't done anything all that different from what you could do in a text frame. Sure, you have a few more special effects to play with, but the text still marches across the page in a nice straight line—even if that line slants up or down. Is this all you can ask of text?

No. Straight lines are only one possibility in WordArt, because there's one other formatting option available to you in WordArt that's also one of the most powerful: shapes.

At the left end of the Formatting toolbar is the Shape list box. When you first draw your WordArt frame, it shows a straight line and the words `Plain Text`. Click the arrow of the Shape list box to see a list of available shapes (see fig. 14.16).

Fig. 14.16

The shapes give you an idea of what your text would look like. Again, the best way to find out for sure is to try each one.

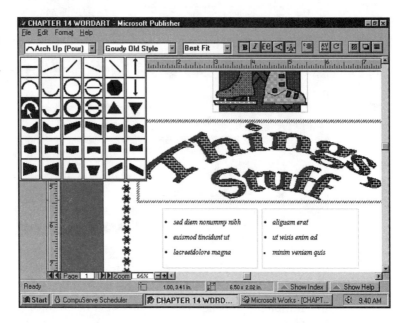

Just decide what shape you want and click it. The list closes and the shape applies to your text. It's that easy.

Applying appropriate shapes to text can give that text added emphasis. A cautionary sign, for example, could have text in the shape of a stop sign; a "banner headline" could be in the shape of a banner floating on the breeze; an important announcement could emerge from the mouth of a megaphone. The possibilities are limited only by your imagination.

CAUTION   **WordArt shapes are some of the most powerful tools for giving** your publication a unique look—but like all tools, use them in moderation. Because WordArt shapes distort the normal shape of characters, they can sometimes make characters difficult to read. So, too, can the colors, shadows, and other effects you add to text in WordArt.

Remember that your publication's purpose is to effectively communicate with a reader. Unless the main thing you're trying to communicate is the fact that you have a fancy computer, printer, and software, use WordArt's more elaborate effects sparingly, and always know exactly what you're striving to achieve with them. That will stop you from giving in to the temptation to use special effects just because they're available. (Now if someone could just stop Hollywood from doing the same thing!)

Can I use regular graphics tools with WordArt?

After you perfect your WordArt text, you can return to the workspace to work on other elements of your Publisher publication. Just aim the mouse pointer at anything on the page outside the WordArt frame, and click once. The WordArt toolbar disappears and the normal Publisher toolbars re-establish themselves.

But that doesn't mean you've exhausted all the possibilities for improving your WordArt frame. Far from it. If you now select the WordArt frame by clicking it, you don't re-open the same editing controls you just used. Instead, the WordArt frame sprouts black handles, just like any other Publisher frame—and that means all the formatting possibilities available to you in a regular graphics frame, from resizing to recoloring, are now available for your WordArt frame. That includes options like borders and background patterns and gradients. See Chapter 10 for more details.

Editing your creation

Say you've finally used every formatting tool you can on your WordArt frame, and ended up with something that looks like figure 14.17.

Trouble is, you don't like it. Oh, you like the BorderArt and gradient—you've just decided you don't like the WordArt itself. How do you get your WordArt editing and formatting tools back so you can change it?

You have two options, both of which begin by selecting the WordArt frame. Choose Edit, Microsoft WordArt 3.0 Object, Edit. This opens the same tools you used to create the WordArt frame and text in the first place. But if your final choice is Open instead of Edit, you open the dialog box shown in figure 14.18. This pulls together all your WordArt formatting options into one easy-to-use dialog box. Make your changes, click OK, and your WordArt object is finished.

Fig. 14.17

I slightly resized the frame with BorderArt and added a background gradient. See what I mean about it being easy to go overboard with Publisher's formatting possibilities?

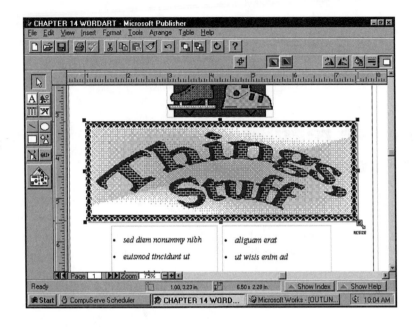

Fig. 14.18

This handy dialog box makes editing every aspect of WordArt easier than using the tools you originally drew the WordArt with.

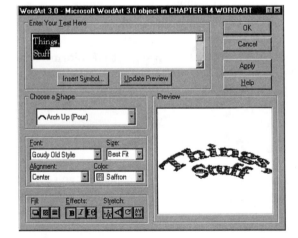

 TIP The dialog box in figure 14.18 is actually easier to use than the regular formatting toolbars, so you might prefer to do all your WordArt creating from there. However, because it doesn't appear by default, you have to take a couple of extra steps to open it when you first draw your WordArt frame. First, click anywhere else in your workspace to deselect the newly drawn frame. Then select it again, right-click the frame, and choose Open. The dialog box in figure 14.18 appears, ready for you to create a new object.

Q&A   ***There's a third option under Edit, Microsoft 3.0 Object. What does the Convert command do?***

Convert changes the fonts in objects created using an older version of WordArt (1.0) to the fonts that are closest to them in WordArt 3.0. This option is necessary because WordArt 1.0 and WordArt 3.0 don't use the same fonts.

15

OLE: Objects Created in Other Applications

● In this chapter:

- What is OLE, and why should I care?

- Sound and video in a publication? Cool!

- Okay, explain the difference between embedding and linking

- Automatic and manual linking

There's bound to come a time when you want to use something Publisher just can't provide. No problem! Create it in another program, then just pop it into your publication. . . ●▶

What good is OLE anyway?

*O*lè of course, is what bullfighters yell as they face the bull. Roughly translated, it means something like, "What the heck am I doing here with this monster?"

OLE, on the other hand, is something Publisher users yell when they face a hole in their publication that none of Publisher's built-in tools can effectively fill. Translated, it means, "**Object Linking and Embedding**!"

That might sound like a mouthful of technical mumbo jumbo, but...surprise! You've already had some experience using OLE objects. Remember those ClipArt Gallery objects? WordArt? How about the Excel spreadsheet you inserted in Chapter 11, or the Microsoft Draw object you inserted in Chapter 9. They're *all* OLE objects: objects you created in a program other than Publisher but embedded or linked to your Publisher publication.

By giving you this capability, Publisher makes it possible for you to create specialized objects in programs designed just for creating those objects, **embed** them in Publisher, and access the necessary tools you need to edit them by just clicking the mouse a couple of times. Even more amazing is this: if you **link** the object, any changes you make to it in another program—say, you're working on your annual report and the spreadsheet tallying up the year's sales figures concurrently—are automatically reflected in Publisher.

 Plain English, please!

An **embedded object** is one you create and edit with another program, but is wholly contained in your publication. An embedded piece of artwork from a graphics program, for example, would exist only in your publication, and the amount of disk space it requires for storage would be added to the amount your publication already requires.

A **linked object** is one that appears in your publication but is actually stored somewhere else. A linked piece of artwork actually exists as a separate program: although you can see it in your publication, and print it as part of your publication, all that is really stored in the file that contains the data for your publication is the linked artwork's name and address. Publisher just "fetches" the artwork from the program that created it (the **source program**) whenever it needs to display it or print it out. **99**

Inserting an OLE object

To add an OLE object to your Publisher publication, begin by clicking the Insert Object button in the Publisher toolbar. This first opens a drop-down list of the OLE programs you used most recently in Publisher. If you click the More button, the Insert Object dialog box appears, which has a complete list of all the programs on your computer that support OLE (see fig. 15.1).

Fig. 15.1
When you're inserting an OLE object, Publisher gives you a list of all the programs currently found on your computer that you can use to create OLE objects.

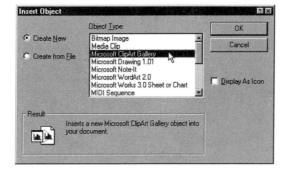

You have several choices to make in this dialog box:

- What type of object you want to add to your publication

- Whether you want to create a new object or insert one from an existing file

- Whether you want to display the inserted object in its entirety or simply as an icon. (For any publication that's meant to be printed, you obviously want the whole object to appear. But if you're, say, sharing the publication electronically with others on a network, you might choose to leave objects as icons; the viewer would simply click the icon to see the OLE object.)

How do I create a new OLE object in Publisher?

If you choose Create New in the Insert Object dialog box, then click OK, one of two things happens (depending on which OLE program you chose): either the pointer arrow turns into cross-hairs, allowing you to draw a frame for your OLE object just as you would draw a frame for text, a graphic, or a table, or the OLE program you chose inserts an object of a default size into your publication. Microsoft Draw, for example, lets you draw the size of the frame you want to fill, whereas Excel simply opens a box without asking you how big you want it.

In figure 15.2, I embedded a Microsoft Works 3.0 chart in a brochure. Notice how the Works menu and toolbar replaced Publisher's. Many OLE programs do the same thing.

You're still in Publisher, but this is the Standard toolbar from Microsoft Works.

Fig. 15.2

Need to add a Works spreadsheet? OLE gives you all the Works tools you need—without ever leaving Publisher.

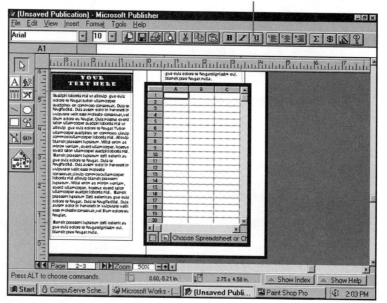

Not all OLE programs just open a box and replace Publisher's menu and toolbars. Some open up full-screen, completely covering Publisher; others (such as WordArt and ClipArt Gallery) open a small window in which you work, although Publisher is still visible in the background.

After you create an object in the OLE program, you return to Publisher either by clicking in the Publisher workspace outside the OLE program's box, or (if the OLE program completely covered Publisher) by closing the OLE program as usual. Make sure you save the object you created if the OLE program asks you to!

After you embed the object in Publisher, you can move or resize it as you can any other object. Other formatting options such as borders and BorderArt might also apply.

Or, create it in the other program, then drop it into Publisher

Another option for creating an OLE object is to open the program you want to create the object in, work on it there, then copy and paste the object into Publisher.

To do so, after you copy the object in the other program and open Publisher, choose Edit, Paste Special. The Paste Special dialog box opens (see fig. 15.3). The As list box displays various options, depending on the source of the object you're pasting. You can also choose to paste the object into your publication as an icon or to paste the object into your publication as a linked object—but only if Publisher supports that option for the program you're copying from. Make your selection, then click OK.

All it takes is a click

If you're using an OLE program that allows you to draw a frame, but you're in a hurry or you're not sure what size you want your OLE object to be, you can create a frame even more quickly by simply pointing the cross-hairs in the general area of where you want the object to appear and clicking once.

This opens a frame of a preset size that varies depending on how close-up you view your publication. In other words, the frame looks the same size on your screen when you're viewing your publication at 400 percent of life-size as it

does when you're viewing it at 10 percent of life-size—but in absolute terms, the frame created when you're viewing at 10-percent scale is much larger than the frame created when you're viewing at the 400-percent scale.

This "one-click" drawing (which you also use when drawing shapes in Chapter 13) works with graphics, text, and table frames, too, but it's probably most useful in conjunction with OLE objects. You're less likely to know exactly how much space you need for something you create in a different program.

Fig. 15.3

Choose how you want an object you copied from another program to be inserted into Publisher from the Paste Special dialog box.

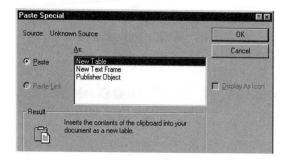

The OLE object appears in your workspace, and you can drag it where you want.

Sound and video? In a Publisher publication?

Among the possible OLE objects you can create in Publisher are some you probably never thought about embedding in a desktop-publishing publication, like sound and video files.

You create these objects using other programs, just as you might create an Excel chart, but the only thing that appears in your publication is an icon. Figure 15.4 shows the icon for a WAV sound object I embedded just below the Works spreadsheet from figure 15.2.

Fig. 15.4

You can even add sound and video to Publisher publications, although all you'll see when you print the publication is an icon.

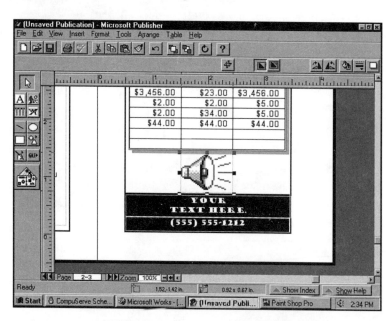

To play a sound or video object,

1 Select the object.

2 Right-click the object, choose the name of the object from the shortcut menu, and then select Play.

The appropriate program opens and you can see or hear the contents.

 Q&A ***All right, I give up. Why would I want to embed sound or video objects into what is essentially a print publication?***

In a large company with networked computers, you could use Publisher to create a publication that would be available to people at their own work stations. They don't have to print the publication; they can just open it on-screen. As long as the sound and video objects you included in the publication are also available on the network, and everyone has the same software and hardware, other people could access the objects by selecting their icons in the Publisher publication. Instead of a print publication, your Publisher publication becomes a multimedia presentation!

For example, you can use this capability in a training publication, where embedded sound files could provide audible help to students and embedded video files could demonstrate the procedures the students have to learn; or to create audio "sticky notes" pointing out problems and asking for feedback on specific areas of a publication before it's converted back into a purely print publication for distribution.

Embedding or linking?

You can embed any of the objects you see when you click the OLE button; you can't link all of them.

The difference is that you if you make changes to an embedded object in Publisher, those changes apply only to that Publisher publication. The original object remains unchanged—unless you go back to the source program and manually save it over the previous version.

Embedding is fine if you're the only one working on the publication.

However, you can link a linked object to several publications and programs. And any changes you make to the linked object in any of those publications or programs are automatically made to all of the links of that object. That's because the object really only exists in one place on the computer, and that makes linked objects useful when there are many different people working on a publication: changes can be made with ease to everyone's copy.

You can only create a linked object using a program that's complete in and of itself, such as Microsoft Word or PowerPoint. Some programs, like ClipArt Gallery, are only "helper" programs that must be called up from within another program. Programs like that can only create embedded objects in Publisher.

To insert a linked OLE object within Publisher:

1 Choose Insert, Object. The Insert Object dialog box opens (see fig. 15.5). Choosing Create New in this dialog box is the same as clicking the Insert Object button; choose Create from File instead.

Fig. 15.5

Choosing Create from File lets you insert an existing file and, if it's from a program that supports it, creates a link to it from your Publisher publication.

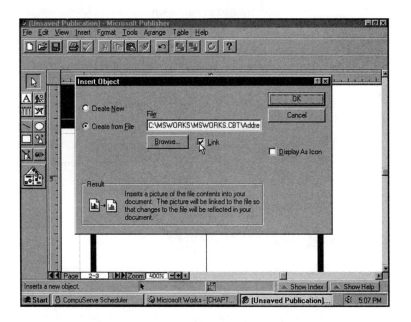

2 Type the name of the file you want to use as a linked object, or use the Browse button. When you find the file you want, select the Link check box.

3 If you don't want the file itself to appear in your publication, but only a representative icon (like the speaker icon that appears when you insert a sound file), select Display As Icon.

4 After you make your choices, click OK. The file you selected appears in your publication as a linked file.

If you ever want to edit the link—update the linked file, for example, to make sure you have the latest changes in your publication—first select the linked object. Right-click it and choose Edit, Links. This opens the Links dialog box shown in figure 15.6. You have several choices:

- **Update Now** takes a look at the selected linked object and its source file, and changes the linked object to match any changes to the source file.

- **Open Source** opens the program you created the linked object in so you can make further changes.

- **Change Source** lets you change the file you linked the object to. For example, you could use this option to update a spreadsheet in an existing brochure from a 1995 file to a new 1996 file.

You can also change the update options in the Links dialog box. If you select Automatic Update, the linked object in your publication automatically changes whenever you make changes to it in the program where you created it. If you select Manual Update, any changes you made to the linked object only show up in your publication when you choose Update Now.

Fig. 15.6
Here you can see, update, and edit all the linked objects in your publication.

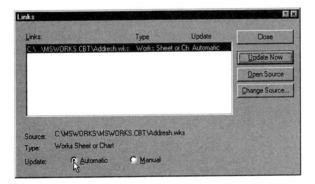

Editing OLE objects

To edit OLE objects, just double-click them. That automatically opens the program you created them in. Make the changes as you normally would, and close the program. (Make sure you save the changes if the program prompts you to do so.)

Part V: Putting It Together

16

When Elements Overlap

● In this chapter:

- ● I have frames on top of frames. How do I keep them straight?

- ● I want to make text flow around objects

- ● I want everything lined up perfectly!

- ● Is there any way to group objects together?

No frame is an island! Frames affect the frames they might overlap. Get them to play nicely together to make your publication look its best! . . . . ❯

Frames on top of frames

reating a Publisher publication would be a cinch if it consisted of a single text frame—but of course it doesn't. Desktop publishing is all about combining a variety of visual elements in an effective way. It's like creating a publication by drawing each individual element on a separate sheet of transparent plastic, then stacking the sheets on top of each other. If you don't stack them in exactly the right way, some things might get covered up that you want to see, while other things you'd prefer to cover up might be visible. You have to shuffle all the sheets until everything looks the way you want it to.

Publisher makes that shuffling process easy by giving you a set of tools to move any element to wherever in the stack of overlapping elements you want it.

Send to back, bring to front

The basic tools for shuffling elements are the Bring to Front and Send to Back buttons in the Standard toolbar.

To see the effect of these buttons, create two overlapping objects, like those in figure 16.1. I put a graphics frame containing a picture of a beetle over a text frame full of text. The graphics frame has a gray background; the text is reversed, white on black.

Fig. 16.1
Here a graphic frame containing a silhouette of a beetle has been placed on top of a text frame.

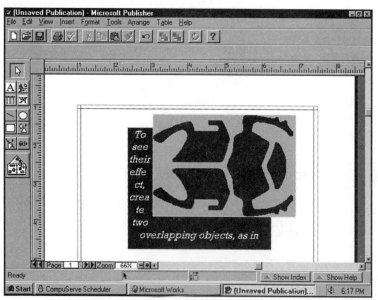

As you can see, the beetle covers part of the text frame. The text has wrapped around the beetle's frame in an awkward, hard-to-read manner (text-wrapping is discussed later in this chapter). To change that, select the beetle's graphic frame, then click the Send to Back button or choose A<u>r</u>range, Send to <u>B</u>ack. Now the text frame is obscuring the beetle (see fig 16.2).

Click here to put the selected —⌐ *Click here to put the object object on top of the stack* | *behind the other elements*

Fig. 16.2

The object you want fully visible should be on top of the stack. In this case, I selected the beetle's frame and made it crawl under the text by clicking the Send to Back button.

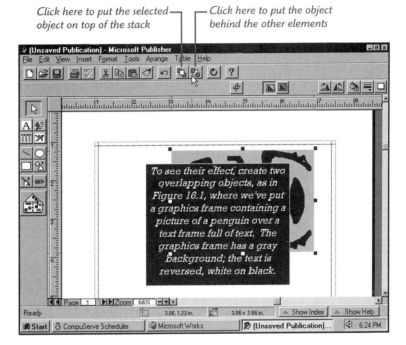

Send farther, bring nearer; when you're arranging more than two frames

Send to Back and Bring to Front are either/or buttons: either the object you selected is clear at the bottom of the stack, or it's on top. If you have more than two overlapping frames, you might want to position a particular frame somewhere in the middle, instead.

In figure 16.3, I added a third frame, a transparent rectangle with BorderArt applied. Right now it's on top, so it's obscuring parts of both the other frames.

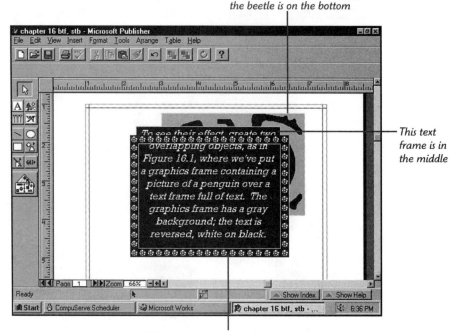

Fig. 16.3
Now there are three
objects overlapping
each other and
interfering with your
view.

*The picture frame containing
the beetle is on the bottom*

*This text
frame is in
the middle*

This empty border is a third element

Of course, if you stack up objects like this, there must be some effect you're
trying to achieve. In this case, I'm trying to create a three-sided BorderArt
border around the text frame, while leaving the beetle barely visible in the
background.

Select the BorderArt frame, then choose A̲rrange, Send F̲arther. This moves
the BorderArt one layer closer to the back, leaving it sandwiched between
the text frame and the beetle (see fig. 16.4). This is the effect I had in mind.

Choose A̲rrange, Bring C̲loser to reverse the effect; or you could select the
beetle and choose A̲rrange, Bring C̲loser to place it between the text frame
and the BorderArt frame.

When it's tough to get to the frame you want to move

It's very easy to say "select this" and "select that," but when you stack several
frames over each other, it can be difficult to grab the one you want. That's
because when you point at a stack of frames and click the mouse button,
Publisher selects the frame on top.

Fig. 16.4

This is the effect I had in mind, but I had to move things around to get to it.

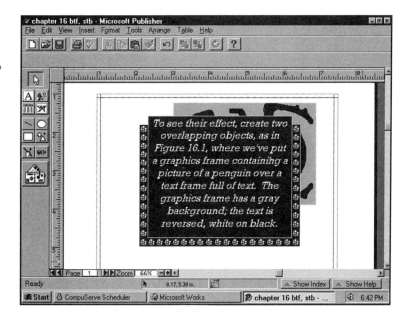

There are two ways to get to the frame you want. One is to make judicious use of the arranging tools discussed in the previous section, sending the top frame to the back, then the new top frame after that, and so on until the frame you want comes to the front. If the frames are all exactly the same size, that's the only option open to you.

If the frame you want is distinctly smaller, or a very different shape, than the other frames in the stack, you might be able to select it by "lassoing." Point your mouse arrow somewhere on the publication where there are no frames, and click the left mouse button. If you now move the mouse, you'll see that your arrow draws a rectangle.

That rectangle is your "lasso." If you draw it around an object, Publisher selects that object. If you can manage to draw it around only the frame you want to select out of a stack of them, Publisher selects only that frame (see fig. 16.5). You can then edit it, bring it closer, send it farther in the stack, move it, or whatever else you have in mind for it.

Using the lasso, you can also select more than one frame at a time: useful if you want to form them into a group. See the section "Organizing objects into groups," later in this chapter for more information.

Fig. 16.5

I carefully lassoed the half-buried picture frame containing the beetle. Because the picture frame is the only object in the stack that was completely surrounded by the lasso, it's the only one that will be selected when I release the mouse button.

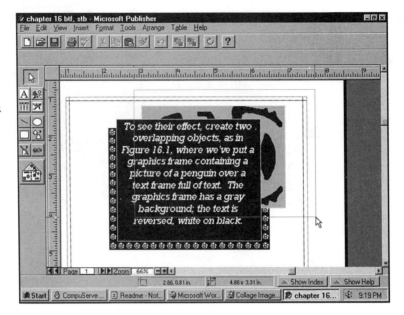

Keeping things straight

There's a general rule of thumb that's true for all desktop publishing jobs. Quickly designing a publication doesn't take long at all. Drawing in the text and graphic and table frames is a snap. Importing text or clip-art? Nothing to it.

But giving everything that final polish, making sure frames are aligned with the margins, that lines meet boxes smoothly, that the text in adjacent columns lines up—*that* takes time.

It would take even more time if Publisher didn't provide you with some useful tools for the purpose.

Lining up objects

Publisher can automatically line up objects with each other or with the margins of your page. You can choose to line up the left edges of some or all frames with the left edge of the object that extends farthest in that direction—or do the same thing to the right. Or you can align their centers—their horizontal axes—with each other.

Rather than aligning objects from left to right, you can also choose to align them from top to bottom: you can align the top edges of all the selected frames with the top edge of the frame that's in the highest position, align the bottom edges with the bottom edge of the frame in the lowest position, or align their horizontal axes with each other.

Or, rather than align objects with each other, you can align them with your margins. To see the difference, compare figures 16.6 and 16.7.

Fig. 16.6
I aligned three different elements along the left edge of the leftmost object.

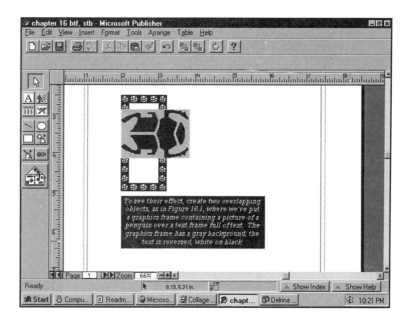

Fig. 16.7
I aligned these objects along the left margin of the page.

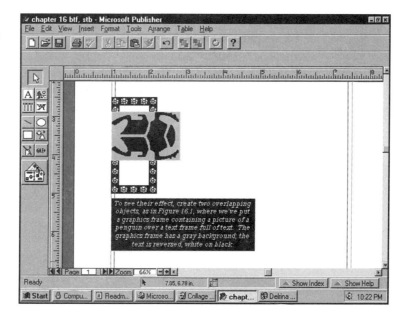

To use Publisher's automatic alignment tools:

1 Select the objects you want to align by clicking them one after the other while pressing and holding Shift. You can also lasso them with the mouse (see fig. 16.8).

Fig. 16.8

To use the automatic alignment tools, select a group of objects by lassoing them with the mouse. If objects ever desperately needed aligning, these do!

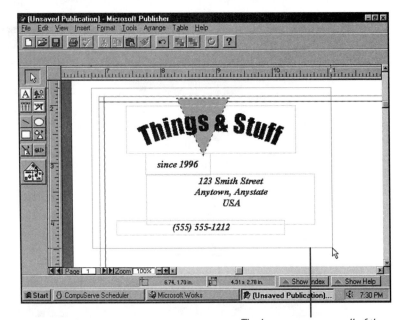

The lasso encompasses all of the frames that need alignment

2 Choose Arrange, Line Up Objects. The Line Up Objects dialog box appears (see fig. 16.9).

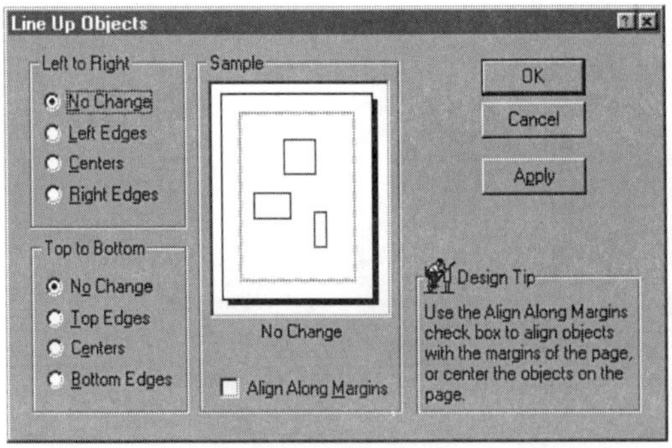

Fig. 16.9

Publisher automatically lines up several objects at once in a variety of ways, saving you a lot of nitpickety labor.

3 Decide if you want to align objects just with other objects, or with the margins. If you want objects aligned with the page margins, select the Align Along <u>M</u>argins check box.

4 Choose the type of horizontal alignment you want to apply to the selected objects. The Sample area shows you how that alignment choice will affect your selected objects.

I choose Centers, which is probably the choice you'll make most often. As you can see in figure 16.10, it can make sense out of even the most uneven collection of objects.

Fig. 16.10
Centers lines up objects along the centers of their frames—making it a very useful tool for publications like this.

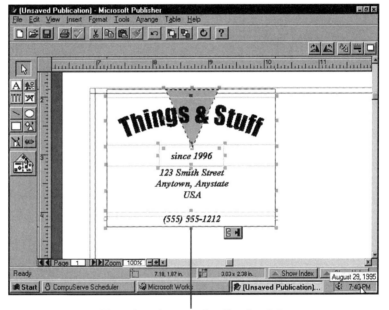

Notice how the center handles of each frame
form a straight line from top to bottom

5 Now choose the vertical alignment, if any, you'd like to apply to your selected objects.

6 Click A<u>p</u>ply to view the results in your publication without closing the Line Up Objects dialog box. (You can undo any alignment changes by choosing No Change in either the Left to Right or Top to Bottom sections.) After you're sure you have the effect you want, click OK.

Nudging objects

The mouse is a wonderful gadget, but it can be a pain to work with when extremely precise movements are called for.

There's no need for that in Publisher; if all you want to do is nudge an object a little closer to another object, or a little farther away, Publisher gives you an easy way.

Simply select the object you want to nudge, and choose A<u>r</u>range, <u>N</u>udge Objects. The Nudge Objects dialog box appears (see fig. 16.11). Just click any of the directional arrows in the Nudge Control area to nudge the object just a bit in that direction.

Fig. 16.11

Clicking any of the arrows will move the triangle selected in the background by .13 inch in the indicated direction.

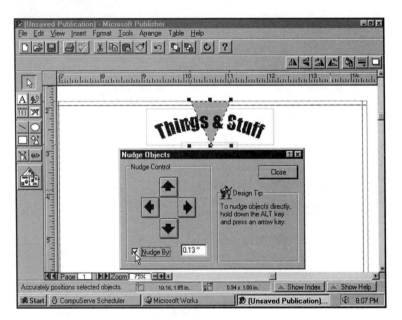

You can adjust how far each nudge moves the selected object by selecting the <u>N</u>udge By check box and entering a distance in the text box (it can be up to two inches). You can enter the distance in centimeters, inches, picas, or points by typing **cm**, **in**, **pi**, or **pt** after the numerals.

TIP   **You don't have to open the Nudge Objects dialog box to nudge** an object. You can simply select the object you want to nudge, hold down the Alt key, and then press one of the arrow keys on your keyboard. Each time you press an arrow key, the object moves the default distance of .13 inch (or the distance you last entered in the Nudge Objects dialog box).

Feeling lost in your own publication? You need a good guide!

Up in the northern part of Saskatchewan, sport fishing is a major industry. People come from all over the world to isolated lakes to try their hand at catching the wily northern pike. And the first thing they do is hire a guide—otherwise they'd waste time fishing in places where there are no fish, or worse, just disappear into the bush.

Publisher has guides, too. They keep you from fishing aimlessly for the goal of perfectly aligned objects and help ensure you don't get lost in your quest for the perfect publication.

In fact, Publisher has two kinds of guides: layout guides and ruler guides.

Layout guides, discussed in Chapter 4, are the lines that show you where the margins of your page and the borders of any rows and columns are. They're generally set when you begin a publication and remain unchanged while you're working on it.

Ruler guides are lines you add to your publication to help you place objects in precise locations. You can draw a horizontal or vertical ruler guide: just point at either the vertical or horizontal ruler, hold down Shift, and click and hold the left mouse button. Your mouse pointer changes to the ADJUST pointer. If you point at the horizontal ruler and drag the mouse down, a horizontal line that stretches clear across your publication will follow; point at the vertical ruler, and you drag a vertical line (see fig. 16.12).

These lines don't print; they're just to help you align objects in your publication.

Snap to it!

The guides in Publisher might look like ordinary lines, but they actually have a secret power. With the Snap To command, you can make them sticky, and you don't have to smear glue on your monitor to do it. They give you another option for aligning objects; if the left edges of all the objects you've drawn are stuck tight to the same guide, you know all those objects are aligned. In fact, if you have the Snap To options activated when you first design your publication, you might not need to use Publisher's automatic alignment tools at all, because any frames you draw that are in contact with the guides will already be aligned.

Fig. 16.12

You can add as many ruler guides as you want to help you precisely position objects in your publication.

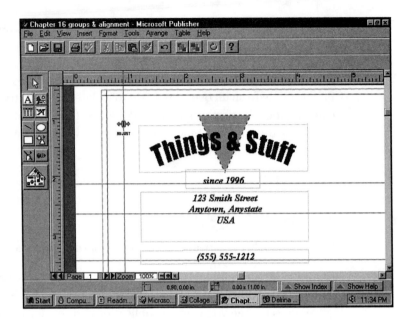

The guides aren't the only things you can make sticky with Snap To commands. You can also make the invisible lines indicated by ruler marks sticky, or objects themselves. You can use all of these options to keep objects aligned while you draw them.

There are three Snap To options on the Tools menu:

- **Snap to Ruler Marks.** If you drew lines down and across the page from the marks on the vertical and horizontal ruler, you'd create a grid. With this option selected, Publisher acts as if that grid were there and made up of sticky lines. In fact, it won't let you position an object anywhere where its left border and top edge aren't perfectly aligned with a ruler mark. This can help you align objects at precise distances from margins or other objects.

- **Snap to Guides.** When you select this option, objects snap to ruler guides or layout guides when you move them close enough. This is particularly useful if you're viewing a full page; the small size of the image can make it difficult to tell whether you have things properly aligned. With Snap to Guides active, you can simply shove objects up against a guide to ensure their alignment. And even if you make the guides invisible so you can see what the printed page will look like (by choosing View, Hide Boundaries and Guides), objects continue to snap to them.

- **Snap to Objects.** You can make objects magnetic, too—not just guides. When you select this option, the edge of one object snaps to the edge of another if you bring them close together. This is helpful if you want objects to bump up smoothly against another without any unsightly gaps.

Only turn on the Snap To options when you really need them; otherwise you'll soon find yourself annoyed by frames' tendency to stick to everything in sight: the margins, the ruler guides, each other, and so on.

Although precision has its place in desktop publishing, so does aesthetic sense, and occasionally you'll want to deliberately fudge an alignment to make a little more room for a graphic or another bit of text, or just because you think it looks better. The Snap To options are like grammar checkers on a word processor: helpful up to a point, but downright annoying when you know what you're doing and have some special effect in mind that doesn't fit in the software's view of how things should be.

Objects of a feather group together

When you first design a publication, you spend most of your time working with individual frames. You have to create each one, fill it with text and graphics, and properly format it.

But suppose you created a complex advertisement for a newsletter that contains graphics and WordArt—and you suddenly realize you have to make space on that page for one more story you forgot. Your only option is to shrink the size of the ad—but shrinking all the frames that went into making it is going to take forever.

Publisher has the solution: it offers you a way to group related object together and manipulate them all at once—in this case, you can resize all of them at the same time and by the same amount.

 CAUTION **When you resize a group containing text frames, the size of the** text in the frames is not affected. If you make the group smaller, the text might no longer fit in its frame. After resizing a group containing text frames, make sure you check each text frame individually and adjust the size of any text as required.

Organizing objects into groups

To form a group, select all the objects you want it to include by holding down Shift and clicking each object in turn, or by lassoing them all with the mouse. Notice that a blue box surrounds all the selected objects. At the bottom of this box is the Group button. You might have spotted this button before; it always appears when you select more than one object.

When you place the mouse arrow over this button, it turns into a pointing hand. Click the Group button with the finger of the hand, and the objects you selected group together. Essentially, they become one large object whose dimensions are determined by how far the various member objects extend in all directions.

In figure 16.13, I grouped the items I worked with earlier.

Fig. 16.13
With a click of a button, you can lump together objects of different types in a single group.

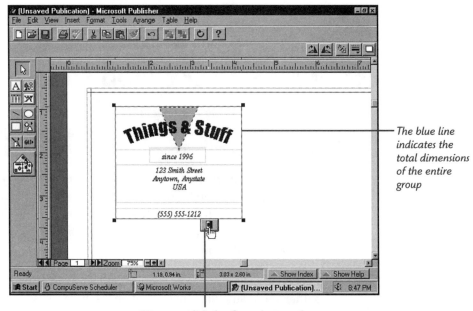

The blue line indicates the total dimensions of the entire group

When you click the Group button, the black and white pieces come together

To dissolve the group, simply click the Group button again.

Group therapy

Now that you put all those objects into a single group, you can work with that group as though it were a single object. You can move or rotate it just as you would any other object.

You can copy, cut, delete, or paste the group using the buttons in the Standard toolbar, or resize it or move it just as you would an ordinary frame (it provides only four handles instead of the usual eight).

You can also click the Shadow button, or the Border button, but any shadows or borders you apply don't surround the group—they surround the individual objects in the group. If you want every object in the group to have a border, that's useful, but if you want a border around the group itself, you'll have to draw the border separately. (Of course, after you draw it, you can add it to the group.)

Q&A *I resized a group containing many different sorts of objects, but I ended up with a mess. Some objects seem to have adjusted to the new size while others didn't. What's going on?*

The key to working with a group is remembering that, although it acts like a single object in many ways, it isn't. It's made up of many different objects. All of those objects maintain their original characteristics when you resize the group. That means that while the graphics and WordArt elements simply adapt to the new size, the text in text frames and tables keeps its original point size, which might be too large or too small for the new size.

So, resizing a group is most useful if the group consists entirely of graphics and WordArt; resizing them as part of the group ensures that they all change in the same fashion.

Going with the (text) flow

When a blizzard is blowing, the wind—carrying millions of snowflakes—rushes along pretty smoothly until it runs into a house or car or some other stationary object. The result is turbulence. A drift forms where the snow, no longer rushing smoothly along, instead tumbles to the ground.

Similarly, your text might flow along just fine through your publication until it encounters another object. The result, if you're not careful, can be turbulence in the flow of your design. In fact, it could bring your publication tumbling to the ground, just like the snowflakes.

Publisher gives you several ways to deal with this situation.

That's a wrap

Whenever you draw a graphic frame or select an existing one, the two text flow buttons become active in the toolbar.

 The Wrap Text to Frame button is selected by default. With this button selected, any text that comes in contact with the graphic flows around the outside of the frame, forming a square around the graphic (see fig. 16.14).

Fig. 16.14
No matter how oddly shaped the graphic, text politely stays outside its frame if the Wrap Text to Frame button is selected.

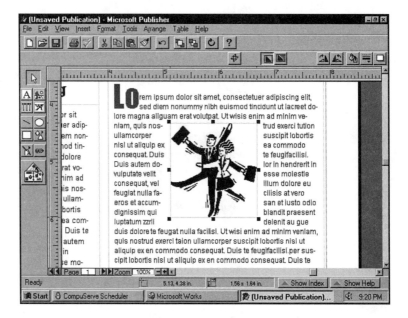

 Click the Wrap Text to Picture button, and the text starts snuggling up against the picture itself, ignoring the margins of the text frame (see fig. 16.15).

Fig. 16.15

The happy business couple from the previous figure looks a little claustrophobic now that the Wrap Text to Picture button is selected.

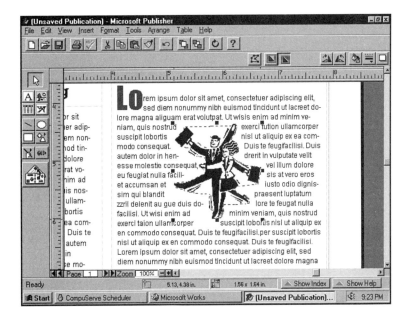

 When you're in Wrap Text to Picture mode, the Edit Irregular Wrap button becomes active.

The Edit Irregular Wrap button allows you to carefully mold text around a picture, ensuring it remains readily legible while better integrating the graphic into the text. Done properly, this can give a publication more of a sense of being a seamless whole instead of a collection of many different parts.

Click the Edit Irregular Wrap button. The usual eight selection handles give way to many more, all around the perimeter of the picture. With these, you can fine-tune the way text wraps around the graphic. Place your arrow on one; the arrow changes to an ADJUST symbol. Click and hold the left mouse button and move the handle wherever you want. The text wrap outline changes its shape accordingly (see fig. 16.16).

TIP **The flow of text around a picture isn't always pretty; you can end**
up with ugly breaks in words, words all by themselves, and other problems.
Don't automatically accept the way the computer chooses to wrap text; use
the Edit Irregular Wrap button freely to fine-tune the flow of text. Nothing
undermines the professional look of your publication more than badly
wrapped text.

Massaging the margins

You can also adjust how close text wraps to a picture's frame or the picture
itself by selecting the picture, clicking the right mouse button, and choosing
Object Frame Properties. The Object Frame Properties dialog box appears
(see fig. 16.17).

Fig. 16.17

You can precisely adjust how close text can come to your picture.

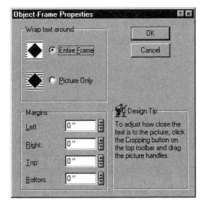

You have the choice of wrapping text around the Entire Frame or around the Picture Only. If you select the former, the Margins area has four text boxes in which you can adjust how close text can come to each side of the frame. As usual, you can enter measurements in centimeters (cm), inches (in), picas (pi), and points (pt).

If you choose the Picture Only option, only one control, Outside, will appear in the Margins area. The margin you enter applies around the entire picture. Return to your workspace to see the effect, then use the Edit Irregular Wrap button to fine-tune it.

17

Checking Your Layout

● **In this chapter:**

- **I want my publication to be perfect! Got any tips?**

- **Can Publisher help me avoid layout errors?**

- **Look out! Widows and orphans at large**

- ***That's* never happened before**

Only you can decide when your publication is perfect, but Publisher can act as a second pair of eyes to help you be sure . . . . ➤

For several years, I was editor of a weekly newspaper. Every story from every reporter flowed through my computer terminal every week, and from my terminal straight into the typesetting machine. I perused every word, every sentence, every paragraph with an eagle eye, determined that this would be the week when not a single typographical error would find its way into print…

…and every week, I was disappointed. Every week, I missed something. Sometimes, the errors were so glaring I cringed when I picked up the paper and wondered how on earth I could have failed to see a mistake that obvious.

It's not easy producing a perfect publication on your own. What you really need is a second pair of eyes to look things over.

Publisher gives you that second pair of eyes; it will look over your publication to check for common layout errors, and as discussed in the chapters on text frames, it will even look over your publication to check for common spelling errors.

But remember, it won't look over your publication to check for factual errors, or names spelled wrong, or just plain ugly design. Content is *your* department.

Need some quality control?
Try the Check Layout command

Suppose you're giving your publication the final once-over before printing. Everything looks great in Full Page view, but when you zoom in to 150 or 200 percent, you begin to notice things that aren't quite right. Surely that story didn't end there, in the middle of a thought! Why are there odd gaps in that headline over there? And how come only half of that graphic is visible?

These are the kinds of layout problems that can easily creep into a publication as you move and manipulate graphics, text, tables, and WordArt. Sometimes the causes of these problems are obscure. That's where Publisher's Check Layout command comes in. Publisher already knows the kinds of problems users commonly run into; it will look at your document, find potential problem areas, and let you know where they are. Then you can look at each potential problem and decide what, if anything, needs to be changed. Check Layout is like having an assistant always at hand whose sole job is to proofread your work.

To activate this tireless assistant, choose Tools, Check Layout. This opens the Check Layout dialog box that asks if you want to check all pages or a range of pages (you have to enter the page range). You can also choose to have Publisher look at background pages.

After you make those selections, click Options to open the Options dialog box shown in figure 17.1.

Just do it—but do it right!

Before you consider your publication finished, give it one more once-over. And even though I don't talk about printing until the next chapter, go ahead and print out a draft copy.

As I know from bitter experience, some mistakes— mysteriously invisible on the computer screen— become glaringly obvious on paper.

Here are some suggestions to consider while looking over your publication for the final time:

- **Check your facts.** Make sure the information is accurate and consistent—especially if it changed at any point during the design process.

- **Check your figures.** Spell check doesn't check numbers, so make sure you do.

- **Check your text.** Is it legible throughout the publication? (Sometimes print in shaded areas that looks fine on the screen becomes hard to read on paper.) Do the fonts enhance the sense of the text? If they don't, consider changing them.

- **Check your writing.** Is it clear and comprehensible? Pretty layout doesn't mean a thing if your publication doesn't communicate.

- **Check your graphics.** Do they look as good on paper as they did on the screen? Do they complement the message you're trying to get across or distract from it? If the latter, consider replacing them.

- **Check the overall impact of the publication.** Try to view it with a fresh eye, as though you're seeing it for the first time. Better yet, show it to someone who really will be seeing it for the first time. Does it communicate what you want to communicate? Does it achieve the goal you set for it?

And when you've done all that...let Publisher take one last look at your publication, too.

Fig. 17.1

Tell Publisher what layout problems you want it to look for.

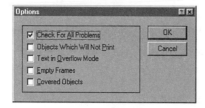

From here, you can choose to have Publisher look at all or some of four common problems:

- **Objects Which Will Not Print.** Choose this option to make sure all the objects you placed in your publication will actually show up on paper when you print. Publisher will find all objects that won't print: for example, objects located too close to the edge of the paper (see fig. 17.2). Most printers can't print right to the edge of a sheet of paper, so if you draw an object to close to the edge, part of it won't print. Some of the problems that the other options find also fall into this category.

Fig. 17.2

This graphic looks fine on the page, but in fact it's too close to the edge, which means part of it will be cut off when you print—a fact Publisher has just brought to your attention.

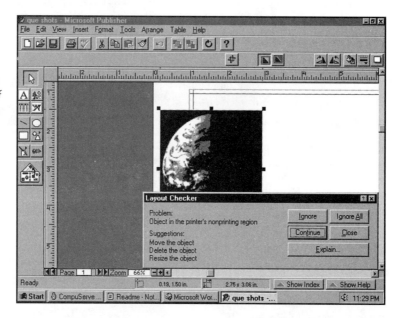

- **Text in Overflow Mode.** Choose this option to make sure you didn't cut off stories prematurely by trying to cram too much text into too small a text frame. If you have, some of the text will be hidden in the text overflow area (see fig. 17.3). You need to enlarge the frame or reduce the text size (or edit the text) to make sure no text is missing when you print. (See Chapter 5 for more information about text frames and the overflow area.)

Fig. 17.3

There's more text here than meets the eye: some of it is hidden in the overflow area. You may not know it's there, but Publisher does!

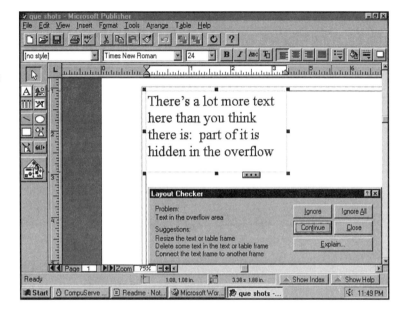

- **Empty Frames.** Choose this option to make sure you don't have any empty frames leftover from the design process. Empty frames don't print, but they can cause other problems with your layout, especially if text tries to wrap around them (see fig. 17.4). In any event, if they're empty, you don't need them, so you might as well delete them. (See Chapter 2 for more information on working with frames.)

- **Covered Objects.** Choose this option to make sure you have the objects you want on "top," and didn't inadvertently cover up parts of other objects you actually want visible (see fig. 17.5). This option allows you to look at each instance of objects on top of each other to make sure they are stacked the way you want them. If you knowingly layered objects on top of each other in several places in your document for a specific effect—several pieces of ClipArt combined into a kind of collage, for instance, or a complicated combination of WordArt, graphics, and text—you might want to turn this option off.

Fig. 17.4
Empty frames like this, left behind by accident during the design process, can disrupt the placement of other elements of your publication.

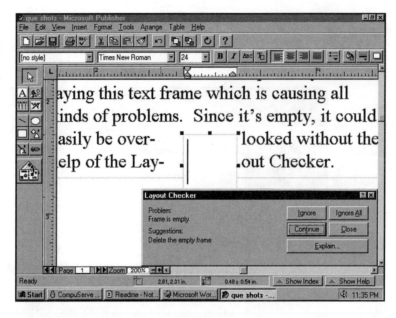

Fig. 17.5
Objects can completely hide other objects, which can not only puzzle you, should a piece of clip art or a bit of text go missing, but also takes up valuable disk space.

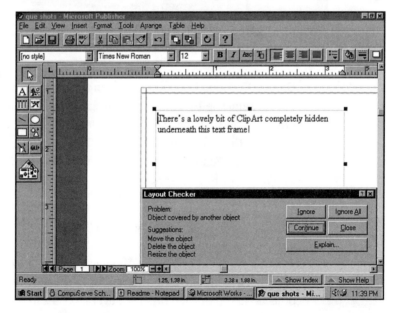

In general, check for all of these problems before you even print a draft copy of your publication. It doesn't take very long, and it just might turn up something you missed. If you go ahead and print a draft copy, Check Layout can help you identify the source of any problems that, even though you didn't notice them on the screen, become obvious on the printed page.

After you choose the layout problems you want Publisher to look for, click OK. If Check Layout finds a problem, the Layout Checker dialog box appears (see fig. 17.6).

Fig. 17.6

The Layout Checker dialog box describes problems found in your layout and offers further explanation of them by linking you to pertinent areas of the Help files.

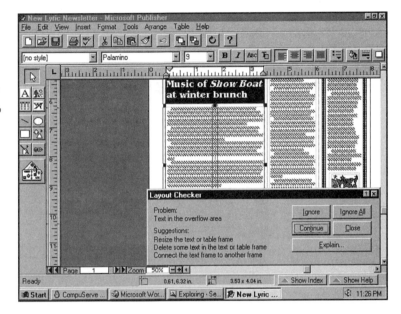

Notice that, behind the Layout Checker dialog box, a story in the publication has been selected. That's the text frame Layout Checker found the problem in. If you want to, you can immediately go to the publication and correct the problem without closing the Layout Checker; just move the dialog box out of the way while you work. All of Publisher's tools remain active even with the Layout Checker dialog box open. This makes it easy to correct each problem as you identify it, then move on to the next.

Sometimes, of course, the "problem" Check Layout turns up isn't a problem at all; it's something you did deliberately to create a specific effect. If you look at the identified problem and like the way it looks, then leave it. *You* are the final arbiter of how your document should be put together.

You can also choose to have Layout Checker Ignore the problem or Ignore All problems of that type, Close the Layout Checker dialog box, or ask Layout Checker to Explain (which opens a section of the help file). Click Continue when you're ready for Layout Checker to continue checking your publication.

CAUTION **Two common problems that Layout Checker won't check for are widows** and **orphans** (single words or sentences that get stranded at the top and bottom of pages due to page breaks). To remove a widow or orphan, add a few words before it to put at least two lines at the top of the page, or take out a few words to drop it to the bottom of the page.

The X-Files: Unexpected side-effects

Finally, when you're giving your layout the *final* going-over, be prepared for the unexpected. A tiny adjustment to a text frame could change the words that flow around a graphic three columns over—and completely mess up your carefully cultivated word-wrap. Making a graphic just a little bit longer can bump the end of the story below it into the never-neverland of text overflow. Altering the point size of a subhead can leave you with blank space at the bottom of the page.

Figures 17.7 and 17.8 illustrate another common example. Here, changing the incorrect spelling of the word "Sunday" using the Check Spelling dialog box has resulted in an extra line of text being added to the end of the story—a change that means the end of this story no longer lines up with the end of the story to the immediate left. You could easily overlook this change during proofreading and Check Layout would not even have caught it.

Fig. 17.7
Of course, you have to change an obviously misspelled word like "Snday"...

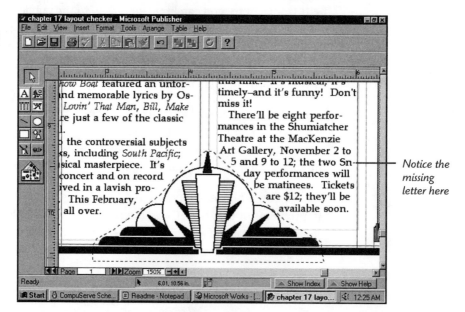

Notice the missing letter here

Fig. 17.8

...but even a tiny change like adding a single letter can have an unexpectedly large effect on some other area of your publication.

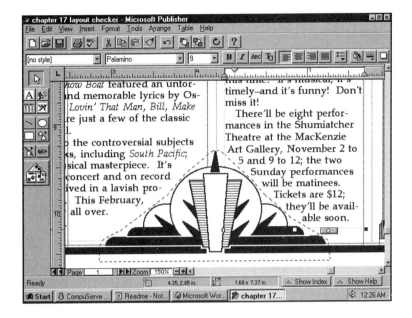

Whenever you make an adjustment, however minor, check to make sure it hasn't created an unexpected side-effect somewhere else.

Unlike *The X-Files* series on TV, you can't blame aliens when something goes wrong with your publication. You're in charge.

18

Printing: The Final Step

● In this chapter:

- How do I get my equipment ready to print?

- This isn't an everyday letter: printing odd jobs

- Uh-oh, something went wrong. Where can I find help?

- My dot-matrix doesn't cut it; I need to take my publication to an outside printer

Whether you print your publication on your own printer or send it to an outside printer, Publisher helps you take desktop publishing's Final Step . . . . ●▶

"A journey of a thousand miles," goes the proverb, "begins with a single step." Your publication's journey into the outside world also begins with a single step, the final step for any desktop publishing job: printing.

Of course, in the process of creating your publication you might actually print it several times, going back and making changes on the computer each time. Eventually, you will have made every change and the time for the Final Printout will come. That's the end of the desktop publishing process.

But you're not there yet. Unlike the single step a human makes at the beginning of a journey, the final step of printing a publication in Publisher can be broken into several smaller steps, which vary depending on who's doing the printing, with what kind of equipment, and the size and shape of your publication.

If you're printing your publication on your own computer printer, then the process beings with Print Setup.

Which printer? What paper? Which direction? Print Setup has the answers

Practically every Windows 95 program that supports printing has Print Setup in some form or another. In Publisher, you access it by choosing File, Print Setup. The Print Setup dialog box appears (see fig. 18.1).

Set your printer choice here

Fig. 18.1
The Print Setup dialog box has three areas: Printer, Paper, and Orientation.

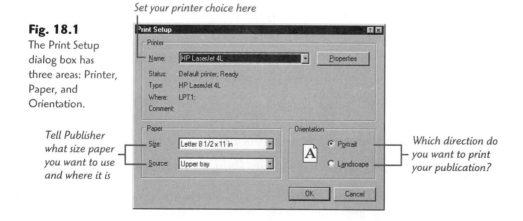

Tell Publisher what size paper you want to use and where it is

Which direction do you want to print your publication?

First, open the Name drop-down list to see a list of all the printers set up on your system to work in Windows 95. When you select a printer (by pointing at its name and clicking the left mouse button once), more information about it automatically appears in the Status, Type, Where, and Comment fields below the Name list box.

Status tells you whether the printer is ready to use (such as, whether it's turned on and if it's the default printer). Type tells you which printer you selected (usually it more-or-less repeats the information in the Name drop-down list). Where tells you which port the printer is connected to (such as LPT1). And Comments might provide additional information entered when you installed the printer in Windows 95.

Click Properties to see the Printer Properties control box. The controls available to you here vary from printer to printer; typical controls include options to set the paper size and source, print resolution, how dark you want your publication to print, and color options.

After you select your printer, check out the Paper area. The Size list box allows you to select what size of paper you want to print the publication on; again, what's available in this list depends on the printer you selected. The same is true of Source list box; it lists the choices for paper feeding your chosen printer has available. Sometimes your publication won't fit comfortably on one of the sizes of paper your printer can use. See the section "All jobs are not created equal" later in this chapter for more information.

Finally, in the Orientation area of the dialog box, you can choose between Portrait and Landscape. If you have trouble remembering that Portrait orientation prints across the narrow edge of the paper, and Landscape orientation prints across the long edge of the paper, don't worry. The Orientation area includes a preview reminder that shows you what direction your choice will print.

When you make all your selections, click OK to return to the workspace.

TIP **Unlike some programs, Publisher doesn't offer you a Print Preview** command, which shows you exactly how the publication will look when you print it.

On the other hand, any time you look at a Publisher publication on-screen, you're pretty well seeing what you'd see if it were printed.

To get an even better idea of what the printed publication will look like, you can turn off all the non-printing elements that might be visible. Choose View, Hide Boundaries and Guides, and (if necessary) choose View, Hide Special Characters.

There's your Page Preview.

But wait! You have even more printing options

If you selected your printer and set it up the way you want it, and you checked over your publication umpteen times and know it's also the way you want it, you might think you're ready to print, and maybe you are—but there are a few more options for you to consider.

Choose File, Print. The Print dialog box stands between you and seeing your publication on paper (see fig. 18.2).

Fig. 18.2

Do you want to print just some of the publication? How many copies should Publisher print? The Print dialog box is where you make these decisions—and more— about the print job.

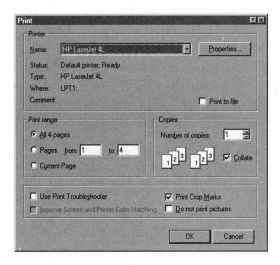

This dialog box has four areas: Printer, Print Range, Copies, and an unnamed section at the bottom.

- The **Printer** area contains basically the same information you set in Print Setup. It gives you another opportunity to change to a different printer. It also contains an additional check box: Print to File. Choose this to "print" the publication to a hard drive or floppy disk, to await printing to paper at a more opportune moment.

- In the **Print Range** area, decide whether you want to print all the pages in the publication or just some of them. The default is All Pages (however many pages you have). If you just want to print some pages—just pages two and three, for example—click the Pages button, enter **2** in the From box and enter **3** in the To box. To change your mind and print all pages after all, just click the All Pages button.

  You can also choose to print just the Current Page. Only the page you're currently viewing in your workspace prints.

- In the **Copies** area, enter how many copies you want to print in the Number of Copies box, and decide whether you want Publisher to Collate them.

 Plain English, please!

To collate pages is to put them in their proper order. If you select the Collate check box and print multiple copies of a multi-page publication, Publisher prints the pages of each publication sequentially: all the pages of the first copy of the publication, then all the pages of the second copy, and so on. If you don't select the Collate check box, Publisher prints each page of the publication individually the number of times specified: 15 copies of the first page, for example, then 15 copies of the second, then 15 of the third, and so on.

- Finally, in the bottom area, you can choose to Use Print Troubleshooter, Improve Screen and Printer Color Matching, or Print Crop Marks. These topics are discussed later in the chapter.

  You can also select the Do Not Print Pictures check box. If you do, Publisher replaces all the graphics in the printed publication with placeholders (light gray boxes crisscrossed by diagonal lines). This is useful for checking layouts because it speeds the printing process.

I'm late! I'm late! Printing on the run

 To quickly print your publication, you don't have to go through the Print dialog box. Just click the Print button in the Standard toolbar. Publisher sends the current page to the printer, using the last settings you entered in the Print dialog box.

All jobs are not created equal

Not all publications are designed to fit on letter-sized paper, legal-sized paper, or even 11-by-17-inch paper. If you're designing a business card, a tent-fold card for a restaurant tabletop, or name cards for a birthday party, your creations are all going to be much smaller than any of those types of paper.

On the other hand, other designs—a poster for a charity circus, for instance, or a banner for a welcome-home party that has to stretch the length of a wall—are going to be much larger than most standard sizes of paper.

Fact is, you'll probably print things in non-standard sizes almost as often as you print things in standard sizes. Fortunately, Publisher can handle even the oddest of odd jobs like these, large or small.

Printing publications smaller than your paper

When you design a publication that's smaller than a standard-sized sheet of paper, Publisher doesn't show you how it will fit on that paper. Instead, it shows the publication as a distinct unit, like the business card in figure 18.3.

Fig. 18.3

Publisher displays small publications like this business card as they will look when finished, not as they will look when printed on a larger piece of paper.

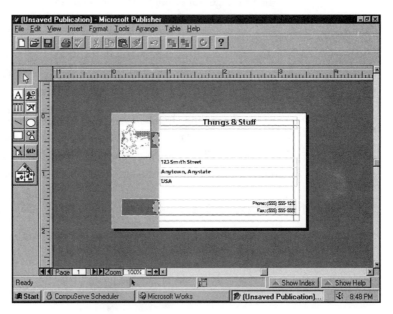

When you choose File, Print to print this kind of publication, however, notice that the Print dialog box has a Page Options button. Click it to open the Page Options dialog box (see fig 18.4).

Choose this if you just want a sample to take to an outside printer

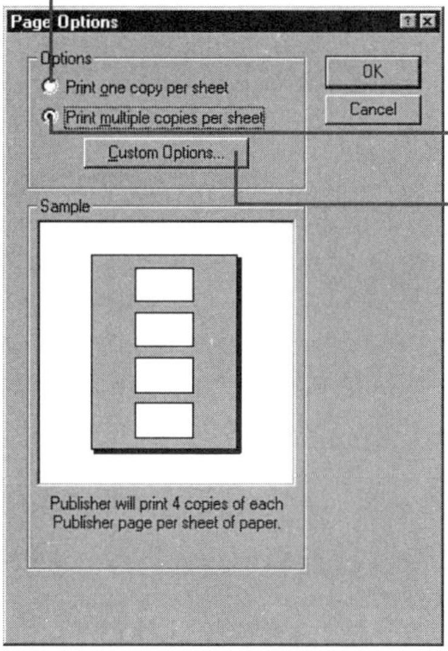

Fig. 18.4

In the Page Options dialog box, you can choose whether to print only one copy of your small publication per page or multiple copies.

If you're printing the entire job yourself, choose this option

Click this option if you want to change the arrangement of the multiple copies

If you choose to print only one small publication per page, you're done; if you choose to print more than one, you activate the Custom Options button. The Sample area shows how Publisher arranges the multiple copies on the page, but you can change it if you want. In figure 18.4, it certainly looks like I could get more business cards on that page than just four, so I'll click Custom Options to open the Custom Options dialog box (see fig. 18.5).

The top area is called Type in Spacing, and that's exactly what you do here: type the amount of space in inches you want in each Side Margin, Top Margin, Horizontal Gap, and Vertical Gap (use the drop-down arrows to switch to centimeters, picas, or points). The preview shows you what you're accomplishing; in this case, it looks like I doubled the number of business cards I can print on the page by making the gaps and margins half an inch all the way around.

Fig. 18.5

Here's where you can fine-tune the way Publisher arranges small publications on the page for printing.

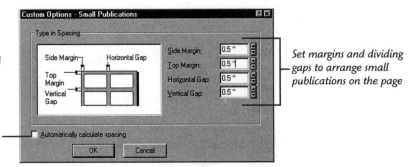

Set margins and dividing gaps to arrange small publications on the page

If you change your mind, click here to restore the automatic spacing

On the other hand, I also made it harder to cut the cards out after they're printed—a good reason to reconsider. To restore the default spacing, just click Automatically Calculate Spacing.

Click OK to return to the previous dialog box, whose Sample area now shows the effects of the changes you made in the Custom Options dialog box. Click OK again to return to the Print dialog box, and click OK one more time to finally start printing.

It's too big! Printing publications larger than the paper in your printer

To print publications that are larger than any size of paper you can use in your printer, such as banners and posters, you also have to use a unique dialog box. For example, suppose you used Publisher's PageWizard to design a poster, and you're ready to print it. Choose File, Print to open the Print dialog box. Now there's a button called Tile Printing Options.

66 *Plain English, please!*

Publications larger than the paper in your printer can be printed on several sheets of paper, each of which has part of the publication on it. You assemble these sheets to create the whole publication, just like tiles fit together to create a pattern on a floor: hence, this method of printing large publications is called **tiling**. 99

Click the Tile Printing Options button to open the Poster and Banner Printing Options dialog box, and you'll see in the Sample area how your publication will be divided among several sheets of paper (see fig. 18.6). The large white rectangle in the Sample area is your publication; the transparent rectangles drawn on top of it represent the separate pieces of paper it will be printed on.

Fig. 18.6

Just as individual tiles create a complete picture in a mosaic floor, you can assemble a complete publication from pieces of paper that each contain only part of it.

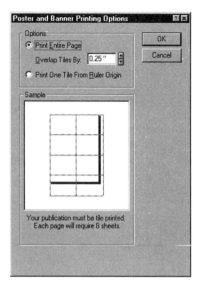

If you print the publication with these settings, it will take eight pages, as shown in the Sample, to cover the whole design.

Notice that two of the pages, near the bottom, will end up having very little of the design on them. You can change that by adjusting Overlap Tiles By. You can change how much each tile will overlap the others by clicking the arrows to the right of the box, or typing in a new number (again, in centimeters [cm], inches [in], picas [pi], or points [pt]).

TIP **Changing the overlap distance can make it easier to assemble the complete publication from the tiles.** A larger overlap gives you more leeway as to where you put the seam: you can trim around entire letters and graphics, for example, rather than having to try to perfectly match their halves.

Adjusting the overlap can also ensure that the outside edges of the publication perfectly match the outside edge of tiles. This can help you line up the printed tiles and make copying the finished publication much easier.

The Overlap Tiles By box is only active if you choose the Print Entire Page button. Choose Print One Tile From Ruler Origin and the Sample changes to show only one regular-sized sheet of paper overlaying your oversized publication (see fig. 18.7).

Fig. 18.7

If you only need to print part of a large publication, perhaps to check how a particular graphic will look when printed or to avoid a nasty seam through a bit of WordArt, use Print One Tile from Ruler Origin.

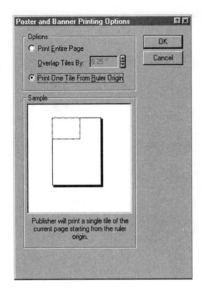

Publisher lines up that single tile with the zero markings on the vertical and horizontal rulers. Normally, those marks align with the upper-left corner of your publication, so that's where the single tile appears by default (refer to fig. 18.7). However, you can change the position of the tile by changing the location of zero on one or both of the rulers. To do that, point at either ruler or at the intersection of the two. Your mouse arrow changes to a two-headed arrow. Press and hold the Shift key, and drag the mouse to the point you want the zero markings to align to (see fig. 18.8).

If you return to the Tile Printing Options dialog box and select Print One Tile From Ruler Origin, you see the single tile has now moved into the middle of your publication in the Sample area (see fig. 18.9).

Click OK to return to the Print dialog box, and OK again to print your publication.

Fig. 18.8
Relocating the zero marks on the rulers, as I'm doing here, and printing a single tile at a time can help you avoid awkward seams when assembling your publication—and you save time by checking just a portion of it for errors during the design process.

After you release the mouse button, zero on each ruler will relocate to where these lines have been dragged

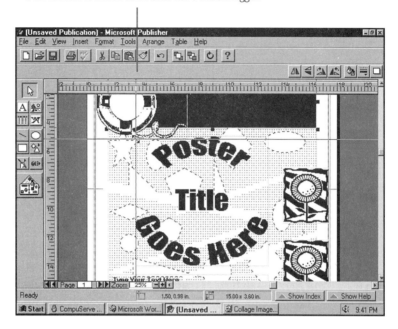

Fig. 18.9
Now that we've moved the zero marks of the ruler, the single tile you'll print has also moved, as you can see in the Sample area.

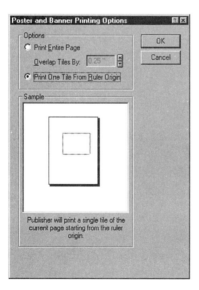

What if I want to print in color?

Publisher offers lots of great tools for using color with text, graphics, WordArt, and tables. But color doesn't do you much good unless you have a color printer. Even then, you might be disappointed; often the color you print doesn't match the color on the screen.

Publisher can help avoid that disappointment: it offers you a couple of ways to ensure that the color on the monitor and the color on the printer are as close as possible.

CAUTION **To access the tools in this section, your color printer must support** Image Color Matching, so check your printer documentation before continuing with the rest of this section. If you don't have a color printer, this section isn't going to do you much good either!

So you finished your design, you carefully chose just the right colors, and you're ready to print. To access Publisher's color-matching tools, first choose Tools, Options. In the Options dialog box, choose Improve Screen and Printer Color Matching (see fig. 18.10).

Fig. 18.10
The first step to successful color printing is to choose this check box in the Options dialog box.

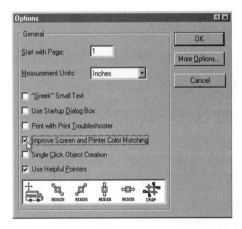

After you activate this option, other tools become available to you. For example, select an object and click the Object Color button, then More Colors. As you can see in figure 18.11, the Mark Colors that Will Not Print Well on My Printer check box is now available. If you choose this, Publisher grays out all the colors in the color palette that will not work well on your printer.

Fig. 18.11
Publisher provides you
with friendly advice on
using the colors that
will work the best.

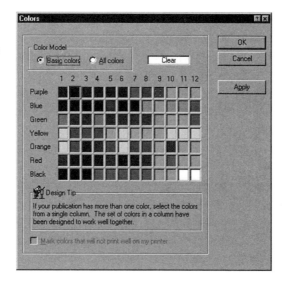

 The second option that Publisher provides that can help you match monitor colors to printer colors is in the Print dialog box that comes up whenever you choose File, Print. Select the Improve Screen and Printer Color Matching check box—which does exactly what it says.

Individual color printers might offer other choices, including a selection of methods for matching screen and printer colors. From the Print dialog box, choose Properties and explore the various options your color printer provides.

Publisher's Print Troubleshooter is here to help

If you've worked with other software packages very much, you already know that printing can be a tricky business. Sometimes, when you finally get through all the options pertinent to your publication and you're ready to print, you click OK for the final time, sit back…

…and something goes wrong.

Maybe nothing prints at all. Maybe your fonts look funny. Maybe graphics don't show up or don't look like they should.

Some problems will require you to check your printer and computer and Windows 95 documentation, but Publisher does its best to give you a helping hand with print problems via the Print Troubleshooter (see fig. 18.12). You can set up Publisher so that Print Troubleshooter opens every time you print, or you can choose to activate it only when you have a problem. Either way, it can provide valuable hints that can lead to a successful resolution of your printing problem. I suggest keeping it active all the time, because you never know when things will go wrong.

Fig. 18.12

If this looks familiar, it should; Print Trouble-shooter is simply a part of the built-in Help feature.

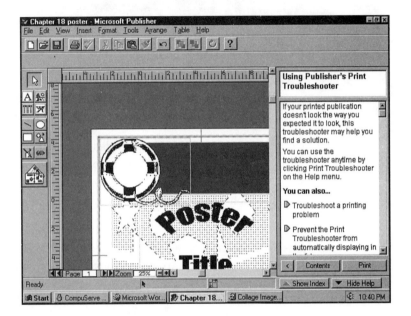

To keep Print Troubleshooter active all the time, choose Tools, Options, then check the Print with Print Troubleshooter check box. Now Print Trouble-shooter will open every time you print.

If you prefer to only activate Print Troubleshooter once in a while, you can click the Use Print Troubleshooter check box in the Print dialog box. As long as it's checked and you're using the same printer, Print Troubleshooter will appear whenever you print.

Or, you can simply choose Help, Print Troubleshooter when you need a printing tip.

When Print Troubleshooter appears, click Troubleshoot a Printing Problem to see the list in figure 18.13. More specific problems branch off from here; with any luck, one of them will not only match the problem you're having, it will also offer the correct solution.

Fig. 18.13
The first step to finding an answer to a printing problem using Print Troubleshooter is to decide which of these general problems most closely matches the one you're having.

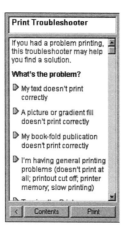

This has to be perfect: sending publications to outside printers

Your ink jet or 300 dpi laser printer might be good enough for your personal use, but if your publication is destined for greater things, such as full-color printing or appearing as an ad in a magazine, you might have to send it to an outside printer.

An outside printer can bring to your project expertise and more specialized equipment than you might be able to afford. In particular, an outside printer will have high-resolution printers that can give your publication that final professional polish. An outside printer can also help you with color choices and even design.

In this section, you'll look at taking the necessary steps to prepare a publication for printing by an outside printer.

Outside Printer Setup

To prepare your publication for printing by an outside service, first choose File, Outside Print Setup. This opens the Outside Print Setup dialog box (see fig. 18.14).

Fig. 18.14
Professional printers offer many more options for printing your publication than the typical home or office computer system.

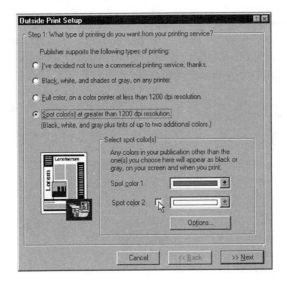

Here you're offered four options:

- **I've decided not to use a commercial printing service, thanks.** So what are you doing opening this dialog box? Choose Cancel.

- **Black, white, and shades of gray, on any printer.** You'd choose this one if you wanted to print your publication at a higher resolution than is available from your desktop or office printer.

- **Full color, on a color printer at less than 1,200 dpi resolution.** If you don't have a color printer or have only a low-resolution color printer, you might want to send your publication out for full-color printing of this sort. Publisher doesn't support full-color printing at greater than 1,200 dpi resolution.

❝ *Plain English, please!*

Printer **resolution** determines how sharply text and graphics will print. Resolution is measured in **dpi**, which stands for dots per inch. Although the letters in a laser-printed font look like they're drawn with lines, they're actually made up of tiny dots. The more dots per inch there are in printed material, the smaller the dots are, and the finer the printer's resolution. ❞

- **Spot color(s) at greater than 1,200 dpi resolution.** Publisher *does* support the use of up to two colors, plus black and shades of gray, at greater than 1,200 dpi. Spot color can be a highly effective way to add color to your publication and generally costs less than full color.

If you choose this option, you must select your spot colors from the two boxes that become available. Click the Op̲tions button just below the color controls to open the Spot Color Options dialog box in figure 18.15.

66 *Plain English, please!*

The kind of full-color printing you see on the cover of this book, which faithfully reproduces everything from skin tones to the color of someone's sweater, requires four different versions of the same image, each designed to be printed in a different color (red, cyan, yellow, and black). When these four colors in varying shades are printed on top each other, they can produce any color. This kind of color printing is called **process color**. Any other kind of color printing, which doesn't involve all those inks or (necessarily) overprinting one color on another, is called **spot color**. The color used to highlight captions and other elements in this book is an example of spot color. Because spot color is so much easier, it's also less expensive, which makes it a popular choice in publication design. 99

Fig. 18.15
Specify the way
Publisher handles
black objects and
text overlying colored
objects with these
controls.

If you select Overprint Black O̲bjects, black objects overlying colored objects print on top of the color, so you have black ink over colored ink on the page. If you don't select this box, no colored ink prints in areas masked by the black.

Similarly, if you select Overprint Black T̲ext under, text smaller than the size specified in the box prints over colored objects; the color under text larger than that size doesn't print.

Disabling overprinting can lead to gaps on higher resolution color printers, so you should discuss the best settings for these controls with your outside printing service.

After you choose the type of outside printing you're interested in, choose Next. That moves you to the next page of the Outside Print Setup dialog box, which asks if you want to use Publisher's outside printer drivers, or select a specific printer.

If you're setting up a publication for an outside printer, you'll probably want to check the first option; you can't select a specific printer unless it's installed on your system.

Click Next again (if you're preparing a black-and-white or spot-color publication) to move to the next page of the Outside Print Setup dialog box, which gives you two more options: Automatically Choose "Extra" Paper Sizes and Show All Printer Marks.

Outside printers frequently print publications on oversized paper to accommodate various printing marks and special effects, such as bleeds—colors that go right to the edge of the page. So you should usually select the Automatically Choose "Extra" Paper Sizes check box.

Selecting the Show All Printer Marks check box means that crop marks, registration marks, and information about the publication will print with the publication. Again, you should usually select this check box.

 Plain English, please!

Crop marks are not mysterious circles that appear in farmers' fields overnight, but marks that tell the printer where to trim the page. They appear as short horizontal and vertical lines that stop just short of intersecting. Each line marks one edge of the page; the invisible intersection marks the corner.

A printing press doesn't print color all at once; each color is laid down on the page separately. **Registration marks**, cross-hairs outside the printing area of the page, are lined up to ensure that each color prints exactly where it should.

Crop marks and registration marks are collectively known as **printing marks**. 💬

The outside printing checklist

Dealing with printers of the human sort can be just as confusing as dealing with printers of the computer sort. Publisher offers you a helping hand in the form of the Outside Printing Checklist, which is also available on this final screen of the Outside Print Setup dialog box. Click Print Outside Printing Checklist, and your printer will spit out a very thorough five-page checklist that takes you through the whole process of using an outside printer.

Part A gives you a series of questions to ask printers, which vary depending on what kind of printing you want done and urges you to call several different printing services before settling on one.

Part B is a list of more detailed matters you need to get settled with the printing service you choose before you finalize your publication.

Follow this checklist and, even if it's the first time you've printed something anywhere but on your own desktop, you'll have the printing service thinking you're a pro.

The outside printing info sheet

Publisher also prints an information sheet that answers many of the questions an outside printer might ask, including the fonts and colors used, the resolution, what kind of printer the proof was printed on, and more. To print this sheet, choose File, Print Infosheet.

Installing Microsoft Publisher 3.0

● **In this appendix:**

- **What do I need to run Publisher on my computer?**

- **Install the whole thing, or just bits and pieces**

- **Thanks but no thanks; get it off my system!**

Knowing how to use Publisher is all well and good, but you can't do much of anything if you haven't installed the soft-ware. Here's how . . . . ▶

Before you begin

The requirements for running Microsoft Publisher 3.0 are not as onerous as you might imagine. According to Microsoft, you need:

- A personal computer with a 386DX or higher processor

- Microsoft Windows 95 or Microsoft Windows NT Workstation operating system version 3.51 or later (Publisher 3.0 won't run on earlier versions of Windows)

- A minimum of 6M of memory for Windows 95 and 12M for Windows NT Workstation

- A minimum of 6M of free space on your hard drive (maximum of 30.2M if you're installing from floppies; 60.9M if you're installing the CD Deluxe version)

- A CD-ROM drive and/or a 3.5 inch high-density disk drive

- VGA or higher-resolution video adapter and monitor

These are, of course, minimum requirements; and operating any software package with just the minimum requirements is frequently an exercise in frustration. To really use Publisher to the best of its capability, you need at least a 486 computer (the faster, the better), 8M of RAM in Windows 95, and a CD-ROM player—because the CD version of Publisher contains more clip art and fonts than the floppy-disk version.

To see what kind of system you have, click Start and choose Settings, Control Panel, then double-click System. Windows 95 automatically examines your system and displays its findings.

After you know you have everything you need to run Publisher effectively, the rest of the installation procedure is smooth sailing.

Installing Microsoft Publisher

Installing any software in Windows 95 is usually a reasonably painless process—that's certainly true of installing Microsoft Publisher 3.0.

With Windows 95 running, click the Start button, choose Settings, Control Panel and, finally, double-click Add/Remove Programs. From the dialog box that appears, click Install. If you're installing from a CD, insert it in your CD-ROM drive at this point; if you're installing from floppy disks, insert the first one in your floppy disk drive; then click Next.

Windows 95 searches for the installation program, called SETUP.EXE. When it finds it, you are asked to confirm the choice by clicking Finish. Do so, and after searching your drive for previously installed components of Publisher, Setup presents you with the Setup dialog box shown in figure A.1.

Fig. A.1

You can install all of Publisher's options, choose to install only some of them (to save disk space), or install some of the options on your hard drive while saving disk space by keeping some items only on the installation CD.

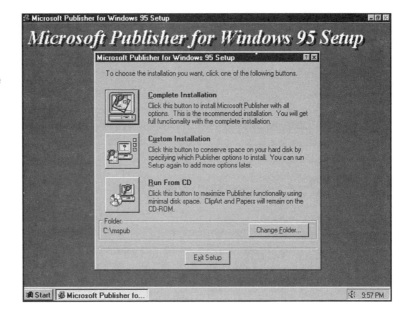

Here you can choose from three options:

- **Complete Installation.** This is recommended. All of Publisher's options will be available to you, and all ClipArt and other support files will be added to your hard drive.

- **Custom Installation.** If you choose this option, you can pick and choose among Publisher's options to minimize the use of disk space, but you can't make use of everything Publisher has to offer (see fig. A.2).

- **Run from CD.** If you choose this option, you can save some disk space by leaving some of Publisher's support files on the CD and accessing them from there when you need them. Publisher will be fully functional, but occasionally slow.

Fig. A.2
From here, you can install some or all of Publisher, which is useful if you want to conserve disk space.

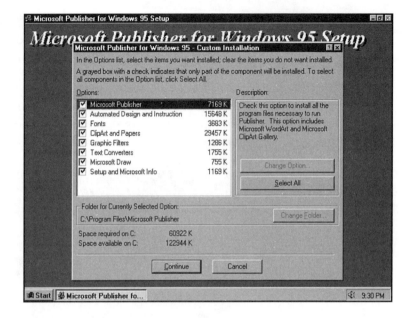

Choose your weapon

CAUTION **The following assumes that you're installing from CD-ROM.** Although the process of installation is the same, some of the details of the setup options in this section might be different if you're installing from floppies. In particular, the CD-ROM version of Publisher includes much more clip art and many more fonts.

If you choose Custom Installation, the Custom Installation dialog box in figure A.2 opens. Here, Setup breaks Publisher into eight segments. You can choose to install any or all of the following:

- **Microsoft Publisher**. These are the essential system files for Publisher. If you're installing the program for the first time, you have to install these. ClipArt and WordArt are included. Disk space required: 7,169K (or 7.1M).

- **Automated Design and Instruction**. This is the largest segment; it includes the PageWizards and the built-in demonstrations of features. These elements are not required, but they can be extremely helpful, especially for novice users. Disk space required: 15,648K (or 10.5M).

- **ClipArt and Papers**. Publisher comes with a large selection of clip art (to go with ClipArt Gallery, installed as part of the basic Publisher files along with WordArt) and templates that help you design applications intended to be printed on special papers that already include various design elements. I think you can never have too much clip art, but if you think otherwise, you can save a lot of disk space by not installing the art that comes with Publisher. Disk space required: 29.5M.

- **Graphic Filters.** When you import a graphic into Publisher, it has to be able to change that graphic into a format Publisher can read. That's the job of these filters, which are available for most of the common picture formats. If you want to install only a few graphic filters—say you only plan to import graphics in PC Paintbrush format and Windows Bitmap format—choose Graphic Filters and click the Change Options button. This opens the Graphic Filters dialog box. Select the filters you want to install, then click OK to return to the Custom Installation dialog box.

- **Text Converters.** Just as Publisher has to convert pictures to a format it can use, so it has to convert text. Because most people prefer to create large documents in their favorite word processor, then insert those documents into Publisher, Publisher has to be able to recognize text generated by many different programs. To save disk space, you might want to only install converters for word processors you have installed on your system. To access them, choose Text Converters and click the Change Options menu. You see the Text Converters dialog box shown in figure A.3. Choose the converters you want to install and click OK to return to the Custom Installation dialog box.

Fig. A.3

Not surprisingly, Publisher has text converters for several Microsoft word processors, as well as their chief (but very popular) rival, WordPerfect.

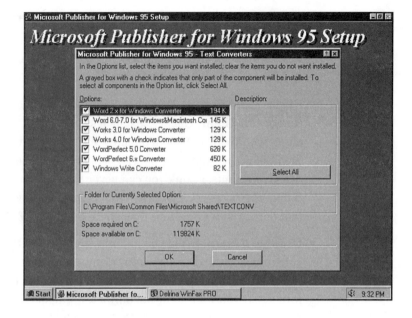

- **Microsoft Draw.** If you've previously installed a Microsoft software package such as Word or Works, you probably already installed this basic drawing program. If not, you have to decide whether you want it, which probably depends on how willing you are to draw your own graphics when you can't find what you need.

- **Setup and Microsoft Info.** You don't need Setup and its support files to run Publisher, but you need them if you're planning to customize your installation in the future by adding or removing components—say, if you buy a larger disk drive and decide you want the full Publisher package installed.

At the bottom of the Custom Installation dialog box (and the Graphic Filters and Text Converters dialog boxes), Publisher keeps track of how much space your selected options require in total, and reminds you of how much space you currently have available.

After you select the components you want to install (or simply click Select All), choose Continue. Publisher then asks if you want to install the Windows 95 PostScript driver—you need this to activate the Outside Printing features discussed in Chapter 18.

CAUTION If you choose to install the Windows 95 PostScript driver, make sure you have your Windows 95 installation CD-ROM or floppies handy, because Setup requires them.

Finally, Publisher will prompt you for the floppy disks or CD-ROM it needs as it needs them, and keeps you apprised of how the installation is progressing with a bar that shows you the percentage of the installation complete.

You can cancel installation at any time; Setup simply warns you that Publisher was not installed properly. You can return to Setup later.

If you do return to Setup after installing part or all of Publisher, you see a slightly different dialog box (see fig. A.4).

Fig. A.4

You can install some or all of Publisher for the first time, reinstall it (to add segments you didn't install the first time), or remove it from your hard drive altogether.

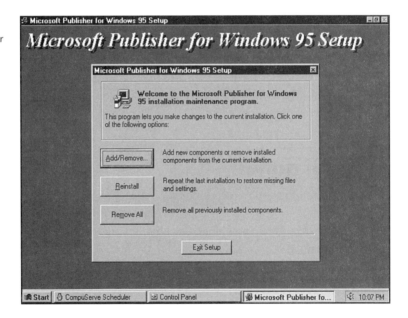

Here you can choose from three options:

- **Add/Remove.** If you're installing Publisher for the first time, or if you have previously installed Publisher but want to add or remove certain segments of it, click this button. You see a Maintenance Installation dialog box similar to the Custom Installation dialog box described earlier where you can choose which segments you want to add or remove.

- **Reinstall.** If you've previously started to install Publisher but had to quit before you finished, or you installed Publisher but elements of it didn't install properly, click this button to repeat and complete that previous installation.

- **Remove All.** If you've previously installed Publisher and wish you hadn't, or desperately need to free up disk space (who doesn't?), click this button.

CAUTION If you've already installed a working version of Publisher and cancel an update in midstream, you might find that your original no longer works properly. Run Publisher Setup again and complete the new installation.

Maybe this wasn't such a good idea

If you're really desperate to free up disk space and don't think you'll be using Publisher for a while, or if you just decide you don't want it any more, choose Remove All from the Setup dialog box. Setup asks you to confirm your choice, then deletes all the installed components of Publisher from your drive.

All done!

Assuming you're installing and not removing Publisher, after the process is complete, you can close Setup and start Publisher by simply clicking Start, choosing Programs, then double-clicking the Microsoft Publisher icon (a big purple P).

Voilà! You're off and running. (I told you it was simple!)

Index